W9-ADV-285

THE

PROBLEM

WITH

WORK

Feminism,

Marxism,

Antiwork Politics,

and Postwork

Imaginaries

KATHI WEEKS

Duke University Press

Durham and London   2011

© 2011 Duke University Press

All rights reserved

Printed in the United States of America on acid-free paper ∞

Designed by Heather Hensley

Typeset in Minion Pro by Keystone Typesetting, Inc.

Library of Congress Cataloging-in-Publication Data appear on
the last printed page of this book.

THIS BOOK IS DEDICATED WITH LOVE TO

Julie Walwick (1959–2010)

Contents

Acknowledgments

I would like to thank the following friends and colleagues for their helpful feedback on versions of these arguments and portions of the manuscript: Anne Allison, Courtney Berger, Tina Campt, Christine DiStefano, Greg Grandin, Judith Grant, Michael Hardt, Stefano Harney, Rebecca Karl, Ranji Khanna, Corey Robin, Kathy Rudy, Karen Stuhldreher, and Robyn Wiegman. Thanks also go to Robert Adelman, Brittany Faulkner, Dennis Keenan, Marcie Patton, the Seattle FOJ, Julie Walwick, Cat Warren and David Auerbach, Diana Weeks, Lee Weeks, and Regan Weeks.

An earlier version of a portion of chapter 2 was published as "The Refusal of Work as Demand and Perspective," in *Resistance in Practice: The Philosophy of Antonio Negri* (Pluto Press, 2005), and a version of chapter 4 appeared as " 'Hours for What We Will': Work, Family, and the Movement for Shorter Hours," in *Feminist Studies* 35, no. 1 (Spring 2009) and is reprinted here with the permission of the publisher.

The Problem with Work

> Though women do not complain of the power of husbands,
> each complains of her own husband, or of the husbands of
> her friends. It is the same in all other cases of servitude, at
> least in the commencement of the emancipatory movement.
> The serfs did not at first complain of the power of their lords,
> but only of their tyranny.
>
> JOHN STUART MILL, *THE SUBJECTION OF WOMEN*

> One type of work, or one particular job, is contrasted with
> another type, experienced or imagined, within the present
> world of work; judgments are rarely made about the world
> of work as presently organized as against some other way
> of organizing it.
>
> C. WRIGHT MILLS, *WHITE COLLAR*

Why do we work so long and so hard? The mystery here is not that we are
required to work or that we are expected to devote so much time and
energy to its pursuit, but rather that there is not more active resistance to
this state of affairs. The problems with work today—my focus will be on
the United States—have to do with both its quantity and its quality and
are not limited to the travails of any one group. Those problems include
the low wages in most sectors of the economy; the unemployment,
underemployment, and precarious employment suffered by many workers; and the overwork that often characterizes even the most privileged
forms of employment—after all, even the best job is a problem when it
monopolizes so much of life. To be sure, if we were only resigned to such

conditions, there would be no puzzle. What is perplexing is less the acceptance of the present reality that one must work to live than the willingness to live for work. By the same token, it is easy to appreciate why work is held in such high esteem, but considerably less obvious why it seems to be valued more than other pastimes and practices.

That these questions are rarely posed within the field of political theory is also surprising. The lack of interest in representing the daily grind of work routines in various forms of popular culture is perhaps understandable,[1] as is the tendency among cultural critics to focus on the animation and meaningfulness of commodities rather than the eclipse of laboring activity that Marx identifies as the source of their fetishization (Marx 1976, 164–65). The preference for a level of abstraction that tends not to register either the qualitative dimensions or the hierarchical relations of work can also account for its relative neglect in the field of mainstream economics. But the lack of attention to the lived experience and political textures of work within political theory would seem to be another matter.[2] Indeed, political theorists tend to be more interested in our lives as citizens and noncitizens, legal subjects and bearers of rights, consumers and spectators, religious devotees and family members, than in our daily lives as workers.[3] And yet, to take a simple example, the amount of time alone that the average citizen is expected to devote to work—particularly when we include the time spent training, searching, and preparing for work, not to mention recovering from it—would suggest that the experience warrants more consideration. Work is crucial not only to those whose lives are centered around it, but also, in a society that expects people to work for wages, to those who are expelled or excluded from work and marginalized in relation to it. Perhaps more significantly, places of employment and spaces of work would seem to be supremely relevant to the very bread and butter of political science: as sites of decision making, they are structured by relations of power and authority; as hierarchical organizations, they raise issues of consent and obedience; as spaces of exclusion, they pose questions about membership and obligation. Although impersonal forces may compel us into work, once we enter the workplace we inevitably find ourselves enmeshed in the direct and personal relations of rulers and ruled. Indeed, the work site is where we often experience the most immediate, unambiguous, and tangible relations of power that most of us will encounter on a daily basis. As a fully political rather than a simply economic phenomenon, work would thus seem to be an especially rich object of inquiry.

There are at least two reasons for the inattention to work within political theory that bear mentioning. The first of these is what I will call the privatization of work. As the pair of epigraphs above suggest, we seem to have a hard time grasping the power relations of both work and family systematically; we often experience and imagine the employment relation—like the marriage relation—not as a social institution but as a unique relationship. Certainly this can be explained in part by the institution of private property that secures the privacy of the employment relation alongside the marriage relation. However, it should also be noted that this mode of privatizing work is not easily maintained: work has long occupied a somewhat vexed position in the private-public economy of liberalism. Thus, even though John Locke could establish the private character of work through both the natural right to property and its integration into the economy of the household, the state's role in defending property rights (and, since Locke's day, increasingly regulating and planning on property's behalf) threatens the status of work as a private relationship, exposing it, by the logic of Locke's scheme, to the purview of properly political power.[4] Work's place within the private-public division becomes even more troubled with the advent of industrialization; as work becomes identified with waged work and separated from the household, it could more easily seem—by comparison to that exemplary private sphere—relatively public. But there are additional mechanisms that secure what I am calling work's privatization. One is its reification: the fact that at present one must work to "earn a living" is taken as part of the natural order rather than as a social convention. Consequently, as C. Wright Mills observes (in one of the epigraphs above), we tend to focus more on the problems with this or that job, or on their absence, than on work as a requirement, work as a system, work as a way of life. Like the serfs who, as John Stuart Mill claims in the other epigraph, "did not at first complain of the power of their lords, but only of their tyranny" (1988, 84), we are better at attending to the problems with this or that boss than to the system that grants them such power. The effective privatization of work is also a function of the way the labor market individualizes work—never more so than today, with the enormous variety of tasks and schedules that characterize the contemporary employment relation. The workplace, like the household, is typically figured as a private space, the product of a series of individual contracts rather than a social structure, the province of human need and sphere of individual choice rather than a site for the exercise of political power. And because of this tethering of work to the figure of the individual, it is difficult to mount a critique of work that is not received as something wholly different: a criticism of workers. As a result of work's subordination to property rights, its reification, and its individualization, thinking about work as a social system—even with its arguably more tenuous private status—strangely becomes as difficult as it is for many to conceive marriage and the family in structural terms.

The second reason for the marginalization of work within political theory's configuration of the political could be attributed to the decline of work-based activism in the United States. In the absence of a worker's party, and with the fickle and sometimes conflicting class alignments within and between the two major parties, electoral politics has rarely served as an adequate vehicle for work-centered activism. The power of union-based politics has also been curtailed by the sharp decline of union membership in the period since the Second World War. Many activists today seem to assume that, besides party-line voting and institutionalized collective bargaining, our best chance for exerting collective power lies in our purchasing power. Ethical buying and the consumer boycott as ways to effect corporate decision making thus rise to the forefront of the political-economic imaginary. Of course, the logic that informs these models of consumer politics is the same one that enables corporations to make the case that low prices for ever more worthy consumer goods is an adequate trade-off for low wages, outsourcing, union busting, and government make-work programs. To the extent that unionization and consumer organizing continue to represent not only two obviously important means, but often the *only* avenues for imagining a politics of work, we are left with few possibilities for marshaling antiwork activism and inventing postwork alternatives.

What amounts in all these instances to a depoliticization of work is precisely what I want to think through and challenge in this contribution to the political theory of work. The brief chapter summaries at the end of this introduction will outline the book's specific points of focus and lines of argument. But first, I want to concentrate on presenting the project's major theoretical lineages and dominant conceptual frames, not to preview the analyses to come so much as to account for their inspiration and explain the kinds of claims and assumptions they presuppose. In terms of theoretical resources, although Max Weber, Jean Baudrillard, and Friedrich Nietzsche will each have a critical role to play at some point in the analysis, the project draws most heavily, albeit selectively, on the fields of feminist theory and Marxist theory, as this introductory discussion will illustrate. I should note, however, that it is not only political theory's disregard for the politics of work that poses obstacles for this endeavor; as we will see, both feminism's and Marxism's productivist tendencies—their sometimes explicit, sometimes tacit pro-work suppositions and commitments—present problems as well. There are, nonetheless, a number of exceptional cases or even whole subtraditions within each of these fields that have much to offer antiwork critiques and postwork imaginaries. But rather than organize this introductory discussion around a rehearsal of the project's more specific theoretical debts, I want to structure it instead in relation to a selection of its key concepts. The analysis begins with two concepts that orient the undertaking and give it direction: the work society and the work ethic. It then proceeds to a series of conceptual pairings—including work and labor, work and class, and freedom and equality—through which I hope to flesh out the text's central themes and further clarify my concerns and intentions. Let me start by articulating some of the reasons why I find the topic of work so theoretically interesting and politically pressing. The concept of the work society is my point of entry into that discussion.

THE WORK SOCIETY

The shift in perspective that I would like to see more political theorists pursue—from state and government to political economy, from cultural products to the sites and relations of their production, from public spaces and marketplaces to workplaces—is reminiscent of something Marx proposed in an oft-cited passage at the end of part two of the first volume of *Capital*. As a way to describe the buying and selling of that very "peculiar" commodity labor power, Marx presents the story of two free, self-interested individuals, each an owner of property and both equal under the law, who enter into an exchange of equivalents: one consents to give the use of his or her labor power for a limited period of time, and in return, the other agrees to pay the first a specific amount of money. But to see what happens after the employment contract is signed, the analysis must then move to a different location, the site where this special commodity will be "consumed" by putting the seller of it to work. "Let us therefore," Marx proposes,

> in company with the owner of money and the owner of labour-power, leave this noisy sphere, where everything takes place on the surface and in full view of everyone, and follow them into the hidden abode of production, on whose threshold there hangs the notice "No admittance except on business." Here we shall see, not only how capital produces, but how capital is itself produced. (1976, 279–80)

By altering the focus of the study in this way, Marx promises, "the secret of profit-making" will be exposed (280). By changing the site of the analysis from a market-based exchange to wage-based production, the labor-process itself—that is, the activity of labor and the social relations that shape, direct, and manage it—will be revealed as the locus of capitalist valorization.

So what are the benefits of this vantage point? What do we see when we shift our angle of vision from the market sphere of exchange to the privatized sphere of production? As the language about revealing secrets suggests, part of what Marx seeks to accomplish by descending into this "hidden abode" is to publicize the world of waged work, to expose it as neither natural precursor nor peripheral byproduct of capitalist production, but rather as its central mechanism (the wage) and lifeblood (work). With this shift in perspective, Marxian political economy recognizes waged labor as central to the capitalist mode of production and claims it as the standpoint from which capitalism's mysteries can be uncovered and its logics laid bare. This recognition of the significance of work remains, I argue, as relevant now as it was when Marx wrote, and it is this observation that my deployment of the category of the work society is intended, in part, to underscore.

Waged work remains today the centerpiece of late capitalist economic systems; it is, of course, the way most people acquire access to the necessities of food, clothing, and shelter. It is not only the primary mechanism by which income is distributed, it is also the basic means by which status is allocated, and by which most people gain access to healthcare and retirement. After the family, waged work is often the most important, if not sole, source of sociality for millions. Raising children with attributes that will secure them forms of employment that can match if not surpass the class standing of their parents is the gold standard of parenting. In addition, "making people capable of working is," as Nona Glazer notes, "the central goal of schooling, a criterion of successful medical and psychiatric treatment, and an ostensible goal of most welfare policies and unemployment compensation programs" (1993, 33). Helping to make people "work ready" and moving them into jobs are central objectives of social work (Macarov 1980, 12), a common rationale for the prison system, and an important inducement to perform military service. Indeed, enforcing work, as the other side of defending property rights, is a key function of the state (Seidman 1991, 315), and a particular preoccupation of the postwelfare, neoliberal state.

But making public the foundational role of work is only part of what Marx achieves with this change in venue. In descending from the sphere of the market—which he satirized as "a very Eden" of equal rights, individual freedom, and social harmony (1976, 280)—into the privatized spaces of work, Marx seeks not only to publicize but also to politicize the world of work. That is to say, the focus on the consumption of labor seeks to expose the social role of work and, at the same time, to pose it as a political problem. Despite Marx's insistence that waged work for those without other options is a system of "forced labor" (1964, 111), it remains for the most part an abstract mode of domination. In general, it is not the police or the threat of violence that force us to work, but rather a social system that ensures that working is the only way that most of us can meet our basic needs. In this way, as Moishe Postone notes, the specific mechanism by which goods and services are distributed in a capitalist society appears to be grounded not in social convention and political power but in human need (1996, 161). The social role of waged work has been so naturalized as to seem necessary and inevitable, something that might be tinkered with but never escaped. Thus Marx seeks both to clarify the economic, social, and political functions of work under capitalism and to problematize the specific ways in which such world-building practices are corralled into industrial forms and capitalist relations of work. This effort to make work at once public and political is, then, one way to counter the forces that would naturalize, privatize, individualize, ontologize, and also, thereby, depoliticize it.

Work is, thus, not just an economic practice. Indeed, that every individual is required to work, that most are expected to work for wages or be supported by someone who does, is a social convention and disciplinary apparatus rather than an economic necessity. That every individual must not only do some work but more often a lifetime of work, that individuals must not only work but become workers, is not necessary to the production of social wealth. The fact is that this wealth is collectively not individually produced, despite the persistence of an older economic imaginary that links individual production directly to consumption.[5] Indeed, as Postone observes, "on a deep, systemic level, production is not for the sake of consumption" (1996, 184). The relationship may appear direct and incontrovertible, but it is in fact highly mediated: the goal of neither party in the work relation is consumption; one seeks surplus value, and the other income. The normative expectation of waged work as an individual responsibility has more to do with the socially mediating role of work than its strictly productive function (150). Work is the primary means by which individuals are integrated not only into the economic system, but also into social, political, and familial modes of cooperation. That individuals should work is fundamental to the basic social contract; indeed, working is part of what is supposed to transform subjects into the independent individuals of the liberal imaginary, and for that reason, is treated as a basic obligation of citizenship. (The fact that the economy's health is dependent on a permanent margin of unemployment is only one of the more notorious problems with this convention.) Dreams of individual accomplishment and desires to contribute to the common good become firmly attached to waged work, where they can be hijacked to rather different ends: to produce neither individual riches nor social wealth, but privately appropriated surplus value. The category of the work society is meant to signify not only the centrality of work, but also its broad field of social relevance (see, for example, Beck 2000).

GENDER AT WORK

Another way to get at the extra-economic role of work that the concept of the work society is intended to evoke is through a further consideration of work's subjectification function, alluded to above. Work produces not just economic goods and services but also social and political subjects. In other words, the wage relation generates not just income and capital, but disciplined individuals, governable subjects, worthy citizens, and responsible family members. Indeed, given its centrality both to individuals' lives and to the social imaginary, work constitutes a particularly important site of interpellation into a range of subjectivities. It is, for example, a key site of becoming classed; the workplace is where, as Marx describes it, the seller of labor power who we are invited to follow into the hidden abode of production "becomes in actuality what previously he only was potentially, namely labour-power in action, a worker" (1976, 283). Class identities and relations are made and remade as some people are excluded from and others conscripted into work, by means of educational tracks and workplace training regimens, through the organization of labor processes and the interactions they structure, via the setting of wage levels, and in relation to judgments about occupational status. This process of subjectification is perhaps best understood in terms of a model not of passive construction but of active recruitment, often less a matter of command and obedience than one of inducement and attraction (West and Zimmerman 1991, 27–29). Along these lines, one can observe that some of the attractions of different forms of work are about joining a relatively advantaged class: becoming a member of the working class rather than the underclass, a middle-class rather than a working-class person, a salaried versus an hourly worker, a professional with a career as opposed to a working stiff and job holder. As a way to build on these logics a little further, let us turn to another dimension of this process of subject making and doing and consider work as a site of gendering.

To say that work is organized by gender is to observe that it is a site where, at a minimum, we can find gender enforced, performed, and re-created. Workplaces are often structured in relation to gendered norms and expectations. Waged work and unwaged work alike continue to be structured by the productivity of gender-differentiated labor, including the gender division of both household roles and waged occupations. But the gendering of work is not just a matter of these institutionalized tendencies to distinguish various forms of men's work and women's work, but a consequence of the ways that workers are often expected to do gender at work. Gender is put to work when, for example, workers draw upon gendered codes and scripts as a way to negotiate relationships with bosses and co-workers, to personalize impersonal interactions, or to communicate courtesy, care, professionalism, or authority to clients, students, patients, or customers. And this is, of course, not limited to waged forms of work. As Sarah Fenstermaker Berk argues, unwaged domestic work too should be recognized for producing not just goods and services, but gender as well (1985, 201). As a result of these activities, work plays a significant role in both the production and reproduction of gendered identities and hierarchies: gender is re-created along with value.

As in the example of class identities noted earlier, gender identities are coordinated with work identities in ways that can sometimes alienate workers from their job and other times bind them more tightly to it. Whether it is the women informatics workers whose pink-collar status and dress code is, Carla Freeman argues, at once a disciplinary mechanism and a source of individual expression (2000, 2), or the specific model of blue-collar masculinity that made industrial work attractive to the working-class boys of Paul Willis's famous study (1977, 150), this gendering of labor—doing men's work or women's work, doing masculinity or femininity as part of doing the job—can also be a source of pleasure in work and serve to promote workers' identification with and investments in the job. This can extend to unwaged forms of labor too; consider, for example, the ways in which conforming to a gender division of household labor might be for some people welcome confirmations of gender and sexual identities and relations. "What is produced and reproduced," in the case of one such example, is thus "not merely the activity and artifact of domestic life, but the material embodiment of wifely and husbandly roles and, derivatively, of womanly and manly conduct" (West and Zimmerman 1991, 30). Sometimes doing gender might be treated as part of doing the job; at other times doing the job is part of what it means to do gender. As Robin Leidner observes in her study of routinized interactive service work, the "degree to which workers accept the identity implied by a job is therefore determined in part by the degree to which they can interpret the job as expressing their gender in a satisfying way" (1993, 194).

But there is more to this story. For an employee, it is not merely a matter of bringing one's gendered self to work but of becoming gendered in and through work. For an employer, it is not just a matter of hiring masculine and feminine workers and putting them to work, but of actively managing workers' gendered identities and relationships. Exploitable subjects are not just found; they are, as Michael Burawoy famously argues, made at the point of production (1979). Even at the level of specific workplaces, individual managers can to some degree fashion the exploitable subjects, including the specific kind of feminized or masculinized subjects they imagine that they have already hired (Salzinger

2003, 20–21). Of course, it is difficult to predict whether various jobs will be segregated by gender in this way, whether they will be considered suitable men's work or women's work, and which particular models of gender such workers will be expected to conform to. In the fast-food franchise that Leidner studied, cooking was understood by managers and workers alike as men's work when it could have just as easily been coded as a feminized activity. Though it is not always easy to foresee if jobs will become gendered—or, if so, which jobs will be treated as more or less appropriate for which specific ideal of gendered comportment— the occupational segregation that is part and parcel of the gender division of labor stands nonetheless as supposed empirical proof of the necessity of gender difference and hierarchy. Thus, as Leidner notes, "the considerable flexibility of notions of proper gender enactment does not undermine the appearance of inevitability and naturalness that continues to support the division of labor by gender" (1993, 196). In her study of gendered labor in the maquiladoras, Leslie Salzinger argues that it is precisely the combination of rigid gender categories with the malleability and variability of their enactments and meaning that explains the resilience of gender as a principle of human differentiation (2003, 25). In this sense, ironically, the tremendous plasticity of gender reinforces rather than undermines its naturalization.

WORK VALUES

The category of the work society refers not just to the socially mediating and subjectively constitutive roles of work but to the dominance of its values. Challenging the present organization of work requires not only that we confront its reification and depoliticization but also its normativity and moralization. Work is not just defended on grounds of economic necessity and social duty; it is widely understood as an individual moral practice and collective ethical obligation. Traditional work values—those that preach the moral value and dignity of waged work and privilege such work as an essential source of individual growth, self-fulfillment, social recognition, and status—continue to be effective in encouraging and rationalizing the long hours US workers are supposed to dedicate to waged work and the identities they are expected to invest there. This normalizing and moralizing ethic of work should be very familiar to most of us; it is, after all, routinely espoused in managerial discourse, defended in the popular media, and enshrined in public policies. The ethic's productivist values are promoted on both the political Right and Left, from employers seeking the most able and tractable workers, and politicians intent on moving women from welfare to waged work, to parents and educators eager to prepare their children or students to embrace the values that might best ensure their future economic security and social achievement.

Let me be clear: to call these traditional work values into question is not to claim that work is without value. It is not to deny the necessity of productive activity or to dismiss the likelihood that, as William Morris describes it, there might be for all living things "a pleasure in the exercise of their energies" (1999, 129). It is, rather, to insist that there are other ways to organize and distribute that activity and to remind us that it is also possible to be creative outside the boundaries of work. It is to suggest that there might be a variety of ways to experience the pleasure that we may now find in work, as well as other pleasures that we may wish to discover, cultivate, and enjoy. And it is to remind us that the willingness to live for and through work renders subjects supremely functional for capitalist purposes. But before the work society can be publicized and raised as a political problem, we need to understand the forces—including the work ethic—that promote our acceptance of and powerful identification with work and help to make it such a potent object of desire and privileged field of aspiration.

Feminism has its own tendencies toward the mystification and moralization of work and has reproduced its own version of this famed ethic. Consider two of the dominant feminist remedies for the gender divisions and hierarchies of waged and unwaged work. One strategy, popular with at least some feminists of both the first and second waves, is to more or less accept the lesser value accorded to unwaged domestic labor and seek to secure women's equal access to waged work. Waged work would be women's ticket out of culturally mandated domesticity. While recognizing the importance of the ongoing struggle to secure equal employment opportunities for women, I want to argue that subjecting feminism's own idealization of waged work to critical scrutiny remains an important task as well. Confronting the present organization of waged labor and its values is especially urgent in the wake of the 1996 welfare reform debate and resulting legislation. Certainly the attack on poor women that was perpetrated in the name of the work ethic should inspire the reconsideration and reinvention of feminist perspectives on waged work —its ever-shifting realities and its long-standing values.

A second feminist strategy concentrates on efforts to revalue unwaged forms of household-based labor, from housework to caring work. Certainly making this socially necessary labor visible, valued, and equitably distributed remains a vital feminist project as well. The problem with both of these strategies—one focused on gaining women's entry into all forms of waged work and the other committed to gaining social recognition of, and men's equal responsibility for, unwaged domestic work—is their failure to challenge the dominant legitimating discourse of work. On the contrary, each approach tends to draw upon the language and sentiments of the traditional work ethic to win support for its claims about the essential dignity and special value of women's waged or unwaged labor.[6] How might feminism contest the marginalization and underestimation of unwaged forms of reproductive labor, without trading on the work ethic's mythologies of work? Feminists, I suggest, should focus on the demands not simply or exclusively for more work and better work, but also for less work; we should focus not only on revaluing feminized forms of unwaged labor but also challenge the sanctification of such work that can accompany or be enabled by these efforts.

The question is, then, how to struggle against both labor's misrecognition and devaluation on the one hand, and its metaphysics and moralism on the other hand. The refusal of work, a concept drawn from the autonomous Marxist tradition, will help to focus the analysis on the question of work's meaning and value. In contrast to some other types of Marxism that confine their critique of capitalism to the exploitation and alienation of work without attending to its overvaluation, this tradition offers a more expansive model of critique that seeks to interrogate at once capitalist production and capitalist (as well as socialist) productivism. From the perspective of the refusal of work, the problem with work cannot be reduced to the extraction of surplus value or the degradation of skill, but extends to the ways that work dominates our lives. The struggle against work is a matter of securing not only better work, but also the time and money necessary to have a life outside work. Although there are a number of important analyses of the most exploited forms of waged and unwaged work performed by workers both in the United States and beyond its borders, the larger systems of labor and especially the values that help sustain them are often insufficiently theorized, leaving one to conclude that all of our work-related goals would be met and the dominant work values justified if only such work were to resemble more closely the employment conditions at the middle and upper reaches of the labor hierarchy. The theory and practice of the refusal of work insists that the problem is not just that work cannot live up to the ethic's idealized image, that it neither exhibits the virtues nor delivers the meaning that the ethic promises us in exchange for a lifetime of work, but perhaps also the ideal itself.

WORK AND LABOR

Earlier I noted the difference between thinking systematically about work and thinking about this or that job. As a way to further clarify my concerns and intentions, I turn here to another distinction—the first of three additional conceptual pairs that I want to explore—that between work and labor. Although the division that I want to register between these categories is not a terminological one, I want to begin the discussion with a brief clarification about my use of the first term. In this book, the label "work" will refer to productive cooperation organized around, but not necessarily confined to, the privileged model of waged labor. What counts as work, which forms of productive activity will be included and how each will be valued, are a matter of historical dispute. Certainly the questions of whether or not various forms of productive activity—including some unwaged forms—will be recognized as work and at what rate they will be compensated have long been at the forefront of class, race, and gender struggles in and beyond the United States.

Which brings me to the relationship between work and labor: for the purposes of this project, I will use the terms interchangeably, thereby running roughshod over a distinction that is frequently, though inconsistently and variably, posed. For Hannah Arendt, to cite one notable theorist, the distinction between labor as the activity that reproduces biological life and work as the creation of an object world serves, among other things, to establish by way of comparison the singularity of a third category, action, as the definitively political activity of being in common (1958). Within the Marxist tradition, by contrast, it is perhaps more often labor—or, specifically, living labor—that figures as the more expansive category and valued practice. Conceived as a collective and creative human capacity harnessed by capital to the production of surplus value, living labor can yield both a critical standpoint from which the alienating and exploitative conditions of modern work can be critically interrogated and a utopian potential that can inform speculations about the revolutionary transformation of those conditions. By this account, the human capacity for labor may be hobbled by the organization of waged work, but as a collective creative potential, can also exceed them.

As far as the classic Arendtian approach to the categories is concerned, the distance it places between both labor and work on the one hand, and the legitimate business of the political on the other hand, renders it less useful for my purposes. As for the example from the Marxist tradition, while I recognize the power of the distinction it poses, I find it ill-suited to a critique that takes aim at both the structures of work and its dominant values. The trouble with the category of living labor deployed in this way as an alternative to work is, as I see it, that it is haunted by the very same essentialized conception of work and inflated notion of its meaning that should be called into question. To the extent that it is imbued in this way with the productivist values I want to problematize, it can neither provide the critical leverage necessary to interrogate the dominant ethic of work nor generate an alternative mode of valuation—a vision of the work society not perfected but overcome.[7] Consistent in this respect with Postone's antiproductivist Marxism, the ensuing analysis intends not to advance a "critique of capitalism *from the standpoint of* labor," but to pursue a "critique *of* labor in capitalism" (1996, 5). My refusal to distinguish between work and labor is thus a wager of sorts: by blocking access to a vision of unalienated and unexploited work in the guise of living labor, one that could live up to the work ethic's ideals about labor's necessity and virtues and would be worthy of the extravagant praise the ethic bestows, I hope to concentrate and amplify the critique of work as well as to inspire what I hope will be a more radical imagination of postwork futures.

In place of the opposition between labor and work, I will employ a number of other distinctions over the course of the argument to secure some critical insight into particular dimensions of work and to imagine other possibilities. These will include the distinction between work time and non-work time, between work and life, between time for what we are obligated to do and time for "what we will," or—to mark differences at yet another level of abstraction—between the category of antiwork used to signal the deconstructive moment of this critique of the work society, and the concept of postwork offered as a place holder for something yet to come.

WORK AND CLASS

Whereas the distinction between work and labor will be suspended for the purposes of this analysis, the relationship between work and class is a link I want to maintain, if only obliquely. Class is, of course, a central category of Marxist political economy, as Marx makes clear in what follows the passage from *Capital* cited above. Consider the first thing we see when we accompany the two owners of property—in one case, money; in the other, labor power—as they descend from the Eden of market exchange where they meet to trade equivalents into the hidden abode of production where one party is set to work. "When we leave this sphere of simple circulation or the exchange of commodities," Marx writes, "a certain change takes place, or so it appears, in the physiognomy of our *dramatis personae*. He who was previously the money-owner now strides out in front as a capitalist; the possessor of labour-power follows as his worker" (1976, 280). Where we had observed two equal individuals, each in possession of a commodity, who agree to make an exchange for the benefit of each, now we witness the inequality that separates the one who steps in front from the one who follows behind; with this shift of the locus of perception from the marketplace to the workplace, the existence of a social hierarchy based on class comes into sharp focus.

Despite the centrality of class in traditional Marxist analysis, work remains my privileged object of study and preferred terrain of political struggle. So let me say something about the relationship between work and class and what might be at stake in different formulations of its terms. There are at least two ways to approach the relationship between the categories: one draws a rather sharp distinction between them, whereas the other finds overlapping concerns. I will start with the first. The difference between the concepts is perhaps most starkly posed when work understood as a process is compared to class conceived in terms of an outcome—that is, as a category (whether explained by reference to ownership, wealth, income, occupation, or forms of belonging) designed to map patterns of economic inequality. To the extent that class is defined and measured in this way, as an outcome rather than an activity, then its utility for my purposes will be limited.

I am, of course, not the first to raise such concerns about this approach to the category of class. For example, the potential shortcomings of the concept have long been debated within Marxist feminism. The original "woman question" was, after all, generated by the disjuncture between the categories of gender and class, and the question this posed for the relationship between feminism and class struggle. But the trouble with class for second-wave feminists was not just that it might be inadequate to broader, extra-economic fields of analysis; the problem was that to the extent that class was conceived—as it typically was—as a gender- and race-blind category, its ability to register the contours of even narrowly economic hierarchies was limited as well. For some of the same reasons that I want to foreground the category of work over that of class, Iris Young once argued in favor of substituting the Marxist category of division of labor for class as a primary analytic of Marxist feminism. In this classic contribution to second-wave Marxist feminism, Young describes at least two advantages of this methodological shift. First, the division of labor has at once a broader reach than class and allows a more differentiated application. Not only can it be used to register multiple divisions of labor by class as well as by gender, race, and nation, but it can, as Young explains, also expose "specific cleavages and contradictions *within a class*" (1981, 51; emphasis added)—not just along the lines of gender, race, and nation, but also, potentially, of occupation and income. Thus the category of the gender division of labor, for example, enables a focus on gendered patterns of work "without assuming that all women in general or all women in a particular society have a common and unified situation" (55). Like the division of labor, the category of work seems to me at once more capacious and more finely tuned than the category of class. After all, work, including its absence, is both important to and differently experienced within and across lines of class, gender, race, and nation. In this sense, the politics of and against work has the potential to expand the terrain of class struggle to include actors well beyond that classic figure of traditional class politics, the industrial proletariat.

Consider too the second advantage noted by Young: "The category of division of labor can not only refer to a set of phenomena broader than that of class, but also more concrete." Unlike class, by her account, the division of labor "refers specifically to the *activity* of labor itself, and the specific social and institutional relations of that activity," proceeding thus "at the more concrete level of particular relations of interaction and interdependence in a society" (51). By this measure, whereas class addresses the outcome of laboring activity, the division of labor points toward the activity itself. Here too there are similarities between Young's interest in the category of division of labor and my focus on work: after all, work, including the dearth of it, is the way that capitalist valorization bears most directly and most intensively on more and more people's lives. This politics of work could be conceived as a way to link the everyday and sometimes every-night experiences of work—its spaces, relations and temporalities; its physical, affective, and cognitive practices; its pains and pleasures—to the political problematic of their present modes and codes of organization and relations of rule.[8] Although the category of class remains analytically powerful, I would argue that its political utility is more negligible. The problem is that while the oppositional class category of the industrial period—the "working class"—may accurately describe most people's relation to waged labor even in a postindustrial economy, it is increasingly less likely to match their selfdescriptions. The category of the middle class has absorbed so many of our subjective investments that it is difficult to see how the working class can serve as a viable rallying point in the United States today. A politics of work, on the other hand, takes aim at an activity rather than an identity, and a central component of daily life rather than an outcome. Once again, the struggle over work in this respect has the potential to open a more expansive terrain than that of traditional class politics, insofar as the problem of work carries the potential to resonate, albeit in very different ways, across a number of income, occupational, and identity groups.

The advantages of work over class extend beyond its breadth and tangibility. Crucial for Marx in his own privileging of labor as the point of entry into the materialist analysis of capitalist society—rather than beginning, for example, with political inequality or poverty—is the relationship between labor and agency that he assumes to be fundamental to anticapitalist politics. Thus in the *German Ideology*, Marx and Engels distinguish their materialist methodology not only from the idealism of the Young Hegelians but also from Feuerbach's "ahistorical" brand of materialism that may have recognized, to borrow another of Marx and Engels's formulations, "that circumstances make men" but not necessarily that "men make circumstances" (1970, 59). Materialism, as Marx and Engels understand it, is a matter not merely of the social construction of subjects but a matter of creative activity, of doing and making, the ontological trajectories of which are equally synchronic and diachronic. By focusing on laboring practices, or "living sensuous *activity*" (64), materialism as Marx and Engels conceive it is a matter not merely of the social construction of subjects but of creative activity, the capacity not only to make commodities but to remake a world. In this way, the focus on laboring practices, on the labor process and the relations of labor, can register the workers' power to act, in contrast, it seems to me, to their relative disempowerment that is registered in the economic outcomes the categories of class are often used to map and measure.[9]

So by at least one way of reckoning, class and work belong to different fields of analysis, and my project pursues the critical study of work instead of class analysis and antiwork politics as a substitute for class struggle. But there is another way to approach class that does not produce such a sharp contrast with the category of work and that yields a different and, I think, more compelling approach to this territory. The distinction between the two fields of analysis becomes rather less clear when class too is conceived in terms of a process rather than an outcome. Process notions of class disrupt the functionalism of static mappings of class formations by attending to the practices by and relations within which they are secured, re-created, and challenged.[10] If class is figured as a process of becoming classed, it may be that work—including struggles over what counts as work—could be conceived as a useful lens through which to approach class; in this way, the struggle against work could be a terrain of class politics.

But let me add one caveat: rather than conceiving class groupings and relations as the ground of antiwork politics, as that which provides its fuel and organizational form, it might be better to think of them as what might emerge from these efforts. By this reading, class formation, or what the autonomist tradition calls class composition, is best conceived as an outcome of struggles rather than their cause. The particular composition of the working class that might emerge from this politics of work—that is, the collectivities that might coalesce around its issues and the divisions that might develop in the interstices of antiwork struggles and in relation to postwork imaginaries—remains an open question. To the extent that the concerns it raises carry the potential to cut across traditional class divisions, a politics against work might serve to de-constitute the field of working-class politics and reconstitute it in a different, perhaps more expansive, way.

So in the end, I am not saying that we should stop thinking about class, but rather that focusing on work is one politically promising way of approaching class—because it is so expansive, because it is such a significant part of everyday life, because it is something we do rather than a category to which we are assigned, and because for all these reasons it can be raised as a political issue. By this account, work is a point of entry into the field of class analysis through which we might be better able to make class processes more visible, legible, and broadly relevant and, in the process, perhaps provoke class formations yet to come.

FREEDOM AND EQUALITY

Whereas my analysis ignores the difference between work and labor and, in the end, defers the question of the precise relationship between work and class, it presumes the significance of another distinction, the one between freedom and equality. To get a sense of how this pair of concepts is conceived for the purposes of this project, let us return yet again to Marx's description of what we see when we descend with the owners of money and labor power from the realm of market exchange to the realm of production. To recall our earlier discussion of the passage, accompanying the change of venue is a visible change in the physiognomy of the dramatis personae: we see the money owner stride out in front as capitalist, while the possessor of labor power follows behind as worker. "The one," Marx continues, "smirks self-importantly and is intent on business; the other is timid and holds back, like someone who has brought his own hide to market and now has nothing else to expect but—a hiding" (1976, 280; translation modified). Whereas we had, as noted above, witnessed the formal equivalence of contractors in the labor market, in the realm of work we discover hierarchy. As the conclusion of the passage suggests, however, it is not only inequality that is revealed, with the capitalist striding in front and the worker following behind, but subordination, with the former smirking and self-important and the latter timid and holding back. In other words, the critical analysis of work reveals not only exploitation but—as the reference to the violence of a hiding serves to amplify—domination.[11]

The domination and subordination experienced at work is not merely incidental to processes of exploitation. Carole Pateman's analysis of the employment contract is illuminating on this point. By her account, the problem with the labor contract is not just a function of the coerced entry that is ensured by the absence of viable alternatives to waged labor, nor is it only a matter of the inequality that is produced as the result of the contract's terms. To translate this into a Marxist vocabulary, the problem can be reduced neither to forced labor nor to exploitation. Rather, we need to pay more attention to the relationship of dominance and submission that is authorized by the waged labor contract and that shapes labor's exercise. Exploitation is possible, Pateman notes, because "the employment contract creates the capitalist as master; he has the political right to determine how the labour of the worker will be used" (1988, 149). This relation of command and obedience, the right of the employer to direct his or her employees that is granted by the contract, is not so much a byproduct of exploitation as its very precondition.

Marx too would seem to be quite clear that the problem with work cannot be reduced to the terms of its recompense, but rather extends into the very heart of the wage relation and the labor process it commands. That is why he insists on describing the program of raising wages as only "*better payment for the slave*" (1964, 118). To focus narrowly on outcomes rather than processes, and on inequality and not also on unfreedom, is to impoverish the critique of capitalism. Marx muses about a comparably inadequate approach in "Critique of the Gotha Program": "It is as if, among slaves who have at last got behind the secret of slavery and broken out in rebellion, a slave still in thrall to obsolete notions were to inscribe on the programme of the rebellion: Slavery must be abolished because the feeding of slaves in the system of slavery cannot exceed a certain low maximum!" (1978, 535).

I am thus interested in adding to the critique of the exploitative and alienating dimensions of work a focus on its political relations of power and authority, as relations of rulers and ruled. My inspiration for this, it should be noted, is not only these readings of Marx, but certain strands of 1970s feminism. A commitment to freedom in conjunction with or beyond equality was what distinguished the more radical sectors of the early second wave of US feminism from liberal feminists of the time. Refusing to honor the "do not enter" sign on the door leading to the so-called private terrains of the family, marriage, and sexuality—a sign meant to ban political judgment of relations that were thought to be governed only by the exigencies of nature or prerogatives of individual choice—the radical elements of the movement sought not women's assimilation into the status quo but a sweeping transformation of everyday life.[12] The goal was not, to use the vocabulary of the day, women's mere equality with men, but women's liberation. What precisely they were to be liberated from and to were, of course, matters of lively debate, but the language of liberation and the project of conceiving a state of freedom beyond equality did serve to open a broader horizon of feminist imagination and indicate new agendas for action.

In addition to 1970s women's liberation, about which I will have more to say below, another resource for this project comes from recent work in political theory that affirms freedom as an important feminist goal. The work of Wendy Brown and Linda Zerilli is particularly valuable for its efforts to take up "the project of feminism in a freedom-centered frame" (Zerilli 2005, 95). Freedom is understood in these accounts beyond the liberal model of an individual possession, something that emanates from the sovereign will and guards its independence such that, to quote a familiar formulation, "over himself, over his own body and mind, the individual is sovereign" (Mill 1986, 16). Instead, freedom is seen as a practice, not a possession, a process rather than a goal. Whether it is drawn from the simultaneously creative and destructive qualities of the will to power in Brown's Nietzschean analysis, or from the inaugural and disordering capacities of human action in Zerilli's Arendtian account, freedom emerges in these texts as a double-sided phenomenon. It is depicted, on the one hand, as an antidisciplinary practice—that is, to use Brown's formulation, as "a permanent struggle against what will otherwise be done to and for us" (1995, 25). But there is more to it: freedom is also a creative practice, what Zerilli describes as a collective practice of world building and Brown characterizes in terms of a desire "to participate in shaping the conditions and terms of life," a longing "to generate futures together rather than navigate or survive them" (1995, 4). Freedom thus depends on collective action rather than individual will, and this is what makes it political. Though freedom is, by this account, a relational practice, it is not a zero-sum game in which the more one has, the less another can enjoy. Freedom considered as a matter of individual self-determination or self-sovereignty is reduced to a solipsistic phenomenon. Rather, as a world-building practice, freedom is a social—and hence necessarily political—endeavor. It is, as Marx might put it, a species-being rather than an individual capacity; or, as Zerilli contends, drawing on an Arendtian formulation, freedom requires plurality (2005, 20). Thus Arendt provocatively declares: "If men wish to be free, it is precisely sovereignty they must renounce" (1961, 165). Freedom in this sense demands not the absence of power but its democratization.

Although political theorists like Brown and Zerilli are helpful in elaborating a notion of freedom that can serve as a central analytic and principle of political aspiration, political theory in general, as noted above, has not attended sufficiently to work. Work has been relatively neglected not only as a practice productive of hierarchies—a scene of gendering, racialization, and becoming classed—but as an arena in which to develop and pursue a freedom-centered politics. Yet at the same time, as Michael Denning reminds us, "the workplace remains the fundamental *unfree* association of civil society" (2004, 224). It is the site of many of the most palpable and persistent relations of domination and subordination that people confront, even if these are not conventionally perceived as potentially alterable enough to be regarded as properly political matters. If, as I maintain, a political theory of work should address the problem of freedom, a political theory of freedom should also focus on work. My interest, then, is in developing a feminist political theory of work that could pose work itself—its structures and its ethics, its practices and relations—not only as a machine for the generation of inequalities, but as a political problem of freedom.[13] Linking the previous distinction between class and work to this conceptual pair might help to clarify my concerns in this respect. Rather than a politics of class focused primarily on issues of economic redistribution and economic justice—particularly a politics that seeks to alter wage levels to redraw the map of class categories—the politics of work I am interested in pursuing also investigates questions about the command and control over the spaces and times of life, and seeks the freedom to participate in shaping the terms of what collectively we can do and what together we might become. If what I am calling a "politics of class outcomes" lodges its central complaint against the inequalities of capitalist society, the politics of work that I would like to see elaborated would also levy a critique at its unfreedoms.[14]

MARXIST FEMINISM REDUX

Although I draw on a variety of sources, the version of 1970s feminism that has been of particular importance to this effort to theorize work in these terms is Anglo-American Marxist feminism.[15] As an attempt to map capitalist political economies and gender regimes from a simultaneously anticapitalist and feminist perspective, the tradition in its heyday was committed to investigating how various gendered laboring practices are both put to use by, and potentially disruptive of, capitalist and patriarchal social formations.[16] Three focuses of this literature are especially relevant to my interests here: publicizing work, politicizing it, and radically transforming it. However, the efforts in all three of these areas require some prodding and pushing if they are to be of use to this project in this moment. The category of the refusal of work introduced above will be used to do some of this prodding and pushing, serving as a tool with which to reconfigure each of these focuses by providing certain correctives and additions.

The Marxist—or, as some prefer to call it, socialist feminist—tradition is an inspiration for this project first and foremost because of its focus on labor, both as a point of entry into the critical analysis of capitalist patriarchy and as a key site of political action. "Socialist feminism," as one analyst summarizes it, "means paying consistent attention to women *in our capacity as workers*, and in all our variety" (Froines 1992, 128). Perhaps its most significant contribution to the critical theory of work in the 1970s was the expansion of the category. Feminists insisted that the largely unwaged "reproductive" work that made waged "productive" work possible on a daily and generational basis was socially necessary labor, and that its relations were thus part and parcel of the capitalist mode of production. What had been coded as leisure was in fact work, and those supposedly spontaneous expressions of women's nature were indeed skillful practices. In their efforts to adapt Marxist concepts and methods to new concerns, these feminists usefully troubled the tradition's definition of work. Nancy Hartsock describes this by way of an addendum to Marx's story about the owner of money and the owner of labor power. To return to that passage one final time, if after descending with the capitalist and worker into the realm of waged work we were then to follow the worker home, into yet another hidden abode of production, we might observe another change in the dramatis personae:

> He who before followed behind as the worker, timid and holding back, with nothing to expect but a hiding, now strides in front, while a third person, not specifically present in Marx's account of the

transactions between capitalist and worker (both of whom are male) follows timidly behind, carrying groceries, baby, and diapers. (Hartsock 1983, 234)

By following the worker not only from marketplace to workplace, but also from the place of employment to the domestic space, we find evidence not only of class hierarchy, but of specifically gendered forms of exploitation and patterns of inequality. By descending into the even more hidden, even more fiercely privatized space of the household, we see men and women who may be formally equal under the law transformed through the gender division of labor into relatively privileged and penalized subjects. Thus, Marxist feminists in the 1970s explored the means by which gender hierarchies deliver unwaged women workers to the domestic mode of reproduction while also ensuring a cheaper and more flexible secondary or tertiary waged labor force. These feminists debated the exact value to capital of women's unwaged domestic labor and exposed the hyperexploitation of women wage earners around the globe. And they studied the interconnections among the family, the labor market, waged and unwaged labor processes, and the welfare state. As we will see, in fact, many of their insights into the conditions of women's labor under Fordism will prove to be more widely applicable to the forms of work typical of post-Fordist economies. By extending these efforts to publicize, politicize, and transform work into the field of domestic labor, feminists usefully complicated and upped the ante of all three projects. What might have at first appeared to be a simple addition to Marxist analyses has in fact required a vast rethinking of its concepts and models, its critical analyses and utopian visions.

Whereas many of these texts are helpful for their emphasis on work, the tradition's productivist tendencies, which it shares with some other versions of Marxist theory, prove more troublesome. As we have already noted, feminism has managed to reproduce its own version of the work ethic, whether in the process of defending waged work as the alternative to feminine domesticity in both liberal feminism and traditional Marxism, or through efforts to gain recognition for modes of unwaged labor as socially necessary labor. Feminism, including much of 1970s Marxist feminism, has tended to focus more on the critique of work's organization and distribution than on questioning its values. The autonomous Marxist tradition is thus useful in this instance insofar as it simultaneously centers its analytical apparatus on work and disavows its traditional ethics. Central to that tradition is not only the analytical primacy accorded to the imposition of work as fundamental to the capitalist mode of production, but also the political priority of the refusal of work—a priority recorded in the call not for a liberation *of* work but a liberation *from* work (see Virno and Hardt 1996, 263). The refusal of work is at once a model of resistance, both to the modes of work that are currently imposed on us and to their ethical defense, and a struggle for a different relationship to work born from the collective autonomy that a postwork ethics and more nonwork time could help us to secure. As a simultaneous way to insist on work's significance and to contest its valuation, the Marxist feminist literature on wages for housework—with roots in an Italian feminism that was, as one participant observed, "characterized, with more emphasis than in other countries, by the *leitmotif* of 'work/rejection of work' " (Dalla Costa 1988, 24)—will be of particular importance to my project in this respect.

Thus work is not only a locus of unfreedom, it is also a site of resistance and contestation.[17] This brings me to the second element of the Marxist feminist literature that I have found instructive: the commitment to work's politicization. Marxist feminists focused not only on exploited workers but, to cite one of these authors, also on subjects that are "potentially revolutionary" (Eisenstein 1979, 8). Within this body of literature, one can find an attention both to structures of domination and to the possibilities for critical consciousness, subversive practices, and feminist standpoints that might be developed in their midst. This investment in constructing collective political subjects on the basis of, or in relation to, work practices, relations, and subjectivities remains for me an aspect of this literature with the most relevance to contemporary feminism. Harking back to the example of a Marxism that conceived the industrial proletariat as a revolutionary class less because it had nothing to lose but its chains than because it had the power to create a new world, many of these authors concentrate on the ways that feminized modes of labor—marginalized by, but nonetheless fundamental to, capitalist valorization processes—could provide points of critical leverage and sites of alternative possibility.

This more capacious understanding of work also entailed a transformation of what might be recognized as a terrain of anticapitalist politics, pushing beyond orthodox Marxism's industrial model of productive cooperation that centered on the factory, in which the proletariat was once imagined as the singularly revolutionary subject, to a more expansive set of sites and subjects. The focal point of analysis for this expanded political terrain might best be described as the contradiction between capital accumulation and social reproduction.[18] Capital requires, for example, time both to "consume" labor power and to produce (or reproduce) it, and the time devoted to one is sometimes lost to the other. The competing requirements of creating surplus value and sustaining the lives and socialities upon which it depends form a potential fault line through capitalist political economies, one that might serve to generate critical thinking and political action. Under the conditions of Fordism, for example, this meant that capital was dependent on a family-based model of social reproduction, one that was in some respects functional to its purposes but was in other ways a potential hindrance to its hegemony. Thus we find in a body of management literature and practice that spans the Fordist and post-Fordist periods an expressed need to locate and preserve some kind of balance between work and family—a relationship that many feminists, on the contrary, struggled to expose as a product of normative imposition rather than natural proclivity and a site of flagrant contradiction rather than mere imbalance.

But just as Marxist feminism's critical study of work was limited, at least for the purposes of this project, by its productivist propensities, so too the focus on locating and cultivating revolutionary possibilities in relation to work was sometimes compromised by a susceptibility to functionalist logics. The temptation of functionalism is, of course, not peculiar to feminist theory. Indeed, its presence at some level reflects a methodological and political choice: whether to concentrate on how social systems persist over time, or to highlight the ways that they can and do change. Foucault explains it this way: because of the instability and unpredictability generated by the "agonism" of power relations on the one hand and the "intransitivity of freedom" on the other hand, there is always the option "to decipher the same events and the same transformations either from inside the history of struggle or from the standpoint of the power relationships" (1983, 223, 226)—a pair of options between which his own work could be said to oscillate. This same methodological distinction marks a long-standing division within the Marxist tradition as well. Thus, for example, although they both offer systematic mappings of capitalist logics and social formations, Marx's *Grundrisse* approaches the analysis more from the point of view of crisis and conflict, whereas *Capital* tells the story from the perspective of capital's appropriative and recuperative capacities.

To return to the case of 1970s Marxist feminism, the residues of functionalist logics show up in what is, I would argue, a limited understanding of social reproduction. In fact, there are at least two related problems with the analyses from a contemporary perspective. First, whereas these authors arguably succeeded in developing more-complete accounts of the relationship between production and reproduction typical of Fordist political economies than were available elsewhere at the time, these accounts are no longer adequate to the project of mapping post-Fordism. In the classic texts from this period, production and reproduction were associated according to the logic of a dual-systems model with two different spaces: the waged workplace was the site of productive labor, and the household was the site of unwaged, reproductive labor. Reproductive labor in these accounts usually included the forms of unwaged work through which individuals met their daily needs for food, shelter, and care and raised a new generation to take their place.[19] However, under the conditions of postindustrial, post-Fordist, and post-Taylorist production, the always vexing exercise of distinguishing between production and reproduction—whether by sphere, task, or relationship to the wage—becomes even more difficult. The dual-systems model, always problematic, is thereby rendered even more deficient.

The second reason why the older models are no longer tenable brings us to the issue of their functionalism. Here is the problem: when reduced, as it tends to be in these analyses, to a familiar list of domestic labors, the category of social reproduction cannot pose the full measure of its conflict with the logics and processes of capital accumulation. The specific problems that this more limited notion of reproduction serves to highlight—the invisibility, devaluation, and gendered division of specifically domestic labors—could, for example, be responded to (but not, of course, remedied) through an expanded reliance on marketized versions of such services. As the refusal-of-work perspective suggests, the problem with the organization of social reproduction extends beyond the problems of this work's invisibility, devaluation, and gendering. Although I want to register that domestic labor is socially necessary and unequally distributed (insofar as gender, race, class, and nation often determines who will do more and less of it), I am also interested in moving beyond the claim that if it were to be fully recognized, adequately compensated, and equally divided, then the existing model of household-based reproduction would be rectified. A more expansive conception of social reproduction, coupled with the refusal of work, might be used to frame a more compelling problematic. What happens when social reproduction is understood as the production of the forms of social cooperation on which accumulation depends or, alternatively, as the rest of life beyond work that capital seeks continually to harness to its times, spaces, rhythms, purposes, and values? What I am in search of is a conception of social reproduction—of what it is we might organize around—that can pose the full measure of its antagonism with the exigencies of capital accumulation, a biopolitical model of social reproduction less readily transformed into new forms of work and thus less easily recuperated within the present terms of the work society.

The third aspect of the Marxist feminist tradition that I want to acknowledge here is its commitment to thinking within a horizon of utopian potential, that is, in relation to the possibility of fundamental transformation (Feminist Review Collective 1986, 8). Work is not only a site of exploitation, domination, and antagonism, but also where we might find the power to create alternatives on the basis of subordinated knowledges, resistant subjectivities, and emergent models of organization. At least some of this literature focuses on both antiwork politics and postwork imaginaries. This model of utopian politics that can "make the creation of prefigurative forms an explicit part of our movement against capitalism" and challenge the "politics of deferment" that would postpone such innovations to some distant future after "the revolution" is something that I think feminist theory should embrace (Rowbotham, Segal, and Wainwright 1979, 147, 140). The problem with these visions of radical social change from a contemporary perspective is that they were most often conceived of as variations on a theme named socialism, even if some called for "a new kind of socialism" or a socialist revolution that would be equally feminist and antiracist.[20] Today, however, it seems unlikely that socialism can serve as a persuasive signifier of a postcapitalist alternative. There are at least three kinds of problems with the term. At one level, there is the problem of the name itself: it has been some time since the language of socialism could resonate in the United States as a legible and generative utopian vocabulary (even though it continues to serve occasionally as a viable dystopia for the Right). But it is not just a matter of the label; it is about the content of the vision, which has traditionally centered on the equal liability to work together with a more equitable distribution of its rewards. As a certainly more just version of a social form that is nonetheless centered on work, it gestures toward a vision of the work society perfected, rather than transformed.

Beyond the obsolescence of the label and the commitment to work it affirms, there is a third problem with the legacy of socialism. Whereas the Marxist feminist—or, more specifically in this instance, the socialist feminist—tradition was willing to affirm the value of utopian speculation about a radically different future, the use of the label "socialism" often nonetheless seemed to assume that this future could be named and its basic contours predetermined. In this respect—here I anticipate an argument that I will develop in chapter 5—socialist feminists would seem "to know too much too soon." There are advantages, I claim, to more-partial visions of alternatives, fragments or glimpses of something different that do not presume to add up to a blueprint of an already named future with a preconceived content. I will use the label "postwork society" not to anticipate an alternative so much as to point toward a horizon of utopian possibility, as it seems preferable to hold the space of a different future open with the term "post" than to presume to be able to name it as "socialist."

In summary, my project can thus be said to begin with a historical tradition of Marxist feminism that often focused on the category of class, the ideal of equality, the problem of domestic labor, and the socialist struggle for more and better work, which I would like to redirect by way of the sometimes rather different commitments and imaginaries referenced by the categories of work, freedom, social reproduction, life, the refusal of work, and postwork. I will thus use work as a point of entry into the territory of class politics; freedom to supplement and redirect an anticapitalist political theory also committed to equality; the refusal of work to confront work's overvaluation; the field of social reproduction as part of a struggle to wrest more of life from the encroachments of work; and postwork utopianism to replace socialism as the horizon of revolutionary possibility and speculation.

CHAPTER OVERVIEWS

The questions raised and points of focus elaborated above are meant to set the stage for the specific arguments pursued in the remaining chapters. One way to approach the overall structure of the discussion that follows is to separate it into two parts: a first part, encompassing chapters 1 and 2, that concentrates on the diagnostic and deconstructive dimensions of the critical theory of work; and a second part, including chapters 3, 4, and 5, that focuses on the prescriptive and reconstructive aspects of the project. Whereas "refusal" is the animating category of the first part, "demand" anchors the analysis in the second part. The argument thus proceeds from the refusal of the present terms of the work society to demands for remedies and for the imagining of alternative futures.

As noted above, the work ethic is at the center of the political theory of and against work that I want to begin to elaborate. A critique of work that seeks to challenge its dominance over our lives must take on the ethical discourse that gives work its meaning and defends its primacy. The first two chapters seek to develop a critical account of the work ethic and to explore some of the theoretical resources through which it might be interrogated. Chapter 1 concentrates on the nature and function of the work ethic in the United States. In what may be a fitting departure for a text so often indebted to Marxist resources, the analysis in chapter 1 draws on one of that tradition's most famous critiques, Max Weber's *Protestant Ethic and the Spirit of Capitalism*. Tracing the continuities and shifts in the work ethic over the course of its different incarnations—first as a Protestant ethic, and later as an industrial and then a postindustrial ethic—the analysis seeks to map the recent history of the work ethic and to raise questions about its future. Today when neoliberal and post-neoliberal regimes demand that almost everyone work for wages (never mind that there is not enough work to go around), when postindustrial production employs workers' minds and hearts as well as their hands, and when post-Taylorist labor processes increasingly require the self-management of subjectivity so that attitudes and affective orientations to work will themselves produce value, the dominant ethical discourse of work may be more indispensable than it has ever been, and the refusal of its prescriptions even more timely. The analysis thus attempts to account not only for the ethic's longevity and power, but also its points of in-stability and vulnerability.

Chapter 2 explores some theoretical tools with which we might exploit some of these openings. Drawing on Jean Baudrillard's critique of productivism, the chapter explores the limitations of two familiar paradigms of Marxist theory, labeled here "socialist modernization" and "socialist humanism," and then concentrates on an explication of autonomist Marxism's theory and practice of the refusal of work. The critical review of the two earlier models presents an opportunity to confront the pro-work assumptions and values that remain stubbornly embedded within a number of theoretical frameworks, including some Marxist discourses, as well as instructive contrasts to the very different commitments animating the more recent example of autonomist Marxism. As a refusal not of creative or productive activity, but of the present configuration of the work society and its moralized conception of work, the refusal of work serves as a methodological center of gravity and ongoing inspiration for the models of analysis and speculation that occupy the subsequent chapters. The critical practice at the heart of the refusal of work, as I read it here, is at once deconstructive and reconstructive—or, as the autonomists might describe it, a practice of separation and process of self-valorization—an analysis that is committed at once to antiwork critique and postwork invention.

In keeping with this dual focus of the refusal of work, chapter 3 marks a shift in the project from the critical charge I just described to the task of constructing possible alternatives, from the development of an antiwork critique to the incitement of a postwork political imaginary. More specifically, the argument shifts at this point from a focus on the refusal of work and its ethics to the demands for a guaranteed basic income (chapter 3) and for a thirty-hour work week (chapter 4). The category of the utopian demand (a category I explore in more detail in chapter 5) is one of the ways I want to conceive the relationship between antiwork analysis and postwork desire, imagination, and will as they figure in the practice of political claims making. Utopian demands, including demands for basic income and shorter hours, are more than simple policy proposals; they include as well the perspectives and modes of being that inform, emerge from, and inevitably exceed the texts and practices by which they are promoted. Assessments of their value thus need to be attentive to the possibilities and limits of both their structural and discursive effects.

But first: why single out these demands? Certainly there are any number of demands for change worth exploring, proposals that could affect tangible improvements in the present conditions of work.[21] The demand for a living wage is an obvious example; across the United States, campaigns for living-wage reform have mobilized impressive levels of political activity and achieved significant victories. I focus on the demands for basic income and shorter hours for two reasons. First, like the demand for living wages and others, they represent important remedies for some of the problems with the existing system of wages and hours. A guaranteed and universal basic income would enhance the bargaining position of all workers vis-à-vis employers and enable some people to opt out of waged work without the stigma and precariousness of means-tested welfare programs. A thirty-hour full-time work week without a decrease in pay would help to address some of the problems of both the underemployed and the overworked. The second reason for focusing on these demands—which I think distinguishes them from many other demands for economic reform, including the demand for a living wage—is their capacity not only to improve the conditions of work but to challenge the terms of its dominance. These demands do not affirm our right to work so much as help us to secure some measure of freedom from it.[22] For the purposes of this project, I am interested in demands that would not only advance concrete reforms of work but would also raise broader questions about the place of work in our lives and spark the imagination of a life no longer so subordinate to it—demands that would serve as vectors rather than terminal points.[23]

Chapter 3 begins with a rereading of the 1970s movement for wages for housework, the most promising dimensions of which, I argue, have been poorly understood. This instance of Marxist feminist theory and practice is particularly relevant to this project because of its roots in the autonomist tradition and for its commitment to, and distinctive deployment of, the refusal of work. Building on some of this literature's unique analyses of the gendered political economy of work, its mode of struggle against the organization of domestic work, and its treatment of the feminist political practice of demanding, I go on to propose a rationale for a different demand: the demand for a guaranteed basic income. I argue that this demand can deliver on some of the potential of wages for housework while being more consistent with conditions in a post-Fordist political economy. Drawing on a framework gleaned from the wages for housework literature, the demand for basic income can do more than present a useful reform; it can serve both to open a critical perspective on the wage system and to provoke visions of a life not so dependent on the system's present terms and conditions.

This particular understanding of what a demand is and what it can do guides the analysis in chapter 4 of another demand, this one for shorter hours. The chapter explores the demand for a six-hour day with no decrease in pay as at once a demand for change and a perspective and provocation, at once a useful reform and a conceptual frame that could generate critical thinking and public debate about the structures and ethics of work. In contrast both to those who defend a reduction of hours at work in order to expand family time, and to those who fail in their articulation of the demand to address the intimate relationship between work and family, the case for shorter hours developed here focuses on expanding our freedom not only from capitalist command but also from imposed norms of sexuality and traditional standards of proper household composition and roles. Taking aim at, rather than appropriating, normative discourses of the family, the demand for shorter hours is conceived here as a demand for, among other benefits, more time to imagine, experiment with, and participate in the relationships of intimacy and sociality that we choose. This account thus understands the movement for shorter hours in terms of securing the time and space to confront and forge alternatives to the present structures and ethics of both work and family.

Whereas the demands for basic income and shorter hours usefully point in the direction of a critical politics against and beyond work, they could be easily dismissed as utopian. Chapter 5 investigates the case against utopia and, drawing on the work of Ernst Bloch and Friedrich Nietzsche, attempts a response. Rather than rehearse the arguments made in other chapters about why these demands are in fact realistic proposals, chapter 5 pursues another tack. Provisionally accepting the judgment that they are utopian, the discussion explores instead what a utopian demand is and what it might be able to do, arguing that only through a more complicated understanding of the utopian dimensions of these demands can we appreciate their efficacy. To establish the general credentials and specific possibilities and limitations of the demand as a utopian form, the analysis explores its relation to other, perhaps more familiar, utopian artifacts, including the traditional literary and philosophical utopia and the manifesto. The conception of the utopian demand that emerges from this account emphasizes not only its capacity to advance significant reforms, but also its potential as a critical perspective and force of provocation that can incite political desires for, imagination of, and mobilization toward different futures.

The brief epilogue attempts to both reflect on the previous arguments and address some topics that they neglected. I begin with two points of clarification. First, my preference for politics over ethics as the terrain of antiwork struggle and postwork speculation raises a question about the relationship between politics and ethics that the analysis presumes. Also meriting discussion is a second relationship, between the project's radical aspirations to remake a life outside of work and its comparatively moderate demands. This seeming incongruence between ambitious ends and modest means warrants an elaboration of the relationship between reform and revolution that informs the project. In the final section, I take another step back from the material to consider one way to bring the two demands together as part of a broader political effort to defend life against work, the colloquial version of which could be described as "getting a life." The rubric of life against work is, I propose, both capacious and pointed enough to frame a potent antiwork politics and fuel a postwork imagination.

In the epigraph above, C. Wright Mills laments the fact that we measure the satisfaction of jobs only against the standard of other jobs: "One type of work, or one particular job, is contrasted with another type, experienced or imagined, within the present world of work." That is to say, "judgments are rarely made about the world of work as presently organized as against some other way of organizing it" (1951, 229). I want to make a case for the importance of a political theory of work and specifically, a political theory that seeks to pose work as a political problem of freedom. Beyond any particular claim or category—beyond any of the specific arguments about the role of the work ethic in sustaining the structures and cultures of work, the legitimacy of basic income, the need for shorter hours, or the utility of utopian thought—the project is meant to raise some basic questions about the organization and meaning of work. The assumptions at the heart of the work ethic, not only about the virtues of hard work and long hours but also about their inevitability, are too rarely examined, let alone contested. What kinds of conceptual frameworks and political discourses might serve to generate new ways of thinking about the nature, value, and meaning of work relative to other practices and in relation to the rest of life? How might we expose the fundamental structures and dominant values of work—including its temporalities, socialities, hierarchies, and subjectivities—as pressing political phenomena? If why we work, where we work, with whom we work, what we do at work, and how long we work are social arrangements and hence properly political decisions, how might more of this territory be reclaimed as viable terrains of debate and struggle? The problem with work is not just that it monopolizes so much time and energy, but that it also dominates the social and political imaginaries. What might we name the variety of times and spaces outside waged work, and what might we wish to do with and in them? How might we conceive the content and parameters of our obligations to one another outside the currency of work? The argument that follows, then, is one attempt to assess theoretically and imagine how to confront politically the present organization of work and the discourses that support it.

CHAPTER 1

Mapping the Work Ethic

Let us, then, be up and doing,
With a heart for any fate;
Still achieving, still pursuing,
Learn to labor and to wait.

HENRY WADSWORTH LONGFELLOW, "A PSALM OF LIFE"

The idea of duty in one's calling prowls about in our lives
like the ghost of dead religious beliefs.

MAX WEBER, *THE PROTESTANT ETHIC AND THE
SPIRIT OF CAPITALISM*

There are two common answers to the question of why we work so long and so hard. First, and most obvious, we work because we must: while some of us may have a choice of where to work, in an economy predicated on waged work, few have the power to determine much about the specific terms of that employment, and fewer still the choice of whether or not to work at all. Whereas this first response focuses on necessity, the second emphasizes our willingness to work. According to this account, we work because we want to: work provides a variety of satisfactions—in addition to income, it can be a source of meaning, purpose, structure, social ties, and recognition. But while both explanations are undoubtedly important, they are also insufficient. Structural coercion alone cannot explain the relative dearth of conflict over the hours we are required to work or the identities we are often expected to invest there; individual consent cannot account for why work would be so much more appealing than other parts of life. No doubt our motives for devoting so much time and energy to work are multiple and shifting, typically involving a complex blend of coercion and choice, necessity and desire, habit and intention. But although the structure of the work society may make long hours of work necessary, we need a fuller accounting of how, why, and to what effect so many of us come to accept and inhabit this requirement. One of the forces that manufactures such consent is the official morality—that complex of shifting claims, ideals, and values—known as the work ethic.

This chapter develops a critical analysis of the work ethic in the United States. Max Weber's account of the Protestant work ethic will serve as an archeology of the ethic's logics and functions that will guide our brief explorations of two later—and comparably ideal typical—versions of the ethic: an industrial work ethic that dominated US society through the culmination of the Fordist period in the years following the Second World War, and a postindustrial work ethic that has accompanied the transition to post-Fordism. The analysis seeks to recognize the power of the work ethic and to identify some of its weaknesses—that is, the chapter's goal is to attend at once to the coherence and the contradictions of the ethic's elements in a way that can account for both its historical durability and its perennial instabilities. As we will see, the elements that make the discourse of the work ethic so forceful and tenacious also render it always productive of antagonism. The work ethic has proved to be a trap, but it is also sometimes a weapon for those who are subject to its strictures.

I want to advance three general claims in this chapter: first, we cannot take on the structures of work without also challenging the ethics on which their legitimacy depends; second, despite its longevity, the ethical discourse of work is nonetheless vulnerable to such a challenge; and third, a claim that I will make more explicitly toward the end of the chapter, because of its particular significance to post-Taylorist labor processes, our "insubordination to the work ethic" (Berardi 1980, 169) is now more potentially subversive than ever before. In short, I want to argue that confronting the dominant ethic of work is necessary, possible, and timely.

THE PRIMITIVE CONSTRUCTION OF SUBJECTIVITIES

Weber's *The Protestant Ethic and the Spirit of Capitalism* remains a touchstone for studies of the work ethic, including this one, for good reason. As an unintended consequence of the Reformation, the Protestant work ethic, as Weber tells the story, bestowed on work a new and powerful endorsement. This new ethic entailed an important shift in expectations about what work is or should be, and a distinctive conception of what it means to be a worker. What characterized the Protestant ethos in particular was the ethical sanction for and the psychological impetus to work; ascetic Protestantism preached the moral import of constant and methodical productive effort on the part of self-disciplined individual subjects. This was no mere practical advice: "The infraction of its rules is treated not as foolishness," Weber maintains, "but as forgetfulness of duty" (1958, 51). One should set oneself to a lifetime of "organized worldly labour" (83) *as if* (and not, as we will see, precisely *because*) one were called to it by God. Weber's brilliant study of how and to what effect we came to be haunted by the legacy of this Puritan ethic introduces the essential components, fundamental dynamics, and key purposes of the new ethic of work that developed in conjunction with capitalism in Western Europe and North America.[1]

Weber offers an archeology of capitalist development that is in many ways comparable to the one Marx proposed in the brief account of primitive accumulation toward the end of the first volume of *Capital*. There Marx countered the political economists' morality tale about two kinds of people, the industrious and the lazy, with a very different kind of origins story, this one about the violent usurpation by a few of the common property of all (1976, 873–76). In equally polemical fashion, Weber takes on his own enemy, the structural teleologies of the economic determinists, and presents a sharply contrasting analysis that emphasizes the unpredictable emergence and historical force of ideas. Marx and Weber each offer an account of how two classes, the proletariat and the bourgeoisie, came to be; but where Marx focuses on their relations to the means of production as propertied owners and propertyless workers, Weber concentrates on the development of their consciousnesses as employers and employees. Weber explains the ideas that gave the political economists' parable about the ethically deserving and undeserving its authority and insists that this story must be understood as more than an ideological cover for the use of force; it was itself part of the arsenal of historical change in Europe and North America, and part of the foundation upon which capitalism was built. Indeed, the two analyses mirror one another, with the role of consent and coercion reversed: in one, the proletariat must first be forced into the wage relation before its consent can be manufactured; in the other, consent to work must be won before necessity can play its role in inducing compliance. The private ownership of property may be fundamental to capitalist exploitation, but that does not in itself guarantee the participation of exploitable subjects. Thus to Marx's account of the primitive accumulation of private property, Weber adds a story about the primitive construction of capitalist subjectivities.

One could pose Weber's project—as indeed many have—as a historical idealist alternative to Marx's historical materialism, an analysis centered on cultural forces to counter Marx's privileging of economic production. And certainly Weber's insistence on the role of ideas in history is sometimes cast in terms that match Marx's occasionally polemical claims about the primacy of material forces. But both Weber and Marx recognize that, formulated as a dichotomous pair, neither materialism nor idealism is adequate; they may at times serve some rhetorical or heuristic purpose, but they should not be treated as viable methodologies. Weber is clear that neither a "one-sided materialistic" nor "an equally one-sided spiritualistic causal interpretation" will do; thus in the final paragraph of *The Protestant Ethic*, he reminds us that the cultural explanation of economic developments that he has so vigorously defended is insufficient without an economic explanation of cultural developments (1958, 183). For his part, Marx affirms that production involves the fabrication not just of material goods, but also of relationships, subjectivities, and ideas; cultural forces and forms of consciousness are inseparable from, and thus crucial to, whatever we might delimit as a mode of production.[2] "Production thus not only creates an object for the subject," Marx observes, "but also a subject for the object" (1973, 92). Although each thinker may have tarried with a different line of emphasis, neither denies that understanding and confronting the contemporary work society requires attention to both its structures and its subjectivities.

Finally, just as Marx's account of primitive accumulation in *Capital* stands out as a brief historical exploration of a phenomenon he was otherwise dedicated to explaining in terms of its current logics, Weber's *Protestant Ethic* can also be profitably read, rather against the grain of traditional interpretations, as more a critical study of the present and its possible futures than a historiographical narrative of beginnings and ends, or a sociological analysis of causes and effects. In keeping with this line of interpretation, I will treat Weber's famous argument about the

historical relationship between capitalist development and religious belief less as a strictly historical claim than as a genealogical device. Indeed,
what I find most compelling about Weber's presentation is not the argument about the religious origins of capitalist economic institutions, but
the way that putting the analysis in a religious frame enables Weber to
capture and effectively convey both the specificity and the peculiarity of
this orientation to work. The discussion that follows will thus focus
more on the rhetorical force of the causal argument than on the details
of its empirical adequacy. As we will see, posing the historical claim
about the unholy melding of religion and capitalism in terms of a neat
causal argument—with its sharp and definitive contrasts between a "before" to the Protestant work ethic that Weber casts as "traditionalism"
and an "after" that he assumes to be secular—serves to highlight, clarify,
and dramatize this capitalist ethos, to train our attention on and school
our responses to the phenomenon. Each of these transitions—first from
the traditionalist to the Protestant orientation to work, and then from
that religiously informed ethos to a secular one—offers an opportunity
to defamiliarize what was already in Weber's day, and certainly is today,
an all too familiar formulation of the nature and value of work.

Though cast as an elegantly simple and straightforward causal argument, Weber's account nonetheless manages to convey many of the complexities of this animating ethos of capitalist development. The Protestant work ethic is not a single doctrine so much as it is a set of ideas, a
mixture or composite of elements that sometimes work in conjunction
and other times in contradiction. Indeed, it is by Weber's reckoning a
highly paradoxical phenomenon, at once powerfully effective and spec-
tacularly self-destructive. The paradoxical character is nowhere more
evident than in Weber's claim that this Puritan brand of productivism
unwittingly sowed the seeds of its own destruction: the rationalization it
helped to fuel eventually undercut the religious basis of the Protestant
ethic. While the ascetic ethos of work lives on in the spirit of capitalism,
as the "ghost of dead religious beliefs" (Weber 1958, 182) its existence
and effects are now far more mysterious, a haunting that is at once
palpably present and strangely elusive. Weber's analysis is attentive to
several points of instability on which my reflections on the ethic's later
manifestations will build. As we trace its later iterations under the Fordist and post-Fordist periods of US history, we see that some of its elements remain constant while others shift. Indeed, the history of the work

ethic in the United States—from the Protestant to the industrial and then to the postindustrial work ethic—reveals the precariousness of what is at the same time a remarkably tenacious set of ideas, dispositions, and commitments. What makes this normative discourse of work so adaptable also renders it constantly susceptible to contestation and change.

The exploration of the work ethic that follows identifies in Weber's original argument a set of antinomies that continue to animate the work ethic in the United States over the later course of its history, through the industrial and postindustrial periods. Three of these antinomies stem from the content of the ethic's prescriptions as it mandates at once the most *rational* and *irrational* of behaviors, promotes simultaneously *productivist* and *consumerist* values, and advances both individual *independence* and social *dependence*. Two more emerge as we consider the history of struggles over the ethic and its application: how it has served as an instrument of *subordination* but also as a tool of *insubordination*, and functioned as a mechanism of both *exclusion* and *inclusion*. These five pairs are conceived as antinomies rather than contradictions to highlight the effectivity of their internal conflicts without presuming their dialectical resolution and teleological trajectory.[3] Whether such dynamics will produce disciplinary devices or weapons of the weak, and whether they will generate a progressive historical development, let alone sow the seeds of their own destruction, remain open questions.

DEFAMILIARIZING THE WORK ETHIC

At the heart of the Protestant work ethic is the command to approach one's work as if it were a calling. It is here that we find the first and, perhaps for Weber, most remarkable of the discourse's constitutive antinomies: the unlikely confluence of the rational and the irrational. Arguably the most important message that Weber manages to convey—the central finding and dominant theme of his analysis—is that the work ethic is irrational at its origins and to its core, and yet it is prescriptive of what is taken to be the most rational forms of practical economic conduct. Indeed, this religious doctrine played no small part in the rationalization that is for Weber so distinctive of Western modernity. It is this doubling with which Weber seems so preoccupied. "We are here," he insists, "particularly interested in the origin of precisely the irrational element which lies in this, as in every conception of a calling" (1958, 78). Key to this "irrational element" is, as we will see, the noninstrumental qualities that Weber discerns in what we commonly take to be the most instrumental of endeavors: disciplined, productive work.

This irrationality of our commitment to work as if it were a calling is, however, also the element of this new cultural orientation to work that Weber may have struggled most to bring into focus. This "peculiar idea" of one's duty in a calling, "so familiar to us to-day, but in reality so little a matter of course" (54), has settled into the cultural fabric, making it difficult to grasp on its own terms. The value of work, along with its centrality to our lives, is one of the most stubbornly naturalized and apparently self-evident elements of modern and late, or postmodern, capitalist societies. To examine its social and historical specificity and understand its impact on our lives, this most familiar of doctrines must first be rendered strange. Indeed, given the normalization of these work values, perhaps the most important task and lasting achievement of Weber's analysis is the powerful estrangement from the reified common sense about work that it manages to produce. In this case, the periodizing frame and story of the ethic's religious origins serve Weber well; the alternative historical perspectives they identify provide the reader with the possibility of critical distance. In fact, the ethic is defamiliarized from two directions: first by considering it from the perspective of the "traditionalist" orientation to work that it supplanted, and second from the perspective of the secularized world from which the reader can then look back.

In a genealogical move, Weber finds early in his analysis a point of historical contrast in relation to which the work values now considered so obvious and necessary are revealed to be the product of a specific and indeterminate history. "Traditionalism" is Weber's label for a precapitalist orientation to work that treats it as no more than a means to concrete and finite ends. The "immensely stubborn resistance" of those who prefer working less and meeting their traditional consumption needs to working and having more (60) was, as Weber tells the story, "the most important opponent with which the spirit of capitalism, in the sense of a definite standard of life claiming ethical sanction, has had to struggle" (58). From a traditionalist perspective, the new Protestant ethic of work —the willingness to dedicate oneself to work as an end in itself, living to work instead of working to live—makes little sense. Once it supplants older orientations, however, "economic acquisition is no longer subordinated to man as the means for the satisfaction of his material needs. This reversal of what we should call the natural relationship, so irrational from a naïve point of view, is evidently as definitely a leading principle of capitalism as it is foreign to all peoples not under capitalistic influence" (53). From such a "foreign" and "naïve" point of view, we can perhaps grasp what is so strange about this new way of thinking, this confounding of means and ends, "where a man exists for the sake of his business, instead of the reverse" (70), and begin to appreciate the ways this commitment to work is "so irrational from the standpoint of purely eudaemonistic self-interest" (78).

It was precisely this attenuation of the relationship between work and economic utility, the strange new noninstrumentality of waged work, that made the work ethic a significant spur to capitalist development. According to Weber, the promise of additional wages for longer hours of more intense work was not originally an adequate incentive to adopt new work rhythms and routines. The problem is that although keeping wages low could serve as a reliable way to induce workers to submit to longer hours and greater effort, such a strategy was soon recognized to be incompatible with the long-term viability of the system of waged labor (61). Since wage incentives do not necessarily function as a stimulus to work longer hours at a more demanding pace, and wages can be lowered only so far if labor power is to be reproduced, the Protestant ethic tapped into other sources of motivation. Material need, Weber suggests, is not the only, or even necessarily the most effective, inducement to work. The moral justification for hard work for long hours thus serves to accomplish what neither raising nor lowering wages alone can do.

Not only does the idea of work as an end in itself render the satisfaction of concrete needs less relevant, but it also makes the specific qualities of the work less germane.[4] The Protestant ethic is in this sense a democratizing force: neither the quality nor the status of work is important; what matters is that it is approached with methodical dedication, or, in Weber's formulation, "*as if* it were an absolute end in itself, a calling" (62; emphasis added; see also Muirhead 2004, 106–8). The ethic is thus well-suited to an economic system predicated on labor abstracted from the specificity of the working person and the particular task; it helps to render both the qualities of the work and the satisfaction of concrete needs irrelevant to the logic of now limitless production (Bauman 1998, 8; see also De Angelis 1995, 112–13). To the extent that the quantity of the worker's effort is now more significant than the quality of the work, the ethic is well attuned to a new cycle of capital, production not for finite consumption but for continuous accumulation.[5]

The contrast to traditionalism provides Weber's analysis with an initial distancing mechanism; but we gain even more critical leverage through its estrangement from a different direction, by looking back on the Protestant ethic from the perspective of the secular world for which it served as midwife. Weber's text opens this angle of vision early on by organizing the argument in accordance with the protocols and in the language of social science, addressing us from the beginning as denizens of the rationalized world whose origins we are to explore.[6] The irrational element of the new dogma of work is again highlighted, but this time as we focus our attention on the specific Protestant doctrines that fueled it—the strangeness of which, from a modern perspective, Weber need not belabor. Of these doctrines, Weber singles out Calvin's view of pre-destination, the psychological effect of which he insists was "extraordinarily powerful" (1958, 128). It also stands out for the way that it further compounds the irrational noninstrumentality of the behaviors it prescribes. As Weber explains it, the doctrine encourages the believer to work as if working were an end in itself, but not because by doing so one could earn a place among the chosen; one's fate was predetermined and could not be altered through the performance of good works. Commitment to work is prescribed rather as a way to assuage the anxiety produced by such uncertainty and to strengthen one's confidence in being among the worthy elect (112). This orientation to work was thus less the result of one's faith in the afterlife than constitutive of it; hard work and success are not a means to salvation, but at most signs of it. To the extent that work acquires more meaning as an act of signification than as a production, there is something ritualistic about our adherence to its discipline. As a means to neither concrete material nor spiritual rewards but rather as an end in itself, the instrumentality of work discipline is even further weakened. Not even religiously instrumental, the rationality of the behavior appears increasingly tenuous.

If we pause for a moment to examine the development of productivist norms since the period of Weber's focus, we can get another perspective on this gap between means and ends. Weber's study explained the subjective constitution of the proletariat and bourgeoisie; the story continues once they are successfully converted to the new values and rhythms of industrial discipline, and later still as they adjust to the conditions of postindustrial production. Once the world is made hostile to the religious basis of the Protestant ethic, new rationales emerge for what remains a fundamentally similar prescription: to dedicate oneself, fully and methodically, to work. Where religion in the seventeenth and the early eighteenth centuries may have demanded a life devoted to work, the promise of social mobility—that one could by one's own disciplined effort and persistence pick oneself and one's family up by the bootstraps —had emerged in the United States by the early nineteenth century as the most recognizable rationale of this official ethos of work (see Rodgers 1978, 10–12). This industrial work ethic, as a secular version of the old ethos, focused not on the question of mobility in the afterlife but rather on its achievement in this life. After the middle of the twentieth century, another element, present but not as stressed in the industrial discourse, came to the forefront of the new postindustrial work ethic—an element that characterized work as a path to individual self-expression, self-development, and creativity (see, for example, Bunting 2004, 168; M. Rose 1985, 77–92; Zuboff 1983, 166).[7] Thus the transcendental rationale of the Protestant ethic served historically as what Fredric Jameson calls a "vanishing mediator" between precapitalist and capitalist economies (1973). It was first supplanted by the social rationale of high Fordism, the promise of mobility, and then also by a more individual justification and the promise of an even more immediate gratification—namely, fulfilling and meaningful work.[8] Indeed, the history of the work ethic in the United States demonstrates the adaptability of this ascetic ideal as it spans time and travels across space. As it turns out, the means to the different ends—that is, the behaviors that the ethic prescribes—remain consistent: the identification with and systematic devotion to waged work, the elevation of work to the center of life, and the affirmation of work as an end in itself. The ethic's goal, however, the supposed reward for this ethical practice, has proven surprisingly flexible.

To appreciate the strangeness of this confounding of means and ends, let us return to Weber's critical account. The analysis culminates in the final pages of *The Protestant Ethic*, where he describes the fate—the iron cage—to which the ethic delivered us, and at which point the ethic was drained of its religious content and absorbed into the secular culture of capitalism. Its secularization did not, however, eliminate the irrational qualities of the new economic ethos. Indeed, after the demise of this rather short-lived religious mandate, our continued devotion to the ethic's precepts appears even more difficult to account for in terms of a familiar means-ends rationality. At least the Puritan could explain his or her adherence to work discipline in relation to spiritual practices and meanings. Once the religious rationale loses its force, the continued devotion to work becomes more mysterious. Thus, "where the fulfillment of the calling cannot directly be related to the highest spiritual and cultural values, or when, on the other hand, it need not be felt simply as economic compulsion, the individual generally abandons the attempt to justify it at all" (Weber 1958, 182). Haunted by the work ethic, our commitments remain difficult to defend; attempts to explain them often exhibit more the qualities of post hoc rationalizations than sufficient accounts of our motives.[9] Yet the puzzle of our motivation would seem to be of little practical concern; when we have no memory or little imagination of an alternative to a life centered on work, there are few incentives to reflect on why we work as we do and what we might wish to do instead. Rather, our focus is generally confined to how, to draw on a famous phrase from another text, "we shall set to work and meet the 'demands of the day' " (Weber 1946, 156).

Once again, the religious framing of the narrative serves to amplify Weber's final indictment of the now-secularized spirit of capitalism and the dependence on waged labor that it promotes. By the end of his analysis, one can detect an unexpected nostalgia for the religiously motivated ethic, a phenomenon that the text had prior to that point treated with a detachment that would seem to be fueled by equal parts scientific objectivity and ethical distaste. From the perspective of the Puritan worker, there is a hollowness, a purposelessness, to our secularized "*workaday existence*" (149). The historical trajectory along which this new subjectivity of work develops lends to Weber's final characterization, borrowed from Goethe, a tragic dimension: "Specialists without spirit, sensualists without heart; this nullity imagines that it has attained a level of civilization never before achieved" (1958, 182). Cast as a delivery from the flames of religion to the fire of disenchantment, the secularization of the ethic is greeted with Weber's patented ambivalence as an ambiguous form of progress, at once welcome, calamitous, and inescapable.

A "WORLDLY ASCETICISM": PRODUCTIVISM MEETS CONSUMERISM

Weber's insistence on the religious origins of secular ethics calls our attention to a second antinomy through the improbable pairing of the terms "worldly" and "asceticism." On one hand, the Protestant work ethic is, as Weber emphasizes, a fundamentally ascetic morality, one that "turned with all its force against one thing: the spontaneous enjoyment of life and all it had to offer" (166). "Life" with its wealth of possibilities is subordinated to the disciplinary demands of work. This injunction to delay other gratifications and focus instead on methodical effort for productive ends remains at the core of later formulations of the work ethic. "Of all the pillars of the work ethic," Daniel Rodgers observes, "the predilection to see the moral life as a mustering of the will against the temptations within and the trials without remained the strongest, the least affected by the industrial transformation" (1978, 123). The "sanitizing effects of constant labor" (12) and the focus on work as the arena in which the individual can, with the proper self-discipline, will his or her own self-development and transformation continue to be affirmed today under the conditions of post-Fordist production. Nonetheless, as a worldly asceticism—rather than an otherworldly one—the prescription was and remains rife with difficulties. The worldliness of, for example, unruly bodies, seductive pleasures, and spontaneous enjoyment poses a constant challenge to the mandate for such focused attention to and diligent effort in properly productive pursuits. Ascetic Puritanism sought to fashion—and here the complexities of the project are revealed—a "life *in* the world, but neither *of* nor *for* this world" (Weber 1958, 154; emphasis added).

Thus, on the one hand, this worldly brand of asceticism, with its elevation of productive work and prohibitions on luxury and idle amusements, placed constraints on consumption. "On the other hand," Weber observes, "it had the psychological effect of freeing the acquisition of goods from the inhibitions of traditionalistic ethics" (171). The Puritan ethos serves to restructure our needs and desires as employers and employees, but also as producers and consumers. Its prescriptions were never, by Weber's account, confined to one's practice and comportment as a producer. In fact, it is precisely the ethic's attention to both production and consumption, its potent combination of ascetic denial and worldly desire, that accounts for its powerful contribution to early capitalist development. For "when the limitation of consumption is combined with this release of acquisitive activity," the result is the "accumulation of capital through [this] ascetic compulsion to save" (172). The work ethic forged a functional link between productive and consumptive behaviors, originally by dividing their responsibility between two classes: "The treatment of labour as a calling became as characteristic of the modern worker as the corresponding attitude toward acquisition of the business man" (179). Thus, for example, in addition to encouraging workers to accept the primacy of work over the times and spaces of nonwork, the doctrine also taught workers to respond to wage incentives, to recognize and accept a necessary connection between their contribution as social producers and their corresponding rights to individual consumption. The work ethic continues to affirm the legitimacy of this connection: consumption goods are the reward for and sign of one's contributions and status as a producer. As an antinomy rather than an oxymoron, the "worldly asceticism" of the Protestant ethic functions not despite, but because of, the pairing of terms.

The description that Weber evoked of "specialists without spirit, sensualists without heart" stands as a revealing indictment of the ethic's prescriptions for dedicated production and controlled acquisition at an early stage of capitalist development that depended on hard work for meager rewards from one class, and the accumulation of savings by the other. Yet, as Weber noted early on, this antinomy is at once central to the historical significance of the Protestant work ethic and key to its demise. This worldly brand of asceticism sowed the seeds of its own destruction as, over time, "these Puritanical ideals tended to give way under excessive pressure from the temptations of wealth" (174). But although the Puritan relationship between pleasure and denial at the heart of the Protestant ethic was undercut, similar dynamics serve to animate subsequent versions of the ethic. In the Fordist period of industrial capitalism, with efforts to sustain a level of mass consumption adequate to the exigencies of mass production, a new relationship between production and acquisition was forged. Consumption, rather than savings alone, emerged as an essential economic practice; as opposed to mere idleness, nonwork time was recognized as an economically relevant time, time to create new reasons to work more (Hunnicutt 1988, 46). Instead of one class of producers and another of savers, under Fordism, producers were expected to do double duty as ascetically indulgent consumers. As earning wages gave us the right to spend, working hours authorized leisure time. Thus the producer-consumer antinomy continued to serve as an energizing force under Fordism.

The expansion of consumption and consumer-based identities in the

Fordist period has led a number of commentators to conclude that the work ethic was finally and completely laid to rest, that by the early twentieth century it had been replaced by—depending on the account—a leisure ethic (C. Mills 1951, 236), a hedonistic consumption ethic (Bell 1976, 63), or an aesthetic of consumption (Bauman 1998, 2). According to such accounts, work had once again been reduced—this time by the seductions of commodity culture—to a mere means to an end, and consumption had replaced work as a site of intensive subjective investment. Indeed, the history of the work ethic in the United States reveals many recitations of this claim, usually motivated by a fear that the work ethic is losing its hold on a new generation, with all kinds of potentially dire economic, social, and political consequences.[10] What these arguments fail to recognize is that the work ethic was always already also an ethic of consumption, one that avows the necessary, legitimate, and indeed ethical link between hard work and whatever might count in different economic phases as deserved and responsible spending. The work ethic in its various incarnations helps organize, manage, and justify the changing relationship between production and consumption. It was and remains a way to sustain a functional relationship between the purchase of labor power and the sale of commodities by forging an ethical link between restraint and indulgence. As Weber notes in the case of the Puritan ethic, the enjoyment of wealth was never the problem; the danger, rather, was that one would no longer see the need to continue to work. "In fact," Weber claims, "it is only because possession involves this danger of relaxation that it is objectionable at all" (1958, 157).

Conditions of Fordist and post-Fordist production do not undermine the work ethic, though arguably they do intensify the potential instability of this core antinomy. As the mandate for one class to acquire savings becomes a Fordist prescription for the rationalization of mass consumption, the tensions at the core of the older Protestant ethic—exemplified by its support for a worldly brand of asceticism—are heightened. Under the conditions of post-Fordist production, the relationship between production and consumption that the ethic helps to manage is rendered even more fractious and fragile. More specifically, the claim that the relationship between work and income is necessarily and legitimately mediated by the wage becomes more difficult to maintain. The growth of immaterial forms of postindustrial service, cognitive, and communicational labor ensures that the relationship between a worker's contribution and his or her reward are more difficult to measure; the expansion of part-time, temporary, and insecure forms of employment renders the relationship between employment and income more precarious; and the decline of Fordist and Keynesian ideologies that insisted on and managed the wage-consumption connection at the industry and national levels makes the relationship between a worker's labor and his or her wage even more tenuous. I will explore the implications of these developments further in chapter 3. Here, I want to emphasize that the work ethic functions, as Weber originally recognized in the Protestant case, to stimulate consumption in some relation to production; it prescribes both productivist and consumerist values, insisting only on their necessary connection, their mutual dependence. Though a constant source of the ethic's instability, prescriptions for whatever may be conceived at any particular moment as "rational acquisition" or "legitimate" consumerist indulgence remain at the heart of, rather than beyond the purview of, capital's productivist ethic.

AUTONOMY AND COMMAND: MANAGING INDEPENDENCE

A third antinomy at the heart of the work ethic that Weber's analysis suggests is its promotion of work as a path to independence and the fact that the individual is thereby subject to dependence on waged labor and delivered to the sovereignty of employers. Although the wage relation has come to be considered the hallmark of self-sovereignty, it nonetheless remains a relation of subordination, and the autonomy that work is expected to ensure maintains an uneasy relationship to the ongoing subjection that it also authorizes. This produces a tension that must be carefully managed, as both the independence of the worker and his or her submission to the wage relation fuel social production. It is this paradoxical figure of what we might call the sovereign individual subject of exploitation that is increasingly the source of surplus value.

Work is often understood and experienced as a field of individual agency and as a sign of and a path to self-reliance. The Protestant work ethic hailed the individual as a moral agent, responsible for achieving the certainty of his or her own salvation (see Weber 1958, 115). Work was in this sense a mechanism of *spiritual independence*: rather than relying upon religious institutions and authorities, "the conscientious Puritan continually supervised his own state of grace" (124). The link between waged work and independence was solidified in the industrial period, when work became lauded as a means to *social and political independence*. Wages freed the worker from dependence on state aid and family support. Waged work thus became seen as the sine qua non of self-reliance. By this account, the "free" labor market provides the institutional setting—"a very Eden of the innate rights of man"—in which individuals can seize control of their own fate; individuals meet in this realm as buyers and sellers of a commodity, labor power, and "contract as free persons, who are equal before the law" (Marx 1976, 280). Of course, the progress of industrialization posed many challenges to the claim that waged work was best characterized as a state of independence rather than dependence. And yet, as Nancy Fraser and Linda Gordon argue, it was in this period that waged labor became increasingly synonymous with independence. Whereas individual—or, more precisely household—independence had been a status that only property ownership could confer, over the course of the industrial period it became increasingly identified with wage-earning. Indeed, whereas working-class activists had previously decried waged labor as a form of "wage slavery," they now claimed "a new form of manly independence within it" (Fraser and Gordon 1994, 315–16). In the process, dependency is redefined in such a way that it does not include capitalist relations of subordination in its field of relevance (325).[11]

As Weber points out, the work ethic—and this remains consistent over the course of its historical transformations—is an individualizing discourse. The individual's economic achievement or lack of achievement depends on and is reflective of his or her character. What could be seen as the responsibility of a collective becomes the duty of every individual; thus, refracted through the lens of Puritan ethics, "St. Paul's 'He who will not work shall not eat,'" once understood to be relevant to the community as a whole, now "holds unconditionally for everyone" (1958, 159). That is, moral responsibility now lies with the individual rather than the community, and rich and poor alike "shall not eat without working" (159–60). This becomes even more applicable over the course of the industrial era, once waged work becomes normative; and it is especially true in the postindustrial period as the breadwinner norm becomes increasingly universal, an expectation not just of household heads but of every adult citizen. With fewer instances of "legitimate" economic or political dependence, "whatever dependency remains, therefore, can be interpreted as the fault of individuals" (Fraser and Gordon

1994, 325). Independence becomes less a matter of the types of relationships one finds oneself subject to and more a quality of one's character (332). "Postindustrial dependency" thus becomes at once increasingly illegitimate and "increasingly individualized" (325).

As an individualizing discourse, the work ethic serves the time-honored ideological function of rationalizing exploitation and legitimating inequality. That all work is good work, that all work is equally desirable and inherently useful is, as William Morris once noted, "a convenient belief to those who live on the labour of others" (1999, 128). The Protestant ethic also "legalized the exploitation of this specific willingness to work," Weber observes, insofar as it "interpreted the employer's business activity as a calling" (1958, 178). From the perspective of the work ethic, governments are seen to protect the welfare of citizens by defending their right to work, while employers are not so much extracting surplus value as they are meeting the concrete needs of their employees for work. Just as the Protestant ethic gave the bourgeois businessperson "the comforting assurance that the unequal distribution of the goods of this world was a special dispensation of Divine Providence" (177), the work ethic offers in all periods a powerful rationale for economic inequality (see Beder 2000, 48; Bauman 1998, 65). Comparable to the way that the "unwillingness to work is symptomatic of the lack of grace" (Weber 1958, 159), today the morally suspect state of poverty can be attributed to the lack of individual effort and discipline. After all, "God"—today we could add the market—"helps those who help themselves" (115). As an individualizing discourse, the work ethic eschews institutional support for what is supposed to be an individual responsibility and obscures the structural processes that limit his or her field of opportunity.[12]

But the work ethic serves more than simply the classic ideological function of passing off the values and interests of one class as the values and interests of all. It also serves a more disciplinary function: beyond manufacturing common meanings, it constructs docile subjects. The work ethic thus possesses not just an epistemological force but an effectiveness that is properly ontological. Indeed, what is essential about the work ethic, as Weber originally described it, was what it could do: deliver workers to their exploitation, not just by manufacturing subjects' consent to capitalist exploitation, but by constituting both exploiting and exploitable subjects. By Weber's account, the subjectification function of the ethic is crucial. More than an ideology, the new discourse of work is a disciplinary mechanism that constructs subjects as productive individuals.[13] The impact of the Protestant ethic was comparable to monastic existence insofar as this worldly asceticism sought "methodical control over *the whole man*" (119; emphasis added). It was and remains, in this sense, a biopolitical force, one that renders populations at once productive and governable, increasing their capacities together with their docility. As Foucault once described the production of disciplinary individuality, "discipline increases the forces of the body (in economic terms of utility) and diminishes these same forces (in political terms of obedience)"; it produces "both a productive body and a subjected body" (1979, 138, 26). The individuated subject is both more useful and more manageable; "the individual is not, in other words, power's opposite number; the individual is one of power's first effects" (Foucault 2003, 30).

The Protestant ethic was so effective because it was not merely imposed on the individual from the outside, by the state or by the church. We "must take account," Weber remarks, "of the great difference between the results of the authoritarian moral discipline of the Established Churches and the corresponding discipline in the sects [generally more typical of Protestant communities] which rested on *voluntary submission*" (1958, 152; emphasis added). For example, the Calvinistic state churches may have "enforced a particular type of external conformity, but in some cases weakened the subjective motives of rational conduct" as well as that "liberation of individual powers" that was the focus of Weber's interest. Rather than enforcing conformity, the Protestant ethic is effective to the extent that it is internalized by the individual. The effect, moreover, is not just to shape the individual's beliefs and values but to promote the individual's constitution in relation to and identification with productivist norms. The ethic is advice not just about how to behave but also about who to be; it takes aim not just at consciousness but also at the energies and capacities of the body, and the objects and aims of its desires. The ethic's mandate is not merely to induce a set of beliefs or instigate a series of acts but also to produce a self that strives continually toward those beliefs and acts. This involves the cultivation of habits, the internalization of routines, the incitement of desires, and the adjustment of hopes, all to guarantee a subject's adequacy to the lifetime demands of work.[14]

So on the one hand, work is conceived in this discourse as a field of individuation and independence. On the other hand, of course, the wage relation is a hierarchical one, which requires individuals to submit to command and control. This antinomy—that work and its ethical discourse produce both independence and dependence, captured by Weber in that strange *self*-discipline he struggles to account for—renders the wage relation always potentially unstable. The ideal of independence can always serve as a critical standard against which the organization of the labor process and the conduct of its managers can be assessed, and a demand around which workers can organize for reforms. In fact, the ideal of individual independence has been invoked over the course of US history to inform struggles against everything from wage slavery to bureaucratic unionism. Even the hard-won reforms of the Fordist period— the laws governing wages and hours, and social wage provisions that offered new opportunities for many workers to advance into the middle class and mitigate their immediate dependence on the whims of employers—were accompanied by new concerns about the state of independence that they secured. The critique of the iconic "organization man" of high Fordism and the standardized individuality of the 1950s called into question the quality of the freedom that such progress entailed. And although new forms of white-collar employment were seen to afford new autonomy for some workers, by the early 1950s, critics like C. Wright Mills were calling into question whether this new middle-class worker—as "the servant of decision, the assistant of authority, the minion of management"—had achieved or relinquished his or her individual independence (1951, 80). These critiques in turn helped to inform the struggles against worker alienation of the 1960s and 1970s and the consequent reorganization of work and its management under post-Fordism.

But the precariousness that the antinomy generates is not only due to the static contradiction between the ideal of autonomy and the reality of submission, or because of the conflicting interests of capital, which demands dependence, and workers, who clamor for independence. A deeper source of conflict stems from the fact that capital needs individuals whose control poses ongoing problems. Even Taylorism, that science of management with its utopia of the assembly line, recognized that workers are more valuable as individuals. That is, the Taylorist organization of work processes in the industrial factory was not just about homogenizing a mass workforce and standardizing its output; it was also promoted by its early boosters as a method that attended to the specificity of each job and the monitoring and measurement of each individual worker (see Rodgers 1978, 56). Indeed, much of management theory and practice is focused on precisely this task: managing capital's dependence upon independence, engineering profitable modes of individuality. Again the example of Taylorism proves instructive. Although Taylor is usually remembered as the architect of a labor process typically thought not to depend on the subjectivity of workers, but to concentrate instead on organizing the work process down to its last detail so that employers can be less concerned about their voluntary compliance and enthusiastic participation, even he sought to fashion productive subjectivities. As Leslie Salzinger notes in her reading of Taylor's account of his success in raising the productivity of the iron worker Schmidt, this was accomplished in part by asking Schmidt over and over again if he was a "high priced man," using this interpellation as a way to motivate Schmidt to work faster and to accept Taylor's detailed control over his work. "Taylor creates the very subject he ostensibly recognizes," Salzinger writes, "giving him a power over Schmidt that goes beyond that of controlling his behavior to that of defining Schmidt's self" (2003, 17).

The dependence on independence and the tensions it produces intensify under the conditions of post-Taylorist production. I will develop this point in more detail later in the chapter. Here I will just note that even more than in industrial production, profits in the service- and knowledge-based economy depend increasingly on simultaneously activating and controlling, on releasing and harnessing, the creative, communicative, affective, and emotional capacities of workers. "As it is no longer possible to confine subjectivity merely to tasks of execution," Maurizio Lazzarato observes, "it becomes necessary for the subject's competence in the areas of management, communication, and creativity to be made compatible with the conditions of 'production for production's sake.'" The task of fashioning productive forms of subjectivity, workers who are simultaneously self-directed and manageable, poses an ongoing puzzle for capitalist—and particularly post-Fordist—management techniques: "Thus the slogan 'become subjects,'" Lazzarato continues, "far from eliminating the antagonism between hierarchy and cooperation, between autonomy and command, actually re-poses the antagonism at a higher level, because it both mobilizes and clashes with the very personality of the individual worker" (1996, 135). The individual autonomy and independence that work is supposed to, and to some degree must, enable thus coexists uneasily with the subjection and dependence that it nonetheless secures (see also Gorz 1999, 38–39).

THE WORK ETHIC AND THE LABORING CLASSES

Whereas *The Protestant Ethic* provides insight into the first three antinomies, the final two require that we move further beyond the historical territory of Weber's account. Specifically, they require special attention to the industrial period and the dynamics of class struggle, antiracism, and feminism that emerged in that period and continue to shape our own. The antinomic relationship between subordination and insubordination enabled by the work ethic can be demonstrated through the example of class struggle; I will use a brief consideration of the histories of race- and gender-based struggles in the following section to highlight a final antinomy in the way the ethic has been deployed as a mechanism of both exclusion and inclusion.

The particular limits of Weber's account can be illustrated by returning again briefly to the similarities between Marx's account of primitive accumulation and Weber's story of early capitalist development. As noted above, each author focuses on a different "vanishing mediator" in the transition to a capitalist society: state violence for Marx, religious doctrine for Weber. Whereas Marx insists that "force is the midwife of every old society which is pregnant with a new one" (1976, 916), Weber claims that it was Puritanism that "stood at the cradle of the modern economic man" (1958, 174). Marx's story of primitive accumulation and Weber's history of the Protestant ethic also end on similar notes. According to Marx, once the capitalist mode of production is in place, the "bloody discipline" deployed to create a class of wage laborers is supplanted by a less direct mode of force, the "silent compulsion of economic relations" (1976, 905, 899). Weber's account concludes with the replacement of the self-discipline of the Puritan by an economic order capable of determining the lives of every individual with "irresistible force": "the Puritan wanted to work in a calling; we are forced to do so" (1958, 181).

The problem is that each of the texts wraps up the narrative too neatly. The story does not end with the assisted birth of economic man; this is, rather, when the hard work begins, with the raising and cultivating of productive subjects. Although Weber recognizes that beyond just forcing the wage relationship on those without other options, "victorious capitalism" also "educates and selects the economic subjects which it needs," the *Protestant Ethic* neglects to pursue that line of analysis (181, 55). Thus, in the same way that many have since revised Marx's original analysis—which had confined the techniques of primitive accumulation to a founding moment—in order to account for the ongoing use of violence and dispossession as means of accumulation throughout capital's history, we need to amend Weber's story line to register more clearly the imposition of waged labor as a continual process.

In fact, of course, US history reveals a protracted campaign, particularly over the course of the nineteenth and the early twentieth centuries, to impose industrial work habits and values on both the formerly enslaved and successive waves of immigrants (Genovese 1974, 303; Gutman 1977, 14). Since the ascetic ideal of work did not hold the same attractions for, or have the same power to interpellate, those for whom Protestant doctrine, the industrial period's promise of mobility, or the postindustrial prospect of fulfilling work was less likely to resonate, it was and continues to be an ongoing struggle to spread these work values across divisions of occupation and income. But the history of class struggle in the United States reveals another of the ethic's animating antinomies, showing how it has been wielded as a weapon by both sides. That is, while the ethic has functioned to maintain the subordination of workers to the conditions of abstract labor, it has also served as a weapon of their insubordination.

As we have seen, Weber clearly recognizes the work ethic's function as a mechanism of subordination. Although the gospel of work in its Protestant version was a "specifically bourgeois economic ethic" (1958, 176), and remains in its later secular instantiations most closely associated with the professional and managerial class, this does not mean that the working classes have been exempt from its strictures or immune to its appeal. After all, the Protestant ethic also provided the bourgeois business owner with "sober, conscientious, and unusually industrious workmen, who clung to their work as to a life purpose willed by God" (177). The work ethic was and remains "an ideology propagated by the middle classes for the working classes with enough plausibility and truth to make it credible" (Barbash 1983, 232).

What Weber did not recognize was that it could also serve as a tool of insubordination. Although industrialists and their managers struggled to inculcate the work ethic among laborers, its adoption proved to be something of a double-edged sword. On the one hand, managers often succeeded in expanding the reach of the traditional ethic of work; on the other hand, the ethic was not always adopted in the form or with the results they sought. First, the split between means and ends introduces a certain indeterminacy. To function as a disciplinary force, the industrial work ethic is articulated—contrary in some respects to the original Protestant ethic—in terms of earthly goals and tangible rewards. These then serve as ideals around which workers can struggle for reforms— demanding, for example, higher wages ensuring more social mobility, and better, more satisfying work. Second, the process of inculcation through which willing subjects are fashioned does not establish a mimetic relationship between culture and subject; the norm that is internalized is always in some ways altered or hybridized in the process. The battles fought within the discursive frames set by these competing versions of the ethic operate to continually transform their terms.

Since the nineteenth century, the working class has developed its own version of the work ethic, and this alternative work ethic from below has been useful to the political projects of contesting the structural exclusions and cultural marginalization of the class.[15] This "laborist work ethic" of the industrial period, one of several dissident versions that we will continue to discuss in the following section, draws on a variant of the labor theory of value to celebrate the worth and dignity of waged work and to contend that such work is entitled to respect and adequate recompense (Tyler 1983, 200). Rather than malign the shiftless poor, for example, this version of the ethic takes aim at the idle rich (199). The laborist ethic was a key element of the class composition of the industrial proletariat, both helping to construct it as a class and serving as part of its arsenal. By highlighting and valorizing its productive role, Baudrillard notes how this laborist work ethic helped to constitute the working class as a class, serving to render it legible and appealing as a collective identity: "The ethic of rational labor, which is of bourgeois origin and which served historically to define the bourgeoisie as a class, is found renewed with fantastic amplitude at the level of the working class, also contributing *to define* it as a class, that is to circumscribe it in a status of historical representability" (1975, 155). Defined in terms of a "productivist vocation" to match that of the bourgeoisie, the working class could wage its struggles from a position of dialectical opposition, a position that maximizes both the intelligibility of working-class demands and at another level—as we will see in the next section—their recuperability (156–59).

The laborist ethic was a powerful weapon in the arsenal of the industrial proletariat that helped to secure a host of working-class victories well into the middle of the twentieth century. Taking seriously the familiar descriptions of what work could be and could do, workers have struggled to make waged work live up to its ideals and deliver on its promise of social mobility and individual fulfillment. In this way, the ethic has served to augment the power of the dominant class at the same time that it has served to enhance the counter-power of the working class. Working-class campaigns in the 1930s against exploitation, fueled in part by the laborist ethic, helped to secure the social welfare and regulatory provisions of the Fordist wage relation, not to mention new management efforts at co-optation in the form of the human-relations movement. The postindustrial work ethic, with its new emphasis on work as an avenue for personal development and meaning, was at least in part a response to the rebellions in the 1960s and early 1970s against the disciplinary subjectivity of the Fordist period and the problem of worker alienation that they helped to publicize. The human-resources movement that had come into its own by the 1980s attempted to change work processes in ways that would address, in profitable terms, the problem of work quality posed by activists. Thus the shift from the industrial ethic's focus on work as a path to social mobility to the postindustrial emphasis on work as a practice of self-realization is part and parcel of the confrontation of competing versions of the ethic and the struggles over the organization and meaning of work that they signified and facilitated (see Bernstein 1997; M. Rose 1985; Storey 1989).

Class struggles over the application of the work ethic can produce another unintended effect. As more people demand that their work be recognized as relevant to the dominant ethic of work, the class specificity of the ethic becomes increasingly exposed to view. As always, the work ethic with its various claims about the rewards of work—whether those rewards are coded as social mobility or self-development—shifts from a credible ideal to sheer propaganda depending on the conditions of work and the individual's position within the complex, intersecting hierarchies of the work society. The further the discourse travels, the more its precepts are abstracted from the real conditions of work, and the more often it is reduced to a crudely ideological phenomenon: its universal claims about the benefits and gratifications of a lifetime devoted to work may reflect some of the experiences of one class but mystify those of another.

RACE, GENDER, AND THE PROPAGATION OF THE WORK ETHIC

The history of the work ethic in the United States reveals not only its class inflections but also its instantiations as a racialized and gendered discourse. The previous discussion highlighted the potential dual use of the work ethic as an instrument of class domination and a tool of class insubordination, a utility that has served antiracist and feminist struggles as well. A brief look at the racialization of the discourse, and a longer consideration of its gendering, can reveal another of its contradictory dynamics: the way it has served as a mechanism of both exclusion and inclusion. More specifically, I want to focus here on one way the ethic came to be more inclusive—that is, how it extended its reach beyond the bourgeois class of the industrial period and today's professional and managerial class by being rendered simultaneously exclusive of other groups. This focus on both the inclusions and exclusions that the work ethic sustains recalls Weber's dual emphasis on the egalitarian and hierarchical effects of the new work values. To some extent, the discourse was a democratizing force that elevated all forms of waged work to the status of an ethically worthy practice; at the same time, however, it was a powerful source of hierarchy that played a crucial role in the legitimation of inequality, now read as a reflection of individual character rather than a consequence of the structure of waged employment. This last antinomy is a characteristic of any disciplinary norm, which, as Foucault explains it, is simultaneously a force of homogenization and of differentiation, at once prescribing "a conformity that must be achieved" and tracing "the limit that will define difference in relation to all other differences" (1979, 183).

Consider, for example, how the ethic came to be more inclusive in terms of class by means of its exclusions based on race and gender. In the early industrial period, elements of the white working class came to identify with waged work as a mark of independence and status by way of their racial identities. The legitimacy of and identification with what had been resisted as "wage slavery" in the late eighteenth and the early nineteenth centuries was established "in time and in comparison" to the institution of slavery and those constructed through its sustaining discourses as its abject subjects. The embrace of whiteness, as David Roediger explains, "was a way in which white workers responded to a fear of dependency on wage labor and to the necessities of capitalist work discipline" (1991, 13). The othering of various immigrant groups delivered a similar reward to wage laborers, paying what W. E. B. Du Bois called a "public and psychological wage" to the white working class (quoted in Roediger 1991, 12). Thus the work ethic traveled down the class ladder in part on the energies of racism, ethnicity, and nationalism. The racialization of the work ethic also played a role in the postindustrial economy by facilitating the acceptance of white-collar work. Indeed, C. Wright Mills notes that, despite the fact that most of such work was routinized and unskilled, white-collar workers in the United States could nonetheless claim greater prestige than blue-collar workers on the basis of the whiteness and citizenship status of those in the white-collar occupational niche (1951, 248). Once again, the norm's exclusions based on race, nation, and ethnicity fueled its inclusiveness in terms of class. One's status and comportment as a waged worker, as a member of the working or middle class, was not just a matter of asserting one's moral worthiness and social standing as "a worker," but as a white worker, a working man, an American worker, or, to recall an earlier example, a "high priced man"—that is, via one's relative privilege as a racialized, gendered, national, or classed subject.

These ideals of work continue to receive no small amount of their charge from these marginalizing practices. Regardless of the wages, intrinsic appeal, or status of one's work, it can serve as a means to assert one's moral superiority and thereby legitimate one's economic privilege over a series of racialized and gendered groups. Over the course of US history, there is a continuous calling into question of the work commitments and habits of different immigrant and racialized populations. Whether it was the panic about the inability of US corporations to compete with a more vigorous Japanese work culture or the ongoing debates regarding the supposed inadequacies of the work orientations of "inner city residents," "the underclass," "welfare mothers," or "illegal aliens," the work ethic is a deep discursive reservoir on which to draw to obscure and legitimate processes and logics of racial, gender, and nationalist formations past and present. In particular, as the history of racialized welfare discourse demonstrates, the work ethic continues to serve as a respectable vehicle for what would otherwise be exposed as publicly unacceptable claims about racial difference (see Neubeck and Cazenave 2001).

The work ethic is not only a racialized but a gendered construction; women too have served as the excluded others of its various historical articulations. This was enabled by the historical processes through which work in the United States became equated with waged work, waged work was linked to masculinity, and unwaged domestic work was reconceived as nonproductive women's work. This lack of recognition of feminized domestic labor emerged with early industrialization, as unwaged household work came to stand as the (naturalized and feminized) model of nonwork that served to contrast and thereby sustain a (now masculinized) concept of work. As Jeanne Boydston explains it, the gender division of labor thus morphed into a gendered definition of work (1990, 55). Unwaged women (and those waged women who found themselves judged in relation to this normative model), not subject to the morally purifying and invigorating effects of work discipline, were a justifiably dependent class. The work ethic could then be embraced as a masculine ethic while nonwork—a rather more expansive category including everything from leisure practices and consumption work to unwaged agricultural, household, and caring labor—was devalued by its association with a degraded femininity. Within the industrial gender order that emerged from these processes, blue-collar manufacturing work was defined as men's work, and its masculinization helped to promote acceptance of and identification with it as work not only befitting a man (Fraser and Gordon 1994) but as instrumental to becoming a man (see, for example, Willis 1977, 150–51; Baron 1991, 69).

To take a slight detour from the narrative, it is important to recognize the link between the gendering of the work ethic and the disciplinary norm that governs another site of labor, the family ethic. Indeed, the family ethic functioned as a supplement to the work ethic, serving to discipline not only unwaged women in the household, but waged workers as well. The family ethic as a mechanism of social regulation and control was, as Mimi Abramovitz observes, based on the gender division of labor, and served to articulate and rationalize its terms (1988, 37). But it was not only applied to the field of unwaged domestic work. Throughout the industrial period, the conformity of all workers to the traditional model of the family—a nuclear, heterosexual, patriarchal model—was promoted by employers, politicians, religious leaders, and reformers as a crucial adjunct to work discipline, serving as another sign of the worker's dedication to work and adherence to the productivist ethos. This family ethic emerged in the Fordist period as an important means by which to manage the production-consumption nexus. Thus Henry Ford was convinced that a stable and disciplined labor force was reproduced through the institution of the traditional family, and he required that his employees adhere to the model (May 1987). "Culture of poverty" discourses have long focused their critical sights on family structures—including the "Negro family" of the infamous Moynihan Report—claiming that the traditional patriarchal nuclear family is fundamental to economic success (see Roschelle 1999, 316). The institution of the family has, of course, undergone dramatic changes since the period of high Fordism. But just as the work ethic has managed to survive the transformations of work, the ghost of dead family values continues to haunt us as well (Stacey 1996, 49). As one White House report from the 1980s put it, the family, as the "seedbed of economic skills, money, habits, attitudes towards work, and the art of financial independence," plays a key role in the transmission of work skills and ethics; "neither the modern family nor the free enterprise system would long survive without the other" (quoted in Abramovitz 1988, 350–51). The family ethic endures in this post-Fordist period, serving various family-values campaigns as a tool of political-economic discipline arguably for many of the same reasons it was defended earlier: for the role it plays in reproducing a stable and able workforce with little in the way of public funding—or, to put it another way, because otherwise we might "destroy the golden egg that produced cheap labor" (Kessler-Harris 1990, 39).[16]

To return to the major line of argument, the fact that some are excluded from the dignity and worth conferred by the work ethic can serve to render its prescriptions more attractive to others. Thus the inclusion of more white and male workers in the scope of the ethic's logics was facilitated in part by the exclusion of many black and women workers from the status of hard-working and disciplined breadwinner. However, while these articulations of the ethic in relation to gender, race, and class identities and relations served to facilitate its propagation among, in the examples treated above, broader swaths of the white male working class, it also generated conflict as these various exclusions were contested and resisted on the one hand and—as the discussion that opens the next chapter illustrates—refused and disregarded on the other hand. We have already touched upon the historical importance of the laborist ethic. The work ethic has been a similarly powerful weapon in the arsenal of anti-racist struggles. Demanding recognition of the history of hard work and the commitment to productivist values, the supposed whiteness of the work ethic has been challenged at every turn. Claims about the strength of the work ethic have been enlisted in antiracist discourses and projects of racial uplift from Booker T. Washington's efforts to educate students who "would learn to love work for its own sake" (1971, 148) and Anna Julia Cooper's promotion of not only the economic but the social benefits of black women's unwaged household work (Logan 2002) to William Julius Wilson's argument that unemployed and underemployed residents of the "urban ghetto" are, contrary to those discourses that seek to pathologize their "choices," more likely to share than to eschew dominant work values (1996, 179–81).[17]

Although these demands for inclusion have undeniably been important historically and effective politically, I want to focus here on the limitations of such efforts to secure recognition of the moral respectability of excluded or marginalized workers and the ethical status of their labors. The discussion that follows will focus on feminism's relationship to the work ethic to illustrate some of these limits. Feminist reformulations of the work ethic have abounded since the nineteenth century, when "the work ethic brought its enormous reserves of power to the women's movement" (Rodgers 1978, 184). As noted in the introduction, two general feminist strategies for confronting women's marginalization in relation to work and its dominant ethic emerged to respond to the industrial period's imagination and engineering of the gendered relationship between waged work and household labor. One such response accepts the characterization of domestic work as nonwork and focuses on integrating women into waged work. The tradition of liberal feminism has long praised the virtues and rewards of waged work for women. Thus in 1792, Mary Wollstonecraft decried the enervating and corrupting indolence encouraged by the norms of middle-class femininity, insisting that "trifling employments have rendered woman a trifler" (1996, 77). But the work ethic may have received its most unconditional support within feminism in Betty Friedan's Feminine Mystique, which declared that a woman "can find identity only in work that is of real value to society—work for which, usually, our society pays" (1963, 346). Deluded by the feminine mystique "and the immaturity it breeds," the housewives she interviewed were prevented "from doing the work of which they are capable" and making that "serious professional commitment" she prescribes (253, 349). Although these examples drawn from first- and second-wave liberal feminism exemplify a more white and middle-class discourse, befitting those for whom the ideology of separate spheres and anxiety about feminine idleness resonated most, they no doubt also held attractions for a broader cross-section of women who, as Zillah Eisenstein once observed of Friedan's argument, not only may have identified with that class position even if they did not inhabit it, but may have been attracted to the liberal ideals of equality of opportunity and individual independence upon which the arguments are predicated (1981, 178). This emphasis on the "right to work," what Gwendolyn Mink describes as the "labor market bias" of US feminism (1998, 26), continues to characterize broad segments of mainstream feminism.

One feminist response, therefore, was to adopt the traditional work ethic's singular focus on the value of waged labor and claim that women should have equal access to the virtues that employment opportunities could bestow. A second response to the characterization of women as nonproductive citizens insisted instead on the status of domestic work as real work—that is, on its standing as a comparably worthy form of socially necessary and dignified labor. Thus, for example, the home economics movement of the nineteenth and the early twentieth centuries imported a version of this same ethic into domestic work, insisting that household labor requires a level of discipline, efficiency, and systematic effort comparable to that required of industrial labor (see Rodgers 1978, 200–201; Ehrenreich and English 1975). Besides once again creating more work for women—in the first approach, by adding a second job to women's lives; in the second, by raising the standards of domestic work—there were additional drawbacks to each of the strategies: whereas the first risked perpetuating the invisibility and devaluation of unwaged domestic work, the second threatened to reinforce the discourse of separate spheres and with it what Charlotte Perkins Gilman decried as "domestic mythology" (2002, 36).[18]

Second-wave feminists were particularly interested in this second approach, insisting on revaluing feminized forms of not only domestic labor but pink-collar wage labor as well—including, for example, caring work and sex work. The proponents of the classic gynocentric ethic of care claimed that caring labor was real work and should be recognized and valued as such. Though more interested in finding in caring labor another model of ethical work than in imposing the model of waged work on the practices of care, some of these second-wave authors none-theless echo aspects of the ethical discourse of waged labor in making the case for caring labor's significance and worth. Thus the ethic of care could also be construed as an ethic of work. Beyond the long-standing problem of gender essentialism that haunts the project, this and other efforts to expand conceptions of what counts as work also risk tapping into and expanding the scope of the traditional work ethic.[19]

Feminist analyses of sex work offer an illustrative example of the limitations of certain efforts to claim the title of work when that also involves making use of the legitimacy conferred by its dominant ethic. Introduced originally as a way to intervene in the feminist sex wars, the label "sex work" sought to alter the terms of feminist debate about sexual labor (Leigh 1997). For example, as a replacement for the label "prosti-tution," the category helps to shift the terms of discussion from the dilemmas posed by a social problem to questions of economic practice; rather than a character flaw that produces a moral crisis, sex work is reconceived as an employment option that can generate income and provide opportunity. Within the terms of the feminist debate about prostitution, for example, the vocabulary has been particularly impor-tant as a way to counter the aggressive sexual moralizing of some in the prohibitionist camp, as well as their disavowal of sex workers' agency and insistent reliance on the language and logics of victimization. The other side, however, has produced some comparably problematic representa-tions of work as a site of voluntary choice and of the employment con-tract as a model of equitable exchange and individual agency. More relevant to our topic here, it is important to recognize how much of the rhetorical utility of the label "sex work" stems from its association with conventional work values. For those involved in sex worker advocacy, the term can serve not only as a way to foreground the economic dimensions of such labor practices, but as a way to insist on their essential worth, dignity, and legitimacy, as—in the formulation of one advocacy group—"service work that should be respected and protected" (quoted in Jen-ness 1993, 67). I do not mean to deny the vital importance of these efforts, only to point out that they often tend to echo uncritically the traditional work-ethic discourse. Thus the prostitutes' rights group COYOTE ("Call Off Your Old Tired Ethics") may succeed in calling off one of our old tired ethics, but in the process of doing so, taps into and reproduces another. The approach usefully demoralizes the debates about the nature, value, and legitimacy of sex for wages in one way, but it often does so by problematically remoralizing it in another; it shifts the discussion from one moral terrain to another, from that of a suspect sexual practice to that of a respectable employment relation.

All of these dissident versions—the laborist, antiracist, and feminist appropriations of the work ethic—have proved to be powerful weapons for change. Harnessing the ethic has served to render legible and legitimate a host of demands for equality. The laborist ethic "turned necessity into pride and servitude into honor" (Rodgers 1978, 181), thereby providing a vehicle for the development of class consciousness and a lever of power for the labor movement. Antiracist affirmations of the work ethic challenged racist stereotypes and served as a potent weapon in the struggle to gain access to employment opportunities, as well as bolstering struggles for equal access to and reform within a number of sites and contexts. Feminist articulations of the work ethic similarly served to garner sympathy for and expand the appeal of a broad set of demands for women's rights. There is no question that claiming equal rights and opportunities as productive citizens has proved enormously effective as a way to challenge class, race, gender, and sexual hierarchies.

But all of these demands for inclusion serve at the same time to expand the scope of the work ethic to new groups and new forms of labor, and to reaffirm its power. Thus the laborist ethic may have helped in the struggle to win Fordist concessions, but it did so by affirming the ideal as a lifetime of "dignified" work (see also Rodgers 1978, 181). "The 'class of laborers,'" Baudrillard observes, "is thus confirmed in its idealized status as a productive force even by its revolutionary ideal" (1975, 156). Although opposed to the work society's hierarchies, such tactics were complicit with its ethics. This is a potential problem with both of the long-standing feminist strategies regarding work and its dominant values: the demand for inclusion in the form of "real" (that is, waged) work for women and the demand to expand the category of work to include what has been mischaracterized either as idleness and leisure, or as private, intimate, and spontaneous acts of love—but in any case, as nonwork. Each of the approaches risks contesting the gendered organization of a capitalist work society by reproducing its fundamental values. Claiming one's place as a productive citizen and one's value in relation to the legitimating ethic of work, whether or not the original ethic is thereby altered, remains in this specific sense a mode of rebellion susceptible to co-optation. Struggling only within, rather than also against, the terms of the traditional discourse of work both limits the scope of the demands that are advanced and fails to contest the basic terms of the work society's social contract. For all their successes, few political movements have managed to confront directly what Weber calls the "social ethic of capitalistic culture" (1958, 54).

POST-FORDISM AND THE WORK ETHIC

The political and economic developments associated with post-Fordism exert some new pressures on the work ethic. Current trends suggest that our attitudes toward work are of increasing importance to the continued viability of contemporary modes of work and their governance. One could argue that with neoliberal restructuring and the shift in the balance of power between capital and labor that it signals, the coercive inducements to hard work and long hours are often sufficient to deliver manageable workers to the labor market. Indeed, the increasing mobility of capital in comparison to the ongoing restrictions on labor's movement alters the political landscape. The threat of job loss attributed to the pressures of global competition puts workers on the defensive, while the contraction of social welfare provisions further enforces individuals' dependence on the wage relation. The precarious position that so many workers find themselves in echoes that of Weber's Puritan, whose restless anxiety and uncertainty kept his nose to the grindstone.[20]

In such a climate, one could conclude that capital is—to recall Weber's claim about an earlier period—back "in the saddle" (1958, 282, n. 108) and thus no longer in need of its old ethical supports. But that would be only part of the story; in other respects, the willingness of workers to dedicate themselves to work as the center of their lives and as an end in itself may never have been so necessary. There are at least two reasons why our attitudes toward work take on renewed significance in the context of post-Fordism. First, workers' investment in the work ethic is increasingly relevant because in many forms of work—for example, in many service sector jobs—employers want more from their employees than was typically demanded in the factories of the industrial era: not just the labor of the hand, but the labors of the head and the heart. Post-Taylorist work processes therefore tend to require more from immaterial laborers than their sacrifice and submission, seeking to enlist their creativity and their relational and affective capacities. It is not obedience that is prized, but commitment; employees are more often expected to adopt the perspectives of managers rather than simply yield to their authority (Bunting 2004, 110). Whereas Fordism demanded from its core workers a lifetime of compliance with work discipline, post-Fordism also demands of many of its workers flexibility, adaptability, and continual reinvention.[21] If originally the work ethic was the means by which already disciplined workers were delivered to their exploitation, it serves a more directly productive function today: where attitudes themselves are productive, a strong work ethic guarantees the necessary level of willing commitment and subjective investment. Especially in the context of service work and work with an affective or communications component, the individual's attitude and emotional state are considered crucial skills, along with empathy and sociability.[22] Indeed, the very distinction between a worker's skills and attitudes becomes difficult to sustain, since, as Robin Leidner notes, "the willingness and capacity of workers to manipulate and project their attitudes in the organization's interest are central to their competence on the job" (1996, 46). Thus, Doug Henwood claims, "employer surveys reveal that bosses care less about their employees' candlepower than they do about 'character'—by which they mean self-discipline, enthusiasm, and responsibility" (1997, 22).[23] As Arlie Hochschild observes in her groundbreaking study of interactive service sector work, "seeming to 'love the job' becomes part of the job; and actually trying to love it, and to enjoy the customers, helps the worker in this effort" (1983, 6). Indeed, now more than ever, "workers are expected to be the architects of their own better exploitation" (Henwood 1997, 22).

But it is not only a matter of what kind of labor power is often sought. When workers are given more responsibility and more discretion, and particularly when the job involves providing services and instilling in clients and customers certain kinds of emotional or affective states, the workers' performance is more difficult both to measure and to monitor. How does one determine an individual employee's contribution to increasingly cooperative labor processes, particularly those that draw on workers' affective, cognitive, and communicative capacities? ("This call may be monitored for purposes of quality assurance"—but it probably is not.) When individual contributions to collective production processes are more difficult to discern, employers focus on measuring what they can, increasingly resorting to proximate measures. Personality testing is thus on the rise as one kind of proxy for behavioral assessment, and in this way, "the emphasis becomes the total behavior of the individual rather than the specifically 'productive' behavior" (Townley 1989, 106). Putting in long hours can also be used as an indication of commitment, which can in turn be a signal of productivity. A worker's devotion to work serves as a sign of his or her capacities just as it once served as a sign of his or her status among the elect. Strong work values are thus increasingly highlighted in management discourses as a significant remedy to the new problems of surveillance simply because they render it less necessary. Thus, we see a growing trend in the United States and elsewhere to both select and evaluate workers on the basis of their attitudes, motivation, and behavior. This is becoming increasingly the case not just for workers in the higher-paid reaches of the employment hierarchy but for those in the lower-paid levels as well: these criteria are being used on white-, pink-, and increasingly blue-collar employees, in both the industrial and service sectors (92; see also Ehrenreich 2001).

MANAGING POST-FORDIST INDEPENDENCE: BEING PROFESSIONAL

These post-Taylorist labor processes pose new challenges for management efforts to construct workers who are, to recall an earlier discussion, both independent and dependent, both autonomously creative and responsive to command. The crude subjectification of Taylor's Schmidt is guided now by a myriad of management theories and a major industry that aids in the manufacture of productive corporate cultures: the relatively simple industrial psychology of the Fordist era had been remade into the complex art of cultural fashioning and emotional engineering typical of many managerial regimes today. The problem for many employers is one of encouraging employee self-development, but only as a "human resource"—or, as some critics of this logic of managerial control describe it, "encouraging autonomous employees to use their alleged independence to express their resourcefulness as well as to submit themselves to continuous self-scrutiny and audit in the name of accountability" (Costea, Crump, and Amiridis, 2008, 673–74). The impoverishment of this conception of individual development, tethered as it is to a mandate to produce value, is made painfully clear in the management guru Tom Peters's description of work as an opportunity to maximize one's chances of future employment, as what can "teach you new skills, gain you new expertise, develop new capabilities, grow your colleague set, and constantly reinvent you as a brand" (1997, 94).

Just as the Protestant ethic encouraged workers to treat their work as if it were a calling, today one noteworthy management technique involves asking workers to approach their work as if it were a career. Taylor asked the iconic industrial laborer Schmidt if he were the "high priced man" who embodied the Fordist work ethic of social mobility; the comparable injunction for many postindustrial service workers is to "be professional." The discourse of professionalism today enjoys a wide application, serving as a disciplinary mechanism to manage the affects and attitudes of a service-based workforce that is less amenable to direct supervision. A brief excavation of the category's purposes and applications from the industrial to the postindustrial labor orders can suggest the significance of the increasingly ubiquitous deployment of the figure of the professional and its codes of comportment.

The category of professional work was once defined narrowly. Confined to those jobs that were subject to a measure of self-regulation, required specialized knowledge, and involved a relatively high degree of discretion and judgment, the label was traditionally reserved for the fields of law, medicine, and the clergy. To be a professional was to have a career—a calling—as opposed to a "mere" job: "To the professional person his work becomes his life. Hence the act of embarking upon a professional career is similar in some respects to entering a religious order" (Greenwood 1966, 17). The professional's relationship to his or her calling entailed an erosion of the temporal boundaries between work and life, and a different calibration of the qualities of emotional investment between the times and spaces of work and life outside it. As Lisa Disch and Jean O'Brien observe in the case of professorial labor, the professional regards him or herself as incommensurable and, therefore, is willing to do what needs doing rather than only what he or she is paid to do (2007, 149). Professional socialization has always served as a disciplinary mechanism, one that can induce the effort and commitment, entitlement and identification, and—perhaps above all—the self-monitoring considered necessary to a profession's reproduction as such.

The expansion of the professional strata and of the ideology of professionalism was something C. Wright Mills noted in his early anticipation of the changes in work wrought by the move to a postindustrial labor order and the new ways that subjectivity is put to work in white-collar occupations. Whereas the term once suggested a certain mastery of a field of knowledge linked to a specific skill and expertise, increasingly the mastery that a professional is expected to achieve is over what Mills called "the personality." In other words, whereas the high-priced man of Taylor's narrative was required to discipline his physical efforts, today's professional is supposed to gain control over his or her thoughts, imagination, relationships, and affects. Certainly one purpose of this is to promote the kind of self-discipline and subjective investment long associated with being a professional. And because, like the high-priced man, the professional "wears a badge of prestige" (C. Mills 1951, 138), the practice of hailing a wide range of workers as professionals also serves to cash in on the term's cachet and encourage employees to identify with jobs further up the labor hierarchy. To recall Weber's description of the Protestant work ethic, according to which all waged workers were expected to approach their work industriously as if it were a calling, those in low-waged service-sector jobs under post-Fordism are asked to approach their work professionally as if it were a "career." This professionalization of work, the expansion of what is considered a profession and, more important, the number of workers who are expected to "be professional" is one way this disciplinary subjectification is extended both up and down the labor hierarchy in a post-Taylorist age.

Professionalization in this broader application is more about style, affect, and attitude than about the content of the work. Mills notes that white-collar workers' "claims to prestige are expressed, as their label implies, by their style of appearance" (241). In contrast to the uniforms typically required of blue-collar workers, white-collar employees wear their own clothes, mass-produced and standardized though they may be, both at work and at home. This is, Mills observes, reflected in the amount of money that white-collar workers, especially women, spend on clothes. As the studies of two very different contemporary workforces each affirms, the "collar" metaphor has always been about clothes, and clothes in turn are key signifiers of the professional. Carla Freeman's (2000) study of pink-collar office workers in the Caribbean focuses on how the workers were encouraged to identify themselves as professionals, an identification that centered crucially on styles of clothing. This was a source of many pleasures, even or particularly when there was little else about the work that was comparably satisfying. In this case, the discourse of professionalism links the practices and identities of production with those of consumption; indeed, that is part of the attraction of professionalized work, one of the ways that this ideology of the professional promotes consent to and identification with work. Linking professional status and identity to the practices of consumption taps into the many ways that style and dress can serve as statements of individuality, markers of status, objects of pleasure, and sites of aspiration. The professional look, and the time and resources necessary to achieve it, tie us not only economically and socially but also aesthetically and affectively to work. What Andrew Ross dubs the "no-collar" nonconformist mentality of a higher-paid technoscientific knowledge and informational workforce in the United States is signaled by a fashion style quite explicitly opposed to the dress codes of the organizational white-collar worker of high Fordism. Indeed, the creativity and individuality of this no-collar style serves to capture visually the ideal of work that the post-Fordist work ethic celebrates. The carefully crafted theatricality of style signifies the kind of creativity, risk, and iconoclasm that these Internet industries try to sell to both customers and their own workers, to both their "external" and "internal" clients (see Ross 2003, 3, 32, 50).

The workers described in both Freeman's and Ross's accounts used clothes and style as a way to distinguish their employment sector from others (as pink-collar rather than blue-collar, or as no-collar in contrast to white-collar) and, by the same token, to display their status as individuals within that setting rather than merely as members of a "collared" class fraction. But as Hochschild notes in her study of flight attendants, another iconic pink-collar labor force, by defending the intensive managerial control over the workers' appearance through "continuous reference to the need to be 'professional,'" the standardized results may be imbued with honor and the aura of autonomy, but they nonetheless remain highly regulated.[24] According to the industry's standard of professionalism, "the flight attendant who most nearly meets the appearance code ideal is therefore 'the most professional.'" Consequently, she observes, "for them a 'professional' flight attendant is one who has completely accepted the rules of standardization" (1983, 103).

Today the term "professional" refers more to a prescribed attitude toward any work than the status of some work. To act like a professional —to be professional in one's work—calls for subjective investment in and identification with work, but also a kind of affective distancing from it. A professional invests his or her person in the job but does not "take it personally" when dealing with difficult co-workers, clients, patients, students, passengers, or customers. As an ideal of worker subjectivity, this requires not just the performance of a role, but a deeper commitment of the self, an immersion in and identification not just with work, but with work discipline. The popular injunction to "be professional," to cultivate a professional attitude, style, and persona, serves as one way that the autonomy, especially of immaterial workers, can be managerially constituted up and down the post-Fordist labor hierarchy.

CONCLUSION

The five antinomies we reviewed earlier in the chapter are indicative of both the capaciousness of the discourse and its limits, its seeming unassailability and its vulnerabilities. To return again to the original Protestant ethic, Weber cautions us to remember that Puritanism was not a seamless and monolithic force, but in fact "included a world of contradictions" (1958, 169). Together these antinomies suggest that although the hegemony of the work ethic may be substantial, it is also always incomplete, tenuous, and shifting. First, what is from one perspective often taken to be the most rational of behaviors appears irrational once we probe a bit further: that part of the cultural devotion to work that cannot be explained by simple economic necessity often proves strangely inexplicable. Second, the relationship between the ethic's productivist and consumerist prescriptions may be functional, but the tensions between them also generate instabilities and openings for critique. On the one hand, this relationship serves to coordinate production and consumption; on the other hand, stipulating levels of consumption and production that can be adequate to one another risks stimulating desires for consumption that cannot be met through the available forms of employment. Third, a discourse that prescribes at once dependence and independence proves a constant source of potential disorder. The work ethic may invoke the ideals of individualism, but the subjects of those ideals must be managed in accordance with the strict exigencies of capitalist production and reproduction. Fourth, whereas the work ethic in its different historical instantiations has proven enormously useful in cultivating exploitable subjects, it has also been deployed as a weapon of the weak, serving simultaneously as a resource both for the accumulation of capital and for those who would contest its methods. The ethic's promises about work are instilled as desires, beliefs, interests, and hopes that are never fully met; in that sense, the ethical anchor of the capitalist wage relation can also produce wants and needs in excess of those that are merely functional to its reproduction. Finally, the ethic's means of transmission are also key to some of its contradictory dynamics. Spreading as it does through processes of othering and its oppositions—whereby these others could be constructed as abject but also, potentially, as resistant subjects—introduces another element of unpredictability. My claim is that the antinomies that animate the work ethic account for both the continued authority of its prescriptions and the precariousness of its dominance.

The importance of the ethic persists under the conditions of post-Fordism, as does its vulnerability. The ability of work to harness desires for a life beyond work depends, perhaps now more than ever, on the power of the work ethic. The ethic's consistent prescriptions for our identification with and constant devotion to work, its elevation of work as the rightful center of life, and its affirmation of work as an end in itself all help to produce the kinds of workers and the laboring capacities adequate to the contemporary regime of accumulation and the specific modes of social labor in which it invests. But the changes in the labor processes that make work values more important to capital may also render them less plausible. With each reconstitution of the work ethic, more is expected of work: from an epistemological reward in the deliverance of certainty, to a socioeconomic reward in the possibility of social mobility, to an ontological reward in the promise of meaning and self-actualization. Indeed, for the anxious Protestant of Weber's account, the quality of work and quantity of wages, the nature of the concrete task and the amount of income it earned, were less relevant than the level of effort the worker applied. Today, in contrast, both the quality of the labor process and the quantity of its material rewards are relevant to the ability of the discourse to deliver on its new ideals of work.

With so much at stake, weighed down with so many expectations, it is no wonder that the ethical discourse of work is becoming ever more abstracted from the realities of many jobs. Within the two-tiered labor market, we find new modes of "over-valorized work" at one end of the labor hierarchy and "devalorized work" at the other (Peterson 2003, 76). Making labor flexible results in an increase of part-time, temporary, casual, and precarious forms of work. At one end, as Stanley Aronowitz and William DiFazio note, "the quality and the quantity of paid labor no longer justify—if they ever did—the underlying claim derived from religious sources that has become the basis of contemporary social theory and social policy: the view that paid work should be the core of personal identity" (1994, 302). At the other end of the labor hierarchy, work is expected to be the whole of life, colonizing and eclipsing what remains of the social. At the same time, the work ethic is more insistently—and perhaps desperately—defended. "Never," André Gorz observes, "has the 'irreplaceable,' 'indispensable' function of labour as the source of 'social ties,' 'social cohesion,' 'integration,' 'socialization,' 'personalization,' 'personal identity' and meaning been invoked so obsessively as it has since the day it became unable any longer to fulfill *any* of these functions" (1999, 57). Today we hear once again about the potentially drastic consequences of a weakening work ethic among yet another generation whose members, it is feared, will fail to be successfully interpellated. Given the work ethic's internal instabilities, we might conclude that its advocates and promoters have cause to be concerned. Where attitudes are productive, an insubordination to the work ethic; a skepticism about the virtues of self-discipline for the sake of capital accumulation; an unwillingness to cultivate, simply on principle, a good "professional" attitude about work; and a refusal to subordinate all of life to work carry a new kind of subversive potential. My claims are that, given its role, the work ethic *should* be contested, and, due to its instabilities, it *can* be contested.

CHAPTER 2

Marxism, Productivism, and the Refusal of Work

> If hard work were really such a great thing,
> the rich would have kept it all to themselves.
> UNION ACTIVIST

A cultural dominant the work ethic may be; seamless and incontrovertible it is certainly not. The previous chapter touched on one reaction to the exclusions enacted by the work ethic—namely, demands for inclusion that draw on alternative work ethics as tools of insubordination—and considered both the advantages and limitations of this response. But there are other kinds of approaches: the story of the work ethic in the United States is not only about abject subjects and their struggles for recognition but also about various disavowals of and resistances to the normative discourse of work. There is also a parallel history featuring those who failed to internalize the gospel of work—a history of "bad subjects" who resist and may even escape interpellation. One chapter of this story could center on the protests of sectors of the industrial working class whose class consciousness was articulated not by way of a laborist ethic but, as Michael Seidman describes it, "by avoiding the space, time and demands of wage labor" (1991, 169). Another might feature the perspectives of those in the rank and file who saw leisure neither as a means to recreate labor power and ensure consumption, nor as a way to spread the available employment and drive wages up, but as an end in itself, as the gratifying time of nonwork (see Rodgers 1978, 159–60). This alternate history could focus too on the segments of the black working class whose story Robin Kelley recounts, like the zoot suiters and hipsters who, "refusing to be good proletarians," pursued a different mode of race rebellion, seeking meaning and pleasure in the times and spaces of nonwork (1994, 163); and those second-wave feminists, including feminists associated with the wages for housework movement, who insisted that work—whether waged work or unwaged domestic labor— was not something to which women should aspire but rather something they should try to escape. This history of disidentification with the work ethic might also include various youth subcultures, from beatniks to hippies, punks, and slackers, all constituted in opposition to what E. P. Thompson calls "the Puritan time-valuation" (1991, 401). Today the rebellion against the imposition of work finds expression in the agendas of a number of activist groups and advocacy organizations, with arguably some of the most vibrant examples coming out of the European precarity movements that have responded to the increasing flexibilization and precariousness of work with a call not for the restoration of the stable and reliable—but also one-sided and all-consuming—Fordist wage relation, but rather, for the ability to secure an entirely different relation between life and work.[1]

The work orientations of welfare recipients in the United States are interesting for what they reveal about how the work ethic has been both internalized and resisted. Contrary to the often-deployed "cultural deficiency" discourses, studies of the effects of the 1996 welfare reform (the Personal Responsibility and Work Opportunity Reconciliation Act) find much support among recipients for the idea of reform and for the familiar ethic of work in whose name it was advanced. Indeed, "poor mothers' support for welfare reform is the single most striking indication that welfare mothers are not the social 'outsiders' portrayed in the Personal Responsibility Act," reports Sharon Hays (2003, 215). But the history of the US welfare system also reveals the many ways in which recipients have become politicized in relation to work-ethic discourses. From the mid 1960s through the early 1970s, the National Welfare Rights Organization explicitly refused to accept the view that waged work is the only legitimate means of meeting consumption needs. Working the antinomy between productivism and consumerism, these activists rejected the necessity and legitimacy of the link and fought for the individual's right to an income regardless of his or her participation in waged work (see Kornbluh 1997; Nadasen 2002).[2] Thus, even those so insistently targeted by the ethic's judgments and often disenfranchised by means of its prescriptions have mounted radical and forceful challenges to its legitimacy.

My point is simply that the history of the imposition of waged labor and its dominant ethic is incomplete without a parallel history of rebellions and refusals; the ethic generates not only oppositions and their recuperations but also lines of flight. But rather than continue to recount this history, the analysis that follows attempts to do something else: to identify and explore some theoretical resources that might illuminate and enrich antiwork politics and postwork imaginaries.

MARXISM AND PRODUCTIVISM

These theoretical tools are drawn from the Marxist tradition, admittedly both an obvious and a curious resource for a critical, let alone feminist, analysis of work: obvious for its focus on labor, curious because Marxism is so often understood in terms of its commitment to work's acclamation, to the liberation of work from exploitation and the restoration of its dignity in unalienated form. As noted in the introduction, however, there are alternatives within the tradition, including some that couple the critique of work's structures and relations with a more direct confrontation with its values. Autonomist Marxism is one such approach, and a concept central to that tradition—the refusal of work—is an inspiration for the political theory of and against work that I seek to develop throughout this book and central to the critical analyses, political agendas, and utopian speculations that flesh it out. To understand the refusal of work as a Marxist concept that nonetheless takes aim at a fairly broad swath of Marxist history, the chapter will begin with a brief genealogical account that will situate the refusal of work in relation to a history of conflict within Marxism over the nature, meaning, and value of work, a field of contestation for which the critique of productivism will serve as our point of entry.

The critique of productivism in Marxism was put forth perhaps most succinctly and certainly most provocatively by Jean Baudrillard in *The Mirror of Production*. According to Baudrillard, "a specter haunts the revolutionary imagination: the phantom of production. Everywhere it sustains an unbridled romanticism of productivity" (1975, 17). As he sees it, historical materialism reproduces political economy's fetishism of labor; the evidence of Marxism's complicity can be found in a naturalized ontology of labor and a utopian vision of a future in which this essence is fully realized in the form of an unhindered productivity. Baudrillard finds within this normative ideal—this "sanctification of work"

(36)—an allegiance to the values of worldly asceticism in which the richness, spontaneity, and plurality of social practices and relations are subordinated to the instrumental and rationalist logic of productivity, with its exaltation of activities centered on controlling nature in the service of strictly utilitarian ends. What Baudrillard identifies as Marxism's commitment to productivism, its inability to break from the work values that have developed alongside and in support of Western capitalist social formations, represents a failure of both critical analysis and utopian imagination.

Despite the problems with Baudrillard's totalizing indictment of Marxism in its entirety, his critique provides an opportunity to expose and reconsider the productivist assumptions and values that remain stubbornly embedded within at least some contributions to the field. Think, for example, of the critical treatment that the seductive, distracting, and—so it would seem—inevitably degrading pleasures of consumption sometimes receive. The residues of the traditional ethics of work also appear, I would argue, in the ways that the language of creativity is in some instances deployed as a synonym for labor, at least when it has the effect of not only selectively expanding what counts as labor but also elevating its status as a worthy human practice. Thus, for example, by describing postcapitalist society in terms of a liberation of creative activity, even nonwork can be imagined as a disciplined practice directed toward a laudable goal, and distanced from something that risks association with the sin of sloth. The Marxist commitment to these traditional work values is perhaps most clearly displayed in two examples from the history of the tradition—examples that often still dominate particularly non-Marxist representations of the field—which I will call socialist modernization and socialist humanism. These paradigms' assumptions about work are brought into especially sharp relief when viewed through the lens of their respective utopian speculations about postcapitalist alternatives, one posed as an overcoming of labor's exploitation and the other presented as a remedy for labor's alienation.[3] I have selected these two approaches for brief review because their commitments to the essential value of work that Baudrillard criticizes are so clearly exhibited and because they offer an instructive contrast to the examination of autonomist Marxism's antiproductivist approach to work that follows. In addition, the assumptions of the first two approaches about the nature and value of work are extraordinarily persistent, regularly turning up in the critical frameworks and normative visions of a variety of analyses, both within and beyond the Marxist tradition. Their defenses of work and reiteration of its traditional values have yet to be fully reckoned with.

SOCIALIST MODERNIZATION

The utopia of modernization constitutes the characterization of a post-capitalist alternative most popularly ascribed to Marxism. In this vision, communism is equated with the full realization of the productive potential of the forces of production developed under capitalism. The critique of capital, in this version, centers on the problematic of exploitation and the contradiction between the forces and relations of production. Exploitation proceeds from the private ownership of productive forces and consists of the private appropriation of the fruits of surplus labor. According to this well-rehearsed story of capitalist development, these bourgeois property relations eventually become impediments to the full development of modern productive forces: "The conditions of bourgeois society are too narrow to comprise the wealth created by them" (Marx and Engels 1992, 9). Communism, in contrast, would democratize the economic relations of ownership and control. The relations of production—class relations—would be thus radically transfigured, while the means of production and the labor process itself would merely be unfettered.

Although it is usually associated with the political legacy of state socialism, socialist modernization does have some points of reference in the writings of Marx and the Marxist tradition. For example, in a text from 1918 consistent with this paradigm's theory of revolution, Lenin distinguished between two phases after the overthrow of capitalism: the first, socialist phase, in which "factory discipline" is extended over the whole of society; and the final phase of true communism. The socialist stage—a lengthy period of transition between capitalism and communism whose precise duration is unknown—requires from workers "self-sacrifice," "perseverance," and a commitment to "the proper path of steady and disciplined labour" (Lenin 1989, 223, 226). To ensure that communism is achieved in the future, the offensive against capital must be partially suspended during the transition. Socialism thus involves a temporary intensification of capitalism, whereas communism is imagined abstractly as its pure transcendence. In the meantime, "the task that the Soviet government must set the people in all its scope is—learn to work" (240). This includes the use of piece rates, competition among firms, and time-motion analyses. Nowhere is this utopia of moderniza-tion more clearly prefigured than in Lenin's fascination with and admi-ration of Taylorism, and in his insistence on the need for an iron work discipline to combat petit bourgeois laziness, selfishness, and anarchy (see 240–41, 257). But what Lenin considered to be only a means of dealing with the difficult conditions of the immediate postrevolutionary period became, in the hands of others—as the utopia was either deferred into the ever-more-distant future or declared achieved—an end in itself. Perhaps later Soviet policies and rhetoric provide the purest examples of this ideal of modernization. With its affirmation of the heroic, world-building capacities of disciplined, proletarian labor, the vision depends upon and revolves around a valorization of the creative force of human labor, conceived narrowly as social production.

From a Marxist perspective, the problem with this version of the productivist vision is that because it is founded upon an insufficient critique of capital, its vision of an alternative preserves too many of capitalism's structures and values. This tribute to proletarian labor and to the progressive development of productive forces replicates the funda-mental attributes of capitalist society; in this account, the working class inherits and carries on the historical role of the bourgeoisie, who first revealed to us the "productive forces [that] slumbered in the lap of social labor" (Marx and Engels 1992, 8). Here we find an endorsement of economic growth, industrial progress, and the work ethic similar to the one that can be found in bourgeois political economy, with its natural-ization and celebration of the processes of economic modernization. The figures of Stakhanov and Oblomov offer an official Soviet version of the political economists' parable about the ethically deserving and unde-serving, but with the class positions reversed: the worthy industrious worker and useless lazy nobleman. In this form, the critique of capitalist production does not extend, for example, to the labor process itself, and thus does not account adequately for Marx's many pointed critiques of the mind-numbing and repetitive qualities of factory labor, or his insis-tence that freedom requires a shortening of the working day. This narra-tive limits communism to a transformation of property relations, leaving the basic form of industrial production—and even the mode of capitalist command over production—intact. The future alternative to capitalism is reduced, according to Moishe Postone's critical reading of this logic, to "a new mode of politically administering and economically regulating the *same* industrial mode of producing to which capitalism gave rise" (1996, 9). Accordingly, communism could be understood as the rationalization of capitalism, the taming and mastery of its processes.

SOCIALIST HUMANISM

A second example from the archive of Marxist history that sets itself against the modernization model but that nonetheless shares its fundamental commitment to work gained popularity among many Anglo-American Marxists in the 1960s. Whereas the modernization discourse originated in the context of revolutionary movements in Europe during the late nineteenth and the early twentieth centuries, the development and popularization of this model of humanist Marxism coincided with the rise of the New Left. Erich Fromm's *Marx's Concept of Man*, published in 1961 as an accompaniment to the first US publication of Marx's *Economic and Philosophic Manuscripts*, presents a classic statement of this reading of Marx. It is an attempt to rescue Marxism not only from its association with existing socialist regimes, but also from its more economistic and determinist tendencies. Drawing on the *Manuscripts* (which were first published in the 1920s and first translated into English in 1959), Fromm reconstructs a counter-Marx: a philosophical Marx grounded in a humanist tradition and centered on a commitment to the creative individual as unit of analysis and motor of history. Whereas the earlier model, Marxist modernization, gravitates toward *Capital* and *The Communist Manifesto* as privileged texts, this humanist discourse traces its lineage to Marx's early writings, the *Manuscripts* and *The German Ideology*. While the utopia of modernization is conceived as a response to the critique of bourgeois property relations and the problematic of exploitation, the humanist utopia grows out of the critique of alienated labor. Whereas the former focuses on notions of social progress, social justice, and social harmony, the latter privileges the individual as a crucial category and fundamental value. Indeed, according to Fromm, Marx's philosophy "was aimed at the full realization of individualism" (1961, 3). There is a romantic dimension to this as well, which is evident in Fromm's descriptions of Marx's philosophy as "a movement against the dehumanization and automatization of man inherent in the development of Western industrialism" (1961, v) and a "spiritual-humanistic" alternative to the "mechanistic-materialistic spirit of successful industrialism" (72). Together, the utopia of modernization and the humanist utopia present a

Marxist gloss on the two faces of modernity: an ideal of social and economic progress grounded in the continuing development of science and industry and the romantic revolt against the forces of rationalization accompanying that ideal.

The two visions of the future—socialist modernization and socialist humanism—are in some ways opposed to one another, but they are based on a similar commitment to labor as a fundamental human value. In the first, labor is conceived as social production and lauded as the primary mechanism of social cohesion and achievement. In the second, labor is understood as an individual creative capacity, a human essence, from which we are now estranged and to which we should be restored. Drawing on Marx's *Manuscripts*, Fromm insists that the self-realization of man, which he understands to be Marx's central concern, is inextricably linked to the activity of work: "In this process of genuine activity man develops himself, becomes himself; work is not only a means to an end— the product—but an end in itself, the meaningful expression of human energy; hence work is enjoyable" (1961, 41–42). The problem with capitalism is that it estranges us from our essential nature, our authentic selves; alienation is in this sense the negation of productivity (43). "For Marx," Fromm argues, "socialism meant the social order which permits the return of man to himself, the identity between existence and essence" (69). Unalienated labor, as the reigning ideal around which a future utopian society is to be organized, is imagined as the primary means of individual self-realization and self-fulfillment. Fromm presents a long quote from the third volume of *Capital*—a famous passage in which Marx envisions a realm of freedom above and beyond a realm of necessity—and insists that all the essential elements of socialism can be found therein (59–60). In Fromm's reading of this passage, we find the key to the humanist vision of unalienated labor: a transformation of the world of work into a cooperative process that is controlled by the individual producers. It is not the planned economy that produces freedom, but participation in the activity of organizing and planning that enables one to be free: freedom is a matter of individual independence, "which is based on man's [the individual's] standing on his own feet, using his own powers and relating himself to the world productively" (61).

Fromm's cure for capitalism is not more work, as Lenin once prescribed, but better work. "The central theme of Marx," Fromm insists, "is the transformation of alienated, meaningless labor into productive, free labor" (1961, 43); this is the means by which we can finally realize our true humanity. It is interesting to note that in Fromm's discussion of that famous passage from the third volume of *Capital*, the passage that he characterized as expressing all the essential elements of socialism, he quotes the passage at length up through the part where Marx states that the realm of freedom can flourish only with the realm of necessity as its basis but omits the next and concluding sentence of the paragraph, in which Marx adds that "the reduction of the working day is the basic prerequisite" (Marx 1981, 959). Later in his book, Fromm quotes a shorter section of the same passage, this time including the final sentence about the need to shorten the working day. Yet his lack of interest in the ideal of work reduction is still clear: he adds italics to emphasize every part of the quote except the final sentence, upon which he again neglects to comment (1961, 76). Why work less if work in its unalienated form as socialized production is the expression of and means to self-creation? The goal is to restore work's dignity and worth, not to contest its status as the pillar of social value.

Unlike the modernization model, which rejected private property and the market while accepting and adapting the basic contours of capitalist discipline, the humanist paradigm incorporates a more extensive critique of work. This critique is, however, hindered by a tendency toward nostalgia for an earlier time, a romanticization of craft production that informs its visions of an alternative. Fromm argues that alienation is greater now than it was in the earlier stage of capitalism when handicraft production and manufacturing prevailed (1961, 51). Concrete labor in the production of use values is sometimes suggested in these analyses as the alternative to the abstract labor that produces exchange values. Thus, for example, in an essay that fits solidly within this humanist rubric, David McLellan presents another reconstruction, drawn largely from Marx's early writings, of communism as an unalienated society in which we have a direct and personal connection to the products of our labor (McLellan 1969, 464): as objectifications of our laboring essence, the objects we create would serve as confirmations of our being. Instead of producing superfluous things to sell on the market in order to produce surplus value, we would produce useful things for immediate consumption. As opposed to abstract labor as both a conceptual abstraction that reduces different kinds of concrete labor to labor in general and a practical process that transforms the concrete laboring activities of individuals according to the exigencies of large-scale social production, this romantic-humanist perspective tends to valorize concrete labor as an alternative.

As I noted above, at least some of these assumptions about the nature and meaning of work and the kind of speculative visions they inform can be found in sites outside the tradition of socialist humanism represented here by Fromm. Both Maria Mies and Neala Schleuning, for example, present Marxist feminist critiques of industrial capitalist modernization and visions of an alternative economy that resonate with this humanist paradigm. Mies, for example, explicitly rejects what she takes to be the Marxist view that freedom exists beyond the realm of necessity and requires a reduction or abolition of necessary labor (1986, 216). Some forms of work, she argues, should be recognized not as a burden but as a source of enjoyment and self-expression (217), including the work of mothering, peasant labor, and artisanal production—provided that they are not completely submerged in commodity production and beholden to market logics. Schleuning's critique of modern alienated labor is grounded similarly in a model of "good work," this one gleaned from pre-industrial reproductive labor (1990, 90–92). What makes these forms of work so fulfilling in the view of these authors is that they are all involved in the direct, immediate production of life rather than the production of things or wealth (Mies 1986, 217); they produce for use rather than for consumption (Schleuning 1990, 85).[4] We need to have a sense of necessity and purpose in our work; to find this, we should produce useful products (Mies 1986, 218). The goal is to envision a community in which work is once again integrated with life (Schleuning 1990, 45). The length of the working day would then be irrelevant: "a long working-day and even a lifetime full of work, will not then be felt as a curse but as a source of human fulfillment and happiness" (Mies 1986, 217).

Despite the importance of these authors' critique of unsustainable patterns of consumption and their interrogation of a commodity fetishism that functions to deflect questions about the relationship between consumer goods and the conditions under which they are produced, the link the authors affirm between support of productivism and opposition to consumerism reiterates one of the central tenets of the traditional work ethic. One of the problems with these accounts is their tendency to tether individual consumption to individual production. Affirming one of the more direct and unyielding of the links between production and consumption, the authors hold that the ideal is to consume only that which we produce as individuals or members of a community. According to Mies, "only by *consuming* the things which we produce can we judge whether they are useful, meaningful and wholesome, whether they are necessary or superfluous. And only by *producing* what we consume can we know how much time is really necessary for the things we want to consume, what skills are necessary, what knowledge is necessary and what technology is necessary" (219). Production for direct use and consumption for clear need: each places strict limits on the other. Insisting that we must produce in order to consume and consume only what we produce is a prescription for worldly asceticism of the first order.

HUMANISM REVISITED

Just as the humanists stood opposed to the modernization model, we can get an initial sense of the autonomist tradition through its critiques of the kind of interpretive practices and utopian visions that sustain the humanist paradigm described above. In some ways, the critique of alienation that is central to the humanist critique of capitalism in its Fordist incarnation seems even more applicable to the conditions of post-Fordist labor that the autonomists, representing a more recent theoretical project, attempt to address. When more jobs require workers to supply not only manual effort but also emotional skills, affective capacities, and communicative competencies—that is, when more of the self is drawn into labor processes and managed in accordance with the exigencies of profit maximization—the problem of alienation, from both self and others, arguably grows more acute. Yet there remain problems with the critique. For example, particularly when the individual is the unit of analysis, as in many of the arguments noted above, the critique of alienation becomes attached to a prior claim about the nature of the human subject. As Baudrillard describes it, this model of the human founded in a transhistorical capacity for labor mimics the standardization and generalization of work that was established under the conditions of industrialization. To put it in other terms, the abstraction from the concrete and particular that allows one to grasp labor quantitatively is what also allows one to conceive the commensurability of its qualitative instances as the expression of an essential humanity. In this way, Baudrillard explains, "the abstract and formal universality of the commodity labor power is what supports the 'concrete' universality of qualitative labor" (1975, 27). There are two points to emphasize here: first, rather than a critical standpoint outside capital, the notion of man as producer is part and parcel of the practical and ideological imposition of abstract labor; second, and more important, the notion is a mythology internal to and, with its confirmation of work's existential rather than merely practical necessity, ultimately supportive of the work society.

Despite Baudrillard's polemical indictment of Marxism *tout court*, the critique he levels at this type of analytical practice is not uncommon within the Marxist tradition, with the claim about human nature being perhaps the most widely contested. The autonomist theorist Antonio Negri, for example, expresses no interest in the problematic of alienation as a discourse of interiority, of the loss and restoration of an essential human nature. The "so-called humanism of Marx," in which actual historical tendencies are corralled into a predictable narrative of "the organic unfolding of human nature (even if it is defined historically)," is the product of an "impatience with theory, a usage of positive utopia destined to homogenize transition and communism" (1991, 154). Possible futures are, by this means, circumscribed by ready-made visions and predictable outcomes. Baudrillard describes the practical limits of such a move in bold terms: "What an absurdity it is to pretend that men are 'other,' to try to convince them that their deepest desire is to become 'themselves' again!" (1975, 166). How can we be empowered to act on the basis of desires deemed "inauthentic"? There is, by Negri's reading of the *Grundrisse*, no concept of work to restore or to liberate (1991, 10); rather, the organization and meaning of work remains open to radical reinvention. As we will see, autonomists tend to shift the analytical frame from the question of individual nature to the possibilities of collective constitution, from a self to restore to selves to invent.

The vision of an alternative that rests on the paradigm of concrete labor is also problematic from the perspective of other Marxist analytics. To see, as Schleuning and Mies do, concrete labor as a utopian alternative to abstract labor and the production of use values as a replacement for the production of exchange value is to once again imagine as outside a critical standpoint that is in fact inside. The pairings that Marx uses to develop his analysis—use value and exchange value, concrete labor and abstract labor—are part of a critical strategy, not elements of an alternative vision. Nietzsche's pairing of noble morality and slave morality offers an instructive comparison: although he makes use of the distinction by measuring one against the standards of the other, he does not present a return to noble morality as either possible or desirable; the category of noble morality serves as a tool by which to advance the critique of slave morality, rather than as a vision of a better past or future. In a similar way, Marx's categorical distinctions do not provide a remedy to the system he critiques. An alternative to capitalist society would require that we move beyond both abstract labor under capitalism and the modes of concrete labor that are also shaped by it. As another autonomist theorist, Harry Cleaver, reads Marx, "to speak of postcapitalist 'useful labour' is as problematic as to speak of the post-capitalist state" (2000, 129).[5] Again, the problem is that this affirmation of labor—in this case, the useful work of particular individuals—reinforces one of the critical supports of the system it seeks to overcome.

Indeed, as Gayatri Spivak observes, posing use value against exchange value is "far too Luddite a binary opposition" to account for Marx's argument (2000, 2). The Marx that some other interpreters, including autonomists, build on is the one whose description of life in a communist society—where one could "hunt in the morning, fish in the afternoon, rear cattle in the evening, criticise after dinner, just as I have a mind without ever becoming hunter, fisherman, shepherd or critic" (Marx and Engels 1970, 53)—was not an affirmation of artisanal production, but at once a critique of the division of labor and an ironic jab at the kind of pastoral, pre-industrial visions advanced by the utopian socialists.[6] This is the same Marx who argues explicitly in favor of the virtues of cooperation on a mass scale, a form of social labor that he distinguishes qualitatively from handicraft production. The power of social production "arises from co-operation itself," Marx claims in *Capital*: "When the worker co-operates in a planned way with others, he strips off the fetters of his individuality, and develops the capabilities of his species" (1976, 447). Beginning with this stage of cooperation, the individual privileged in the humanist model is no longer the proper unit of analysis; the vision of an individual worker who produces a specific useful product is inconsistent with processes that come to incorporate general technical and scientific knowledge that cannot be attributed to specific individuals. According to Marx in the *Grundrisse*:

In earlier stages of development the single individual seems to be developed more fully, because he has not yet worked out his relationships in their fullness, or erected them as independent social powers and relations opposite himself. It is as ridiculous to yearn for a return to that original fullness as it is to believe that with this complete emptiness history has come to a standstill. The bourgeois viewpoint has never advanced beyond this antithesis between itself and this romantic viewpoint, and therefore the latter will accompany it as legitimate antithesis up to its blessed end. (1973, 162)

This development points not back to an older mode of organization centered on independent individuals, but rather forward to new ways of organizing work and production and new models of subjectivity.

AUTONOMIST MARXISM

The attraction of work as a model behavior and human value exerts a powerful hold not only on the liberal but also the Marxist imagination. Thus, it is not only capital that moralizes, normalizes, and mythologizes work; as Negri notes in a text from 1977, the "official socialist movement" also treats the imposition of work as if it were a "title of nobility" and continually attempts to suppress its refusal (2005, 263, 269). Autonomist Marxism's concept of the refusal of work represents a particularly cogent and timely alternative to such productivist tendencies. The tradition of autonomist Marxism originated alongside and in response to the Italian social movements from the late 1960s and the 1970s, and although the movements that inspired the original work were crushed, the theoretical approach—together with some aspects of the political project—live on (see Dyer-Witheford 1999, 64).[7] Since the refusal of work, both as a theoretical framework and a political agenda, grows out of the broader methodological orientation that characterizes the tradition, I will start with the more general terrain before moving on to the specific.

One way to begin is to situate the autonomist tradition in relation to the two paradigms reviewed above: socialist modernization and socialist humanism. The particular texts they tend to privilege offer one such point of contrast. Whereas *Capital* was key for classical Marxism and the *Manuscripts* was a principal text for the humanists, the *Grundrisse* is a particularly important resource for the autonomists. In his study of that text, *Marx beyond Marx*, Negri explains his attraction to it in terms of his own political situation. Rather than a simple precursor to or early draft of *Capital*, the *Grundrisse* was written in light of a specific crisis in 1857 and is best understood as an attempt to theorize its revolutionary possibilities. Thus, in this case, "there is no possibility . . . of destroying the dynamism of this process by hypostatizing it, by rigidifying it into a totality with its own laws of development that one might be able to possess, or dominate, or reverse" (Negri 1991, 9). The autonomist theorists took their lead from the revolutionary agitation of a loose coalition of workers, students, feminists, and unemployed people that roiled Italy in the 1960s and 1970s. "We find ourselves," Negri writes in 1979, "in a phase where the revolutionary movement is seeking new foundations, and in a way that will not be that of a minority." In this situation, he explains, "we have nothing to do with orthodoxy" (1991, 17). Although there is a fidelity to Marx in Negri's work that might be construed to be as orthodox as any other, what is arguably unorthodox is the willingness to invent a Marx beyond Marx—that is, to move beyond Marx's own analyses in order to keep up with the changing forms of capitalist development and the modes of rebellion generated within. The *Grundrisse*, in Negri's reading, restores Marx as a theorist of crisis rather than equilibrium, of subjective agency rather than objective tendencies, of antagonism and separation rather than opposition and synthesis. Perhaps what characterizes the autonomist tradition more than anything else is its attempts to restore the methodological and political primacy of subjectivity. In this sense, autonomist Marxism can be linked to that broader subtradition within Marxism that seeks to theorize not from what Michael Lebowitz describes as the "one-sided" perspective of capital and its reproduction, but from the perspective of the workers and their potential to subvert that power (1992).[8] This insistence on the power of active subjects requires a dismantling of some of the analytical and organizational apparatuses within Marxist theory and practice that held these subjective forces in check, from the metaphysics of labor, to the Leninist party and the traditional labor union. This restoration of the primacy of subjectivity also involves a rejection of determinism, teleology, and, as we will see, a refusal of the recuperative logic of the dialectic.

The focus of this approach is on the collective as unit of analysis and locus of political agency. The thesis that exemplifies this approach—sometimes called the "leading role of the proletariat" or the "autonomist hypothesis"—concentrates on class struggle as the primary engine of change. As Jason Read explains this thesis, which has served in some respects as the autonomist tradition's methodological center of gravity, working-class resistance precedes and prefigures developments in capitalist production (2003, 13); workers are to be conceived not primarily as capital's victims but as its antagonists (see Tronti 1980). By this estimation, neither capital nor labor power is the primary creative element; rather, working-class insubordination is the dynamic force in history. The hypothesis is perhaps most compelling not as a historical law or even a sociological generalization, but as a methodological rule of thumb that forces us to look for disequilibrium where we might expect to find stability, that scrambles traditional assumptions about who is active and who is reactive, and that encourages recognition of the working class not primarily in terms of its economic role but as a political agent. According to this reading of Marx, "the *working class is defined by its struggle against capital* and not by its productive function" (Zerowork 1975, 3).

Who might be included in this category of the working class remains an open question. It is not a sociological category but a political one, and its boundaries depend on its particular composition at specific times and places. The concept of class composition affirms the "historical transformability of the composition of the class," and, in Negri's view, also the expansion of who might be included in the political formation of the working class over time (1988, 209). That is, the notion of class composition both sets the category of the working class in historical motion and broadens its reach. In terms of historical dynamics, forms of political solidarity that workers achieve provoke a reaction on the part of capital, a reorganization that has the effect of breaking the composition of the class and restoring it in a more functional mode. So, for example, Taylorist mass production was a way to destroy the labor aristocracy that had itself served to break up an earlier pattern of worker solidarity, but mass production also produces new possibilities for mass organizing (Baldi 1972, 11; Negri 1988, 205). Rather than equate the working class with the industrial proletariat, the concept of class composition also designates a broader and more open constituency of capital's subjects, the specific formations of which are mutable (see Zerowork 1975, 4; Cleaver 2003, 43). Negri, for example, describes the changing composition of the working class in terms of a series of shifts—from the professional worker in the early industrial period; to the mass worker of high Fordism, which joined together a broader constituency of waged workers inside and beyond the factory; to the social worker of post-Fordism, a composition that is no longer limited to waged workers but can also include those necessary to its existence and organization, like the unemployed, domestic workers, and students; and, most recently, to Hardt and Negri's multitude, a class category that, in extending across the circuits of biopolitical social production and reproduction, realizes more fully the postworkerist commitments of the project as it developed over time (see, for example, Negri 1988, 235; Dyer-Witheford 1999, 72–76; Hardt and Negri 2000). What counts as work or social productivity and who might organize politically—together or in proximity to one another—in relation to its conditions change over time and space.

The "autonomy" of its namesake is multidimensional, referring to a number of its critical, political, and utopian commitments. The label "autonomist Marxism" refers historically to its autonomy as part of the Italian extraparliamentary Left in relation to other leftist parties and unions, as both specific historical actors and organizational forms. Autonomy in this sense refers to a double relation: an independent relationship with outside groups, but also an internal relationship among autonomist groups imagined in terms of an organizational ideal of a coalition that could encompass a plurality of participants with a variety of agendas. But perhaps more important, it refers to an affirmation of a collective capacity for autonomy vis-à-vis capital.

Three terms are critical to this last dimension of the project of autonomy: self-valorization, antagonism, and separation. The first of these, self-valorization, is one way that the collective dimension of political action has been understood within a tradition that is perhaps more attentive than others to questions of organizational form and practice. As an alternative to capitalist valorization—that is, to a system of values grounded in the production of surplus value—self-valorization is, as Cleaver describes it, not mere resistance to processes of capitalist valorization but "a positive project of self-constitution" (1992, 129; see also Virno and Hardt 1996, 264). Political organizations are aimed at both deconstructive and constructive projects; they are at once agents of critique and of invention. As sites of self-valorization, political collectivities are recognized as constitutive machines rather than merely representational vehicles. The production of autonomous self-valorization depends on the struggle for a separation from the object of critique. Separation is conceived as something different from dialectical conflict;

resistance born of separation is imagined more along lines of flight than lines of opposition. Its task is to organize struggles that neither take the form nor mirror the logic of what they contest. Separation is the path of difference—not an antithesis to be subsumed in a synthesis, but a singularity that might invent something new. Negri describes this as a rejection of a relationship between capital and its antagonists on the model of the dialectical opposition of that which is the same and that which is different, an opposition that he describes as lacking a conception of singularity (Casarino and Negri 2008, 46). Finally, antagonism must be added as a key term: an antagonistic logic of separation stands in contrast to a dialectical logic of contradiction. Whereas dialectical contradiction is an objective category, the product of a system of structures, antagonisms arise from the expressed needs and desires of historical subjects. Antagonism can in this sense be grasped as the subjectivization of contradiction. For examples of subjectivized contradictions, think of the difference between, on the one hand, the contradiction between the forces and relations of production and, on the other hand, conflicts between what we have and what we might want, between what we are and what we could become, between what we do and what we can do. Self-valorization, separation, and antagonism are thus crucial to the project of autonomy, and the means of conceiving a Marxist method— whose ideal form, at least—could be "completely subjectivized, totally open toward the future, and creative," one that "cannot be enclosed within any dialectical totality or logical unity" (Negri 1991, 12).

THE REFUSAL OF WORK

The refusal of work as theory and practice emerges out of these methodological commitments and areas of conceptual focus. As an important slogan in the Italian social movements of the 1960s and 1970s, the refusal of work is a fundamental ground of autonomist Marxism's critical analysis and political strategy, a critical element of the project of autonomy characterized above. At one level a clear expression of the immediate desire experienced by working people around the world, the refusal of work has been developed by autonomists into a more variegated concept, one that encompasses several distinct critical approaches and strategic agendas.

The concept's force, it should be acknowledged, comes from a prior understanding of the place of work in the critical analysis of capitalist social formations. That is, fundamental to the refusal of work as analysis and strategy is a definition of capitalism that highlights not the institution of private property, but rather the imposition and organization of work. After all, from a worker's perspective, earning wages—not accumulating capital—is the primary concern. The wage system remains the dominant mechanism by which individuals are integrated, either directly or indirectly, into the capitalist mode of economic cooperation. Cleaver therefore defines capital as "*a social system based on the imposition of work through the commodity-form*"; it is a system built upon the subordination of life to work (2000, 82). Diane Elson's reading of Marx is helpful in fleshing this out. As she explains Marx's theory of value, it is best understood not as a labor theory of value but as a value theory of labor. In other words, the purpose of the analysis is not to prove the existence of exploitation or to explain prices; the point is not to grasp the process by which value is constituted by labor, but rather to fathom how laboring practices are organized, shaped, and directed by the capitalist pursuit of value. "My argument," Elson writes, "is that the *object* of Marx's theory of value was labour" (1979, 123). Whereas socialist modernization and socialist humanism each imagine the possibility of a postcapitalist society in terms of the realization of the constitutive power of labor, as a matter of grasping the centrality of labor to social life or to individual existence, in this alternative reading of Marx, "labor's constitutive centrality to social life characterizes capitalism and forms the ultimate ground of its abstract mode of domination" (Postone 1996, 361). The crucial point and the essential link to the refusal of work is that work—not private property, the market, the factory, or the alienation of our creative capacities—is understood to be the primary basis of capitalist relations, the glue that holds the system together. Hence, any meaningful transformation of capitalism requires substantial change in the organization and social value of work.

Thus, unlike the modernization model, the autonomist tradition focuses on the critique of work under capitalism, which includes but cannot be reduced to the critique of its exploitation. In contrast to the humanists, who also critique work, autonomous Marxists call not for a liberation of work but for a liberation from work (Virno and Hardt 1996, 263). In their insistence on replacing one slogan of worker militancy, "the right to work," with a new one, "the refusal of work," the autonomists certainly follow in the footsteps of Marx—the Marx who, for example, insisted that freedom depended on the shortening of the working day. But perhaps a more appropriate precursor is Marx's son-in-law, Paul Lafargue. Leszek Kolakowski's description of Lafargue as the proponent of "a hedonist Marxism" only makes this genealogy all the more appropriate (1978, 141–48). Of course, Kolakowski intended his label as an insult, meant to signal Lafargue's naiveté and lack of seriousness, but it is also a fitting classification for a Marxist tradition committed to the refusal of work and open to the possibilities of a postwork future. In *The Right to Be Lazy*, Lafargue takes on the capitalist morality that "curses the flesh of the worker" and seeks to reduce the worker's needs, pleasures, and passions (1898, 3–4). But the immediate target is the 1848 right-to-work rhetoric of the French proletariat, which, he complains, echoes and reinforces this ethic of work—evidence to Lafargue that the proletariat has "allowed itself to be seduced by the dogma of work" (8). In a ploy reminiscent of Marx's insistence that alienated labor is the cause of private property, that the proletarians themselves recreate the system through their continued participation, Lafargue admonishes the French workers rather than the bourgeoisie for the shortcomings of capitalist production. "All individual and society [*sic*] misery," he insists, "takes its origin in the passion of the proletariat for work" (8). So, for example, when the manufacturers consume luxuries in excess or when they attempt to build obsolescence into their products, they should not be blamed; they are only trying to satisfy "the crazy desire for work on the part of the employees" (31). Because of this strange and furious mania for work, the workers do not demand enough: "The proletarians have got it into their heads to hold the capitalists to ten hours of factory work." That, he insists, is the great mistake: "Work must be forbidden, not imposed" (37). One of the most striking elements of the text is Lafargue's rather extravagant refusal to rehabilitate nonwork by recourse to productivist values. He disdains the "capitalist creed of usefulness" and claims that once the working day is reduced to three hours, workers can begin "to practice the virtues of laziness" (41, 32). Certainly his passionate tribute to "O, Laziness, mother of the arts and the noble virtues" (41) offers a pointed contrast to seemingly more serious interpreters of Marx like Kolakowski, who supports a very different reading. Although it is true, Kolakowski concedes, that Marx did support shorter working hours, this was not to give the worker more time for "carefree consumption" as Lafargue suggests, but rather, as Kolakowski reassures us in a language resonant of more traditional and respectable virtues, "more time for free creative activity" (1978, 148).

Despite Lafargue's provocative tribute to the merits of laziness, the refusal of work is not in fact a rejection of activity and creativity in general or of production in particular. It is not a renunciation of labor *tout court*, but rather a refusal of the ideology of work as highest calling and moral duty, a refusal of work as the necessary center of social life and means of access to the rights and claims of citizenship, and a refusal of the necessity of capitalist control of production. It is a refusal, finally, of the asceticism of those—even those on the Left—who privilege work over all other pursuits, including "carefree consumption." Its immediate goals are presented as a reduction of work, in terms of both hours and social importance, and a replacement of capitalist forms of organization by new forms of cooperation. It is not only a matter of refusing exploited and alienated labor, but of refusing "work itself as the principle of reality and rationality" (Baudrillard 1975, 141). In this sense, "work which is liberated is liberation from work" (Negri 1991, 165). Rather than conceive the refusal of work narrowly, in terms of a specific set of actions—including strikes or slowdowns, demands for shorter hours or expanded opportunities for participation, and movements for improved support for or altered conditions of reproductive work—the phrase is, I suggest, best understood in very broad terms as designating a general political and cultural movement—or, better yet, as a potential mode of life that challenges the mode of life now defined by and subordinated to work.

The refusal of work can be broken down, analytically if not practically, into two processes, one that is essentially critical in its aims and another that is more fundamentally reconstructive in its objectives. The first of these, the negative process, is what is most readily conveyed by the word "refusal" and includes the critique of and rebellion against the present system of work and its values. If the system of waged labor is a crucial cultural and institutional mechanism by which we are linked to the mode of production, then the refusal of work poses a potentially substantial challenge to this larger apparatus. But the refusal of work, as both activism and analysis, does not simply pose itself against the present organization of work; it should also be understood as a creative practice, one that seeks to reappropriate and reconfigure existing forms of production and reproduction (see Vercellone 1996, 84). This is the special twofold nature of the refusal of work upon which Negri insists (2005,

269–74). The word "refusal" may be unfortunate in the sense that it does not immediately convey the constructive element that is so central to autonomist thought. Negri describes the refusal of work as both a struggle against the capitalist organization of work and a process of self-valorization, a form of "invention-power" (274). Rather than a goal in itself, "the refusal of work and authority, or really the refusal of voluntary servitude, is the *beginning* of liberatory politics" (Hardt and Negri 2000, 204; emphasis added).

The refusal of work thus comprises at once a movement of exit and a process of invention. The refusal can make time and open spaces—both physical and conceptual—within which to construct alternatives. Rather than a simple act of disengagement that one completes, the refusal is, in this sense, a process, a theoretical and practical movement that aims to effect a separation through which we can pursue alternative practices and relationships. "Beyond the simple refusal, or as part of that refusal," Hardt and Negri argue, "we need also to construct a new mode of life and above all a new community" (204). Paolo Virno develops this same idea through the concepts of exodus and exit: "The 'exit' modifies the conditions within which the conflict takes place, rather than presupposes it as an irremovable horizon; it changes the context within which a problem arises, rather than deals with the problem by choosing one or another of the alternative solutions already on offer" (1996, 199). In this sense, refusal, like exodus or exit, is an "*engaged withdrawal* (or founding leave-taking)" (197), a creative practice as opposed to a merely defensive stance. The passage from the negative moment of refusal to its constructive moment of exit and invention marks the shift from a reactive gesture of retreat to an active affirmation of social innovation. According to this reading, the refusal of work serves not as a goal, but as a path—a path of separation that creates the conditions for the construction of subjects whose needs and desires are no longer as consistent with the social mechanisms within which they are supposed to be mediated and contained. This is why, in contrast to both modernization and humanist Marxisms, Negri locates in the refusal of work not just the symptoms of exploitation and alienation, but a measure of freedom (2005, 273). The defection enacted through the refusal of work is not predicated upon what we lack or cannot do, it is not the path of those with nothing to lose but their chains; it is predicated instead on our "latent wealth, on an abundance of possibilities" (Virno 1996, 199).

By this account, the negative and positive moments of refusal can be distinguished analytically, but not isolated practically. Rather than the traditional two-stage model that posits a radical break between the transition, conceived as a negative process of dismantling, and communism, imagined as the positive construction of an alternative, the logic of this analysis suggests the value of a more substantial break between the present logic of capital and the transition—seen in this case as a process by which a different future can be constructed. That is, this formulation of the relationship between means and ends indicates the importance of pursuing more radical strategies that attempt a more significant break with the present. In this way we might also better understand the militancy of the strategy—the call to refuse and transform the present system of work, rather than simply to reconsider or renegotiate a few of its terms and conditions. Although the immoderate character of the phrase "refusal of work" may strike us today as naive or impractical, if we consider such strategies as laboratories—both conceptual and practical—in which different subjectivities can be constituted and paths to alternative futures opened, the utopian aspect of the refusal of work, its insistence that we struggle toward and imagine the possibilities of substantial social change, is essential.

THE ABOLITION OF WORK (AS WE KNOW IT)

The vision of an alternative that marks the transition from antiwork to postwork in autonomist thought is offered as a contrast to socialism, which is defined as a system that would redeem work through public ownership. In this sense, the refusal of work disavows the two visions we reviewed earlier: socialism imagined either as state-planned economy to alleviate exploitation or as small-scale production to remedy alienation—one version "means primarily disciplining the working class," the other is "romantic" (Zerowork 1975, 6). "The problem is not," Jean-Marie Vincent argues, "simply to liberate production, but also for humanity to liberate itself *from* production by ceasing to treat it as the centre of gravity of all social activities and individual action" (1991, 20). Whatever else it may be, the vision of postcapitalism privileged in the autonomist tradition is not a vision of the work society perfected, with its labors rationally organized, equally required, and justly distributed. Rather, it is a vision of the work society overcome—that is, of a society in which work is certainly not eliminated but comes to play a different role in the economies of social production and political obligation. Negri describes this in terms of the abolition of work, with no homology between work as it is experienced in the present and as it might be organized in the future (1991, 165). Posed in this way, the abolition of work serves not as blueprint, not even precisely as content; instead it is a marker of the disjunction between antiwork critique and postwork possibility.

The same logic of imagination that conceives the relation between the refusal of work and its abolition in terms of difference and rupture grounds it also in tendency and potential. Tendencies that point to the possibility of a postwork future include the perennial conflict generated by a system that expands the needs and desires of its subjects while simultaneously striving to minimize their wages and income. These tendencies also include the growing tension between a society that requires work to secure the means of consumption and the possibility—created by accumulated knowledge, technological developments, and expanding capacities for cooperation—of a social form in which labor does not serve this function, a social form in which, for example, working time is drastically reduced and the link between work and income severed (see, for example, Postone 1996, 361, 365; Vincent 1991, 19–20). The temporality of these antagonisms sets the method apart from other critical methods including ideology critique, in which reality is measured against its ideals or the seeming appearance of things probed for their essential truth. Negri also distinguishes this "tendential method" that reads the present in light of the future from the genealogical method that reads it in relation to the past (1991, 48–49). The former finds its critical point of contrast in the connection between the present and the future, conceived as a relation between the actual and the possible. Postone describes this as a model of immanent critique—in this case, a critique of the work society from the perspective of the emergent possibility of a social form in which work does not serve as the primary force of social mediation (1996, 49), an antiwork critique grounded in a postwork potential.

The refusal of work as both a practical demand and a theoretical perspective presupposes an appreciation of the potentially immense productive power of the accumulated capacities of social labor. "What we want," explains another autonomist, Franco Berardi ("Bifo"), "is to apply, totally and coherently, the energies and the potential that exist for a socialized intelligence, for a general intellect. We want to make possible a general reduction in working time and we want to transform the organization of work in such a way that an autonomous organization of sectors of productive experimental organization may become possible" (1980, 157–58). This affirmation of the creative powers of social labor notwithstanding, the refusal of work does not simply replicate the productivist glorification of work (even socialist or unalienated work). The productive powers of cooperation, knowledge, and technology are celebrated because they carry the potential not only to contest the necessity of capitalist control, but to reduce the time spent at work, thereby offering the possibility to pursue opportunities for pleasure and creativity that are outside the economic realm of production. By this measure, "the refusal of work does not mean the erasure of activity, but the valorization of human activities which have escaped from labor's domination" (Berardi 2009, 60).

Theirs is not only a postindividualist vision of the possibility of a postwork organization of production, it is also a postscarcity vision. The productive force of the accumulated powers of social labor has always had the potential to translate into less work, but only if that change is demanded. The twin demands often evoked as strategies of refusal—for more money and less work—mark a rather sharp contrast to what Vincent describes as "the notion that the struggle for a different society must be a form of worldly asceticism" (1991, 27), that workers' demands should echo, not contest, the discourses of poverty, sacrifice, hard work, and self-restraint that are part of the system's rationalization. These demands for more money and less work reveal precisely what Kolakowski recognized—and disparaged—in Lafargue's early articulation of the refusal of work: the disavowal of political asceticism. In response to the usual insistence on scarcity when it comes to such demands and the promotion of austerity as a solution to capitalist crisis, Lafargue argued that the task instead was the expansion of our needs and desires beyond their usual objects, to avoid the fate of both bourgeois overconsumption and proletarian abstention (1898, 37–38). In a similar vein, the conception of the process of liberation that one can find in the autonomist tradition is often coded not in terms of return or restoration but of excess and expansion: the enrichment of subjectivity, the expansion of needs, and the cultivation of an element or quality of desire that exceeds existing modes of satisfaction.

At this point I want to exit the terrain of Marxist theory and linger for a moment on the political agendas that we have encountered along the way. The three theoretical paradigms we reviewed yield three different prescriptions for change: respectively, demands for more work, better work, and less work. This project's preference for less work over more work is clear enough. The demand for more work may very well be necessary in a context in which work is the only option the individual has to secure his or her livelihood, but I am arguing that the struggle for less work is critical as well. Perhaps, however, more should be said about the relationship between the calls for less work and better work, and why I focus on the former and, by comparison at least, neglect the latter. Certainly I affirm the vital importance of struggles to improve the conditions of work. But although in practical, if not in logical, terms none of these demands—including the demands for less and better work—are mutually exclusive, it is useful to recognize some of the complexities of their relationships. A brief exploration of some recent efforts to demand better work can illustrate some of the difficulties here.

Some analysts draft the work-ethic discourse into this effort by calling for a new version of the ethic, one that affirms the necessity, centrality, and value of work, but in the name of which the demand for better work can also be advanced. For example, what we might think of as a humanist work ethic affirms a vision of unalienated labor and argues that the ethical discourse of work offers a means by which to struggle toward its realization.[9] Recent proponents of an ethic that could in this way renew our support for and investments in work but also press for better work are Al Gini and Russell Muirhead. Since, according to Gini, "work is a fundamental part of our humanity" (2000, xii) and thus is rightly at the center of our lives, our jobs should be good ones. Whereas the Protestant work ethic had been used to mystify the conditions of exploitative and alienating labor—the hierarchy, coercion, drudgery, boredom, and dangers of work—the alternative ethic that Gini defends would insist on the cultural valuing of all work and would serve as a way to make work deliver on its promises of meaning, self-fulfillment, and useful outcomes. But since work is so fundamental to what it means to be fully human, more emphasis is placed in Gini's discussion on praising work as noble and ennobling than on urging its improvement, for "even with all of its failings, work must be saved" (209). Ultimately, what is important is "reinfusing all work with dignity" (218) because "although we cannot always change the nature of the work, we can, however, affect the morale of the workers and the attitudes of society" (218–19). In the last analysis, any work is better than no work: "whether we are happy or numbed by what we do, work we must, and, like it or not, our work is the mark of our humanity" (224). The demand for less work receives little attention in this account; visions of postwork futures are dismissed with the claim that "it is not in our nature to be idle" (206), thereby demonstrating at once an essentialist view of labor and an impoverished imagination of the possibilities of nonwork. Muirhead proposes a similar alternative to the Protestant ethic, one that recognizes the importance of work to our lives and makes sense of our current devotion to it, while at the same time serving as a critical standard—a vision of fitting and fulfilling work—by which we can champion the demand for better work. But Muirhead both offers a more rigorous critique than Gini and pays more attention to the value of life beyond work. For Muirhead, the recognition of the ways that work falls short of its promise requires not only that we struggle to improve work, but also that we try to place limits on the work ethic's claims. His solution is an ethic tempered by the recognition that work should not be the whole of life, an ethic that affirms the necessity and inherent value of work but nonetheless seeks to keep it in its place (2004, 175–76).

From the perspective of my project, the humanist work ethic is certainly an improvement on the dominant discourse, casting as it does a critical eye not only on the quantity of work's compensation but on the qualities of its experience. But I want to raise some potential barriers to a practical strategy that draws on the critique of alienation and that calls for better work in a context in which such languages and concerns have been absorbed so comfortably into the warp and woof of contemporary managerial discourses. This is not a new phenomenon. As Jack Barbash reports, the critique of alienation had moved out of its "Marxist baili-wick" and into popular discussion by the early 1970s, perhaps most visibly with the publication in 1973 of a government study that found widespread dissatisfaction and disaffection among US workers: "Dull, repetitive, seemingly meaningless tasks are causing discontent among workers at all occupational levels" (quoted in Barbash 1983, 242). By the mid-1970s, managerial theories and practices were responding to this critique of work that engaged too little of the self by shifting the focus from securing the compliance of the recalcitrant, effort-avoidant Fordist worker described in what the popular management theorist Douglas McGregor called "theory X," to encouraging the commitment of the work-loving, self-directed, and responsibility-seeking model worker posited by McGregor's own "theory Y" (1960). Whereas the older model of human-relations management had been developed to respond to the militant labor movement of the 1930s, the paradigm of human-resource management that emerged in the 1970s addressed a different manner of dissatisfaction and mode of rebellion. Cast in the latter framework as not just vehicles of labor power but, rather, as fully "human resources," workers ideally were to be "empowered" to develop their capacities and maximize value at the same time.[10] McGregor, one of the model's early architects, presents this as a matter of directing individual desires toward organizational objectives: "We seek that degree of integration in which the individual can achieve his goals *best* by directing his efforts toward the success of the organization" (1960, 55). The two goals—better, more engaging work and more efficient labor processes—are imagined as reconcilable, at least in theory; in practice, whether a particular managerial regime puts more emphasis on improving well-being or on maximizing efficiency depends on the industry, the worker's place in the labor hierarchy, and the balance of power between capital and labor at any given moment. For example, at one end of the labor market it may be that routinization, surveillance, and the threat of moving production offshore can suffice to induce the desired levels of effort and cooperation, whereas other sectors may need to rely on cultural engineering and careful training.[11]

In these latter sectors of employment in particular, the dimensions of the self that are considered part of the human resource to develop—and, thus, legitimate targets of managerial concern—continue to expand into new territories of subjectivity. Consider, for example, the new terrains opened up by the recent interest in "wellness." As the authors of a recent overview of contemporary management concepts and regimes observe, "the idea that one's employer provides some sort of totalized care for the worker's wellness opens up a powerful horizon for expanding the boundaries of organized work" (Costea, Crump, and Amiridis 2008, 670). Or consider what Peter Fleming describes as the "just be yourself" managerial discourse that asks workers to bring their "authentic" selves from outside work into work, attempting thereby to incorporate "the whole person into the production matrix" (2009, 38). Traditional distinctions between work and life are increasingly blurred by management in these its most self-consciously biopolitical modes. Whether or not the watchwords of such programs—empowerment, participation, responsibility, flexibility, and enrichment—involve empty rhetoric or meaningful improvements in the experience of work for employees, they do give employers opportunities to induce new modes and degrees of effort, and in some cases of identification. Thus, worker empowerment can boost efficiency, flexibility can serve as a way to cut costs, and participation can produce commitment to the organization, thereby "embroiling the subject in the act of organizational control" and internalizing organizational discipline (Costea, Crump, and Amiridis 2008, 668). In short, often programs presented under the rubric of work enrichment are also methods of work intensification.[12] In a kind of bad dialectic, quality becomes quantity as the call for better work is translated into a requirement for more work.

There are two points I want to make here. The first is that by tapping into the critique of alienation, and offering more work as the solution, management discourses drain the critique of some of its force. The vision of nonalienated labor articulated by critics like Fromm, Mies, and Schleuning, in which work is reintegrated into life, may have been compelling as a critique of modernization's doctrine and practices of separate spheres, but it loses its critical edge in the context of postmodernity's subsumption of life into work. The affirmation of unalienated labor is not an adequate strategy by which to contest contemporary modes of capitalist control; it is too readily co-opted in a context in which the metaphysics of labor and the moralization of work carry so much cultural authority in so many realms. This is not to suggest that we should abandon the struggles for better work, for liberation from mindless and repetitive tasks, dangerous environments, numbing isolation, and petty hierarchies. It is important to recognize, however, that the language and to a certain degree the practices of work humanization have been co-opted. The ideology of human-resource management—with its various programs for humanizing work to make it a place where employees can be expected to dedicate their hearts as well as their hands and brains, with its techniques for producing more productive models of worker subjectivity—should be recognized as an attempt to address by rendering profitable various expressions of dissatisfaction with work. In this regard, Baudrillard's critique of a version of the Marxist critique of alienation seems particularly appropriate: "It convinces men that they are alienated by the sale of their labor power, thus censoring the much more radical hypothesis that they might be alienated as labor power" (1975, 31).

The problem, therefore, is how to advance demands for better work—how to make good on work's promises of social utility and individual meaning—in a way that does not simply echo and reaffirm the prescription for a lifetime of work. The question I want to consider is whether the kind of affirmation of work at the heart of the work ethic can be used successfully in the struggle for better work: is it possible to demand both better work and less work without one demand neutralizing the critical force of the other? Muirhead offers one attempt to combine these efforts. To recall the earlier discussion, both Gini and Muirhead call for new ethics of work that can continue to celebrate and encourage commitment to waged work, while insisting that such work should be adequately compensated and personally satisfying. But Muirhead goes further, recognizing that these two commitments, to the affirmation of work's inherent value and to the improvement of its conditions, can function at cross-purposes. As a way to manage this, he adds a third commitment: to keep work, even good work, in its place so that it does not consume the whole of life, which would moderate the claims about work's value by simultaneously pursuing a politics directed at work's reform and reduction (2004, 12). "Tempering the value of work," Muirhead explains, "also protects against the abuse of that value in the name of practices that are exploitative—an abuse to which the work ethic is particularly prone" (176).

Despite the importance of this reform agenda—the clear need to demand both better work and less work—the initial affirmation of the inherent value of work, now linked to managerial discourses of work improvement, threatens to contradict and eclipse the call for the moderation of the work ethic's power and to overshadow demands for work reduction. Just as affirming the value of work in the same terms as the work ethic makes it difficult to assert the claim that some work must be improved, calling for better work can easily overwhelm the argument for less work. My second point, then, is that rather than offer a revised version of the work ethic, we must make the critique of this ethic a priority if the struggle for less work is to have a chance of success.

CONCLUSION AND SEGUE: FEMINISM AND THE REFUSAL OF WORK

The refusal of work in its broadest sense has the potential to generate some timely critical perspectives and practical agendas. In particular, it offers a challenge to the work values that continue to secure our consent to the current system. The problem is not, to cite Baudrillard's formulation, that the worker is "only quantitatively exploited as a productive force by the *system* of capitalist political economy, but is also metaphysically overdetermined as a producer by the *code* of political economy" (1975, 31). The glorification of work as a prototypically human endeavor, as the key both to social belonging and individual achievement, constitutes the fundamental ideological foundation of contemporary capitalism: it was built on the basis of this ethic, which continues to serve the system's interests and rationalize its outcomes. The contemporary force of this code, with its essentialism and moralism of work, should not be underestimated. "In the last instance," as Baudrillard asserts and the previous chapter argued, "the system rationalizes its power here" (31). My argument is that the metaphysics and moralism of work require a more direct challenge than the critique of alienation and humanist work ethics are capable of posing. The struggle to improve the quality of work must be accompanied by efforts to reduce its quantity.[13] In this context, the refusal of work, with its insistence on a more thorough critique of, and a more radical break with, existing work values offers a particularly valuable perspective. Where attitudes are productive, the refusal of work—understood as a rejection of work as a necessary center of social existence, moral duty, ontological essence, and time and energy, and understood as a practice of "insubordination to the work ethic" (Berardi 1980, 169)—can speak forcefully and incisively to our present situation.

What this has to offer feminism specifically will be addressed in the next two chapters. As a preface to those discussions, I offer two brief observations. The first is that the challenges that the refusal of work poses to the realities of work today are at least as relevant to feminist concerns and agendas. Feminist calls for better work for women, as important as they have been, have on the whole resulted in more work for women. Beyond the intensification of many forms of waged work noted above, the burdens of unwaged domestic and caring work have also increased, both because of the pressures of neoliberal restructuring along with the double day, and because of the increasingly dominant model of intensive parenting presented as what is required to develop the communicative, cognitive, and creative capacities increasingly necessary for reproducing, let alone elevating, the class status of a new generation of workers (see Hays 1996). Given all the ways that the institution of the family—on which the privatization of reproductive labor has been predicated and sustained—is so clearly not up to the task of assuming so much of the responsibility for the care of children, the elderly, the sick, and the disabled, the refusal of the present organization of reproductive labor may have much to offer contemporary feminism.[14]

My second observation, however, is that extending the refusal of work to the structures and ethics of reproductive labor is a far more complicated endeavor. Although what it might mean to refuse unwaged domestic work is something that we will need to explore, it is clear that this would go beyond the claim that such work should be valued differently in relation to waged work—either more or less than it is now. Indeed, extending the refusal of work into the field of unwaged domestic work undercuts some of feminism's traditional critical standpoints: the critique of a normative expectation of domesticity for women from the standpoint of the benefits and virtues of waged work, and the critique of the heartless world of exploitative waged work from the perspective of domestically cultivated caring ethics or nonalienated craft production. Rather than critique either work or family from the standpoint of the other, this feminist version of the refusal of work encompasses both as sites and objects of refusal. This broader project of refusal poses challenges both for antiwork critique and postwork imagination. Feminist antiwork critique would need to accomplish several things at once: to recognize unwaged domestic work as socially necessary labor, contest its inequitable distribution (the fact that gender, race, class, and nation affects who does more or less), and, at the same time, insist that valuing it more highly and distributing it more equitably is not enough—the organization of unwaged reproductive labor and its relationship with waged work must be entirely rethought. For feminist postwork imagination, it raises the following question: if we refuse both the institution of waged work and the model of the privatized family as the central organizing structures of production and reproduction, what might we want in their stead? In the next chapters, I bring Marxist and feminist traditions together to think about how to challenge and begin to reimagine the structures and ethics of both waged and unwaged work within the practical territory of political claims making—or, more specifically, demanding.

....

CHAPTER 3

Working Demands

From Wages for Housework to Basic Income

> Political visions are fragile. They appear—and are lost again.
> Ideas formulated in one generation are frequently forgot-
> ten, or repressed, by the next; goals which seemed necessary
> and realistic to progressive thinkers of one era are shelved as
> visionary and utopian by their successors. Aspirations which
> find voice in certain periods of radical endeavor are stifled,
> or even wholly silenced, in others. The history of all progres-
> sive movements is littered with such half-remembered hopes,
> with dreams that have failed.
>
> BARBARA TAYLOR, *EVE AND THE NEW JERUSALEM*

We have arrived at a crossroads of sorts. At this point, the focus of the
analysis shifts from antiwork critique to postwork politics, moving away
from the earlier concentration on the refusal of work and its ethics
toward an exploration of demands that might point in the direction of
alternatives. In this chapter, I present a reading of the 1970s feminist
demand for wages for housework and then propose its reconfiguration
as a contemporary demand for a guaranteed basic income. As will soon
become clear, the wages for housework perspective—as it was articulated
in a handful of texts published in Italy, Britain, and the United States
between 1972 and 1976—is an important inspiration for many of the
arguments in subsequent chapters as well.[1] Indeed, the two major demands often repeated by proponents of wages for housework, along
with other autonomists—for more money and for less work—guide the
choice of demands that are the subject of this chapter and the next: the

demand for basic income and the demand for shorter hours. Perhaps more significantly, the literature's insights into both the nature of demands and the practice of demanding inform my analyses of the rationales and potential effectivity of these two demands. In light of my investments in this perhaps peculiar artifact of 1970s feminism, it may be helpful, before moving into the heart of the argument, to clarify something about my approach to this historical terrain.

READING THE FEMINIST PAST

Why return to this bit of feminist history? One would be hard-pressed to find a political vision within feminism that has less credibility today than wages for housework; indeed, it is frequently portrayed in histories of feminism as a misguided movement and, when discussed in feminist anthologies, is typically represented as a rather odd curio from the archive of second-wave feminist theory. One should not discount these assessments; although I find inspiration in several dimensions of the project, I too reject what would seem to be its foundational claim and raison d'etre: the demand for wages for housework. So what might this— to borrow terms from the epigraph to this chapter—half-remembered hope and failed dream have to do with contemporary feminism? More specifically, two questions warrant consideration: first, why return to this piece of the feminist past; and second, how might the past be brought to bear on feminism's present and its possible futures?

This return to the 1970s is made difficult by feminism's own historiographical practices, including some of its most familiar periodizing models and classificatory schemes. Two in particular pose obstacles for the kind of return I seek. The first conceives the relationship between the feminist past and present in terms of a dialectical logic that codes the passing of time in terms of eras in succession. The second approaches history in terms of a familial model, conceiving it as a relation between one generation and the next. The first raises the question of why one would bother with the past; the second poses limits on how one might enlist it in the effort to craft a different future. It is not exactly that the former is too dismissive of and the latter too deferential toward this history; the problem, as I see it, is that one can block access to a full and rich engagement with the past, and the other can keep us from a creative reappropriation of its insights.

Perhaps the most familiar way of telling the story of feminist history relies on a dialectical logic to explicate a progressive development of feminist theories over time. For example, in a well-known and oft-repeated taxonomy of the field popularized in the early 1980s, liberal, Marxist, and radical feminisms were posed as competing models of feminist theory that socialist feminism was seen to at once absorb and outshine. In particular, Marxist feminism, a category that includes wages for housework, was positioned as thesis and radical feminism posed as its antithesis, with the shortcomings of each remedied by socialist feminism imagined as their synthesis. Thus, in some of these early histories of second-wave feminist theory, socialist feminism was described as feminism's crowning achievement, succeeding temporally and transcending both methodologically and politically liberal, Marxist, and radical feminisms.[2] Some instances of this same periodizing scheme produced in the 1990s replace socialist feminism with poststructuralist feminism in the privileged position. Clare Hemmings describes one widely disseminated version of this updated story in her critical reading of such models this way: essentialist feminism of the 1970s—a broad category that includes liberal, Marxist, radical, and socialist feminisms—was challenged in the 1980s by feminists of color and third-world feminists, whose critiques were incorporated into and surpassed by poststructuralist feminism of the 1990s (2005, 126).

One of the limitations of such an account is, of course, its reductionism—a perhaps inevitable side effect of any such classificatory project. In the case that concerns me here, wages for housework is contained in the broader category of Marxist feminism, which is in turn inserted into a progressive historical narrative as one moment in a dialectical chain.[3] But the more difficult problem is not that this narrative codes wages for housework as a political vision that failed and was defeated; the trouble is that wages for housework is imagined as part of a history that has been superseded. That is why a return to this 1970s tradition might be understood not only as a distraction, but as a regression, as a return either to the mistakes that were made before socialist feminism's subsumption of Marxist feminism, or to a thoroughly repudiated and now overcome essentialist feminism.

In response to such logics, part of the analysis of wages for housework that follows will be concerned with setting the historical record straight. This will involve both revisiting some existing interpretations of the discourse and recovering certain lost dimensions of the project. There are, for example, a number of misreadings of the literature that a better understanding of its historical connections to the autonomous Marxist tradition can serve to correct. There will also be an effort to recover specific aspects of the project that were not part of socialist feminism's supposedly more perfect union of Marxist and radical feminisms or of poststructuralism's anti-essentialist feminism. These include the concept of the social factory often deployed in the literature, the project's commitment to the refusal of work, and the understanding of political demands and the process of demanding that was central to both the movement and the analysis. Contrary to the model of dialectical history, the story of feminist history is not only a story of progress but also sometimes, as the epigraph reminds us, of forgotten ideas and stifled aspirations.

Despite its value, however, the work of historical recovery is not my primary concern; I am more interested in remaking wages for housework than in preserving its memory. This brings me to a second conception of the relationship among feminist theories through time, another progress narrative that would undermine the kind of return to the 1970s I want to make. This second mode of feminist history relies on a familial logic for its temporal imaginary. Judith Roof aptly describes this as a generational discourse, one popular version of which casts feminist history as a story of mothers bequeathing a feminist legacy to a new generation that then builds on and carries forward its inheritance, a story of a feminist sisterhood that over time evolves into a succession of generations within a larger feminist family (1997, 70). Progress is secured by the steady accumulation of feminist knowledge and an ever-expanding feminist solidarity. One of the problems with this conception is that, as Roof notes, the family model functions to domesticate differences among feminists (73), reducing fundamental and persistent conflicts to the stuff of family quarrels and generational gaps.[4] But perhaps the more important problem with this model is the way it tends to individuate and personalize theoretical discourse and political contestation. In the realm of feminist academic production, the inheritance to be handed down from one feminist to another is a life's work rather than a collection of writings; authors take precedence over texts in this subjectivized framework.[5] The heritage is at once political and personal, a legacy that flows from the consciousness, experience, desire, and commitment of specific individuals rather than theories, strategies, and visions that exceed the paradigm of individual authorship. Whereas the dialectical model treats the past as either a stage leading to the present or as the dustbin of history, the familial model demands more reverence, treating feminism's history as elders to respect and legacies to preserve.

One problem with both of these periodizing frames and historical imaginaries is their historicism. That is, they cast any given theoretical paradigm as not only *of* its time—developed within a particular political conjuncture and conceptual horizon—but as *only* of its time. Each theory is corralled within a span of time bounded by its genesis and death; even when conceived as a living legacy rather than as a dead relic, the theory remains more of a historical artifact than a project. Each contribution is fixed to a linear time by a logic—whether dialectical or familial—that marks, divides, and seals each moment. Within the dialectical scheme, it is not just that the particular theories are homogenized so as to fit a given classificatory framework, but also that each is seen as a finished product consigned to the boundaries of a particular historical period. Within the familial narrative, each theory is represented by individual authors and their perspectives rather than conceived as collective projects animated by common questions and political desires that are not so easily contained within either an individual or a single span of time.

I am interested here in a different temporality, which might sustain a more fruitful relationship among past, present, and future. To borrow Robyn Wiegman's formulation, I want to "think about feminism's political time as nonlinear, multidirectional, and simultaneous" in a way that can open up "the possibility of thinking about the historical as distinct from and other to the present *and* as a present living force" (2000, 824, n. 14). In contrast to the familial model, my focus is on texts rather than authors. To be sure, I will treat these texts as historical artifacts; I am not interested here in contemporary iterations of wages for housework or the later writings of its original authors. Instead, I will focus on a handful of texts produced in the early to mid-1970s—most of which, it is relevant to note, are manifestoes, and as such, clearly of their time: interventions designed to gather and direct the political energies of a specific moment and location. But my project is not for that reason primarily historical; as a work of political theory rather than intellectual history, its primary focus is on how wages for housework might be employed to confront the present and reimagine its possible futures. The reading I seek is at once antidialectical, open to the lost possibilities from which we might still learn, and antifamilial, treating these texts not as a legacy to preserve but as tools to use. So although I am interested in reading the 1970s wages for housework literature within its historical context—in relation to other Marxist theories, and in a particular moment of transition from Fordism to post-Fordism—in the end, the point is to go back in order to bring some of the insights from the 1970s forward, to use them in this time and place.

THE DOMESTIC LABOR DEBATE

A good place to begin our exploration of wages for housework is with one of the feminist literatures with which it was engaged and of which it is typically remembered as a contributor. The domestic labor debate was one major strand of Anglo-American Marxist and socialist feminist theory in the 1970s that focused on the political economy of women's household labor. Enlisting Marxist categories and frameworks in the service of feminist inquiry held the promise of yielding new insights into the relationship between gendered relations and capitalist logics. Participants in the domestic labor debate argued that gender difference and hierarchy are also constituted and reproduced through laboring practices, and that specific gender divisions of labor are part and parcel of contemporary capitalist social formations. The debate produced a sizable body of literature comprising a lively set of exchanges from the late 1960s up through the end of the 1970s.[6]

By the end of the 1970s, however, the domestic labor debate had exhausted itself (Vogel 2000, 152). This was due, in part, to factors external to the literature itself: by the 1980s, many feminist theorists had moved on to other topics grounded in different frameworks. Most notably, the locus of materialist analysis had shifted from the terrain of economics to that of the body (Malos 1995b, 209), and the preoccupation with the constituting force of laboring practices gave way to increasing interest in language, discourse, and culture as forces that shape the lives of gendered subjects. Interest in the debate also declined as both Marxism and Marxist feminism were often eclipsed—rather than inspired, challenged, and transformed—by the rising popularity and efficacy of poststructuralist approaches. But the more important sources of the debate's demise can be located internally. What began as a promising attempt to combine the theoretical energies and political commitments of Marxism and feminism became mired in a debate about how to conceive the relationship between domestic labor and Marx's theory of value. The basic division, to simplify a complex range of positions, was between those in the more orthodox camp who tended to describe domestic labor as a form of unproductive labor that, since it does not create surplus value, is not central to capitalism per se, and less orthodox contributors who posed domestic labor as reproductive or even productive labor that, since it creates surplus value either indirectly or directly, must be conceived as an integral part of capitalist production. At least in the early years of this debate, two important issues were clear: the conceptual issue of how to approach the imbrication of the domestic political economy and the capitalist mode of production; and the political question of whether to integrate or separate feminist struggles with respect to working-class organizations and agendas. Over time, however, these theoretical questions and practical concerns gave way to an ever more technical debate over Marx's theory of value.[7] The conceptual and political point of the exercise was increasingly obscured as the debate frequently degenerated into a contest to locate the definitive passage from Marx that would resolve the dispute once and for all. The early commitment to rethink Marxism from a feminist perspective was largely overshadowed by efforts to rethink feminism from a Marxist perspective, with the latter too often posited as a reified textual legacy to which feminist questions and commitments must be made to conform.

As another scene from the famously unhappy marriage of Marxism and feminism, there are certainly good reasons why we need not mourn the passing of the domestic labor debate. At the same time, however, neither need we discount the possibility that any number of valuable insights and innovative analyses were produced at its margins. In the pages that follow, I want to revisit what was undoubtedly the most unorthodox of the contributions to the debate: the wages for housework perspective, for which Mariarosa Dalla Costa and Selma James's *The Power of Women and the Subversion of the Community* (1973), is often credited as foundational.[8] My interest in this and other texts in the wages for housework tradition from the early to mid-1970s centers on three aspects of the project that I want to recover and then to reconfigure in order to propose a somewhat different and potentially more timely analysis and strategy: an analysis of the family as part of a new phase of capitalist development that the feminists in this tradition tried to capture with the term "the social factory"; the category of the "refusal of work," which serves to critique not just the structures and divisions of work but also its ethics; and the demand for wages for housework—which, I should note at the outset, appeals to me because of the authors' conception of the practice of demanding, of what a demand is, and of what it can do, rather than because of the specific content of the demand. Gathering these three elements together, I will consider toward the end of the chapter an alternative demand: the demand for basic income.

As I mentioned above, to locate and develop what I see as its more timely dimensions, I want to reconsider the wages for housework perspective in light of and in relation to the autonomist Marxist tradition that it drew upon, and whose later developments it helped inspire.[9] Highlighting some of the links between autonomist Marxism and wages for housework accomplishes two things. First, drawing on the broader Marxist framework to which the feminist project was linked can serve to clear up certain misreadings of those elements of the wages for housework texts that I want to reappropriate. Second, setting the discourse in dialogue with more recent autonomist work will help me construct a revised perspective and a very different demand.[10]

REPRODUCING THE SOCIAL FACTORY

To the chagrin of the more orthodox participants in the domestic labor debate, who saw domestic labor as separate from capitalist production proper, Dalla Costa and James insisted that, despite what Marx both did and did not write, domestic labor is essential to the production of surplus value, and the site of its extraction is what they called the social factory (1973, 30–31). This argument, however, has not been well understood; in particular, the concept of the social factory has generated confusion, with some readings casting it as a misguided analogy intended to bring the household under the rubric of a Marxist analysis of industrial production.[11] The concept was, in fact, also used by other autonomists at the time and was deployed here by Dalla Costa and James to particularly generative ends.[12] Rather than a claim about how the household resembles a factory, the concept gestures toward a broader, more compelling, and—as I will explain below—timely analysis of contemporary capitalism. The theory of the social factory rests on the idea that beyond the factory, what Dalla Costa and James sometimes called "the community," or society itself, is involved in capitalist relations. The concept thus signals an alternative to theories that isolate capitalist production in the times, spaces, and relations of waged labor.

Dalla Costa and James generally used the concept of the social factory in a rather limited way to think about some of the interdependencies between two fields of social cooperation, the household and the waged labor economy. The wage relation, understood as the fundamental social relation of capital, was the key point of linkage between the two realms. As Dalla Costa and James explain it, the institution of the family serves as an important though obscured component of the wage system; as a social relation of the waged to the unwaged (12), it is an expansive category that includes "the unemployed, the old, the ill, children, and housewives" (James 1976, 7). The family functions in this sense as a distributive mechanism through which wages can be imagined to extend to the nonwaged, underwaged, not-yet-waged, and no-longer-waged. As a privatized machine of social reproduction, the family serves to keep wages lower and hours longer than they would be if the general assumption were that individuals needed either to be able to secure commodified equivalents to the goods and services produced within private households or to have enough time outside of waged work to produce the goods and services themselves. Although the family continues to serve as a crucial element of the wage system, it remains a hidden partner, its role concealed by all those discourses that naturalize, romanticize, privatize, and depoliticize the institution. Since the wage system, even in this expanded sense, does not of course succeed in incorporating everyone or giving everybody a living wage, the ideology of the family performs a kind of mopping-up function, enabling us to accept the legitimacy of the wage system despite its shortcomings by encouraging us to imagine that it can provide for those capable of living up to its norms of family form and responsibility. By linking the family to the wage system, by describing it as a pillar of the capitalist organization of work (Dalla Costa and James 1973, 33), Dalla Costa reminds us of the ways in which the institution of the family not only helps to absorb reductions in the price of labor and to produce lower-cost and more-flexible forms of feminized labor, but also provides the ideological basis for relieving the state and capital from responsibility for much of the cost of social reproduction.

This focus on the wage, which we find in Dalla Costa and James's analysis as that which sutures the household to the waged labor economy, is something that the authors share with the broader autonomist tradition. Why privilege the wage this way? Because, in keeping with autonomist approaches to Marx, the wage is understood as the dominant mechanism by which individuals are incorporated into the capitalist mode of cooperation: "Since Marx," Dalla Costa insists, "it has been clear that capital rules and develops through the wage" (Dalla Costa and James 1973, 25–26). More important, the wage is a contradictory phenomenon: it is the mechanism by which workers are integrated into the production of surplus value and also a point of leverage and a resource for creating a life outside of work (see Negri 1991, 132; Baldi 1972, 18; Read 2003, 100). The wage is, in other words, one of the most direct expressions of the relation of power between capital and labor and one of the most tangible objects of struggle over its terms. As two proponents of wages for housework, Nicole Cox and Silvia Federici, explain it, "the wage always has two sides: the side of capital which uses it to control the working class by trying to ensure that every raise is matched by an increase in productivity; and the side of the working class which increasingly is fighting for more money, more power, and less work" (1976, 11). The wage can facilitate both the accumulation of capital and the expansion of workers' potentially autonomous needs and desires.

The wages for housework perspective sought to challenge dominant understandings about who is disciplined by the wage and who is involved in struggles over wages. Just as Marx argued that the wage serves to hide the surplus labor expended by waged laborers in the production of surplus value, the wage also obscures the contributions of unwaged labor toward the process of valorization and, consequently, the true length of the working day (Cox and Federici 1976, 9–10). Cox and Federici express it this way: "We know that the working day for capital does not necessarily produce a pay-check and does not begin and end at the factory gates" (4). They offer a more expansive account of not only who is involved in the wage relation and thus who might contest its terms, but also what counts as a wage struggle, in this case going beyond the focus on wage rates to include efforts to secure the provision of social services and reductions of work time.

Dalla Costa and James's argument was one of the early references to the concept of the social factory in the autonomist literature, where it has since been developed further. One could argue that it was the feminist insistence on expanding the concept of labor beyond its waged forms that helped to open the door to a new conceptualization of the structure of capitalist social production, to which the category of the social factory was an early contribution. Later we will return to the concept of the social factory to consider how it has been transformed under the conditions of post-Fordism, and the consequences of this for the project of mapping the social factory's sites and relations. Here I want to continue the review of the 1970s literature and consider a second point of interest: the refusal of work.

THE REFUSAL OF WORK

When authors like Dalla Costa and James maintained that the family is a site of social production and, in a move we will discuss later, demanded that women receive wages for the work that they do there, the point was not to extol the virtues of domestic work. On the contrary, these authors insisted that work is nothing to revere. Departing from those discourses on both the Right and the Left that acclaim and moralize work, the wages for housework movement and analysis is part of a broader tradition— one that I think we should recover and extend—that embraces the refusal of work as part of its project. But this refusal, one of the most provocative and potentially promising elements of the approach, is also one of its most poorly understood. Some readers, including Seyla Benhabib and Drucilla Cornell, have characterized the movement as a prime example of Marxist feminism's commitment to a "utopia of labor," a feminist version of the orthodox Marxist celebration of productive activity (1987, 4). To grasp the specific character of the critique of work that animated wages for housework both in theory and in practice, one must recognize its roots in and resonances with the autonomist tradition. This is one of those instances when historicizing the argument proves critical; otherwise we may fail to understand one of its central analytical orientations and political commitments.

The refusal of work, to recall the discussion of the concept in the previous chapter, is one of the dominant themes of autonomist critical analysis and political practice. As we noted there, it marks an important departure from those elements within Marxism that are beholden to the productivist valorization of work, including both orthodox Marxism's commitment to the model of economic modernization and humanist Marxism's metaphysics of labor. Against such productivist currents, autonomist Marxism rejects both the utopian vision of life made productive and the ontology of man the producer. The refusal of work is not a rejection of productive activity per se, but rather a refusal of central elements of the wage relation and those discourses that encourage our consent to the modes of work that it imposes. It comprises a refusal of work's domination over the times and spaces of life and of its moralization, a resistance to the elevation of work as necessary duty and supreme calling. It is at once a model of resistance and a struggle for a different relation between life and work that a postwork ethics and more nonwork time could help secure.

In this context, then, calling domestic labor "work" was not meant to elevate it but was imagined rather as "the first step towards refusing to do it" (Federici 1995, 191). Seeking paid work was not a viable way to refuse domestic work: "Slavery to an assembly line is not a liberation from slavery to a kitchen sink" (Dalla Costa and James 1973, 33). Given that capitalist economies have responded to the feminist rejection of prescribed domesticity by continually increasing the number of women in the workforce, and that women often do not escape the primary responsibility for unwaged reproductive labor even when they work for wages, a broader critique of work is required. We must, Dalla Costa urges, "refuse the myth of liberation through work"—after all, "we have worked enough" (47).

If the demand for wages was not meant to celebrate domestic work, neither was it intended to sanctify it. These feminists' insistence on the productivity of unwaged domestic work was not a moral claim: "It is only from the capitalist viewpoint that being productive is a moral virtue, not to say a moral imperative" (Cox and Federici 1976, 6). Here we can get a clear sense of the difficulties with and radical ambition of an agenda that sought to contest at once the invisibility of domestic work and its moralization, to redress both its devaluation as work and its overvaluation as labor of love. Indeed, the application of the refusal of work to the field of unwaged domestic work substantially raises the stakes of the project of refusal: it is one thing to refuse waged work, but quite another to contest the institution of the family and the modes of labor it organizes and imbues with meaning. Applied to unwaged domestic labor, the refusal of work means the rejection of its present familial-centered organization and gendered distribution of labor, as well as the refusal to defend such a critique by recourse to some all-too-familiar romanticization of the domestic realm's relations and rituals.

This deployment of the strategy of refusal within the terrain of domestic work not only radicalizes but also clarifies the practice. Refusing work— in this case, refusing domestic work—does not necessarily mean abandoning the house and denying care; rather, it mandates an interrogation of the basic structures and ethics that govern this work and the struggle for ways to make it, as it were, unproductive. In this sense, the feminist refusal of work might serve as an antidote to the cultural obsession with work, thereby opening a space in which to discuss its present terms. In the United States today—where the work ethic reigns supreme, where work is mythologized and exalted, and where even attitudes must be productive—the critique of work and the instigation of what Dalla Costa calls "the struggle not to work" are both more vitally important and more difficult to develop (Dalla Costa and James 1973, 47).

The refusal of housework involves not only the refusal of its present organization and distribution together with its moralization, but also the refusal of the two common alternatives to the family-based model of reproduction: first, the commodification of domestic work, this different kind of privatization that continues to serve as the default solution of mainstream liberal feminism; and second, its socialization—that is, the making public of domestic work by means of state-funded services including child care, public laundries, and canteens or communal eating places proposed by some radical and socialist feminists (see, for example, Benston 1995, 106). That is, the feminists in the wages for housework movement rejected not only the capitalist but also the socialist remedies defended by other feminists at that time. Wages for housework extended the autonomous Marxist critique of socialist production—a vision they saw as nothing more than the substitution of state control for private control over the same structure of production—into the field of reproduction. Socialism was understood as a program intended to rationalize production in the social factory, to perfect rather than transform the work society.[13] Of course, the critique of publicly funded services to support domestic work was not then and is not now unfamiliar. But this critique did not conjure up the specter of motherless children starting fires in regimented, state-run nurseries so much as it sought to advance the argument that making such services public would not truly change things. Along with other autonomists, these feminists saw socialism as more of a managerial project than a revolutionary one; in this case, more a matter of shoring up family-based care and enabling increasing numbers of women to perform waged work than an effort to change the current regime of productive cooperation centered on waged employment and the family. They did not fail to include in their list of demands the provision of various state services, including child care. But these were treated as necessary reforms rather than as radical demands that pointed in the direction of something different. They were more interested in other kinds of demands: demands for time and money. "We want canteens too, and nurseries and washing machines and dishwashers," Dalla Costa writes, "but we also want choices: to eat in privacy with few people when we want, to have time to be with children, to be with old people, with the sick, when and where we choose." To have choices requires having time, and "to 'have time' means to work less" (Dalla Costa and James 1973, 38). By enabling women to avoid a second shift of waged work, wages for housework could buy some of this time.

THE LIMITS OF THE ANALYSIS

Clearly one must be selective in drawing from a thirty-year-old feminist project, especially a movement and collection of manifestoes developed in a specific time and place. It might be useful to pause briefly here in order to acknowledge a few of the limitations of the analysis. None of the shortcomings I will go on to list, it bears mention, is unique to the wages for housework literature of this period; all should be familiar to readers of 1970s feminist theory. These problems include a tendency toward what could be described as a kind of methodological fundamentalism. One can see this in the literature's predilection for the universalizing claim—what Donna Haraway once described as a reluctance to embrace the status of a partial explanation (1985, 78)—but also in its commitment to the primacy of production, its assumption about the greater efficacy of economic forces over those that the authors deem more properly (and often, indeed, "merely") social, cultural, or political.[14] This is accompanied in some cases by a tendency toward reductionism, as exemplified in Dalla Costa's claim that "the role of the working class housewife . . . is *the* determinant for the position of all other women (Dalla Costa and James 1973, 19) and in the various attempts to reduce complex gender formations and identities to the female role that then seems to have been attributed solely to the constitutive force of capital. Related to this is the authors' unproblematized assumption of and commitment to a unified and ultimately global community of women. Symptomatic of this disavowal of differences among women is the frequent insistence that housework is what all women have in common (see, for example, Dalla Costa and James 1973, 19) and hence that wages for housework is a demand that could inspire all women. In its least persuasive form, wages for housework was even described as the *only* revolutionary perspective (Federici 1995, 188).

Perhaps a more interesting problem to consider is one that the demand for wages was originally intended to remedy: a tendency toward functionalism, whereby capital is attributed a kind of monolithic unity and sole agency, and workers are reduced to the victims of its machinations. The explanations of complex social formations such as the family that assume capital—which often takes the place of a person in the narrative—always acts in its own best interest end up overestimating the autonomous power of capital and underestimating the contradictions and antagonisms that its relations inevitably generate. This tendency to attribute too much coherence, foresight, and force to capital—together with too little heterogeneity, autonomy, and agency to women—is in tension with an equally strong commitment to one of the fundamental principles of autonomous Marxism, that of the leading role of the proletariat, a principle that in other respects these feminists clearly seek to advance. According to this assumption, workers should be seen not as capital's victims, but as its potential antagonists and even saboteurs. It is working-class refusals and assertions of need and desire that provoke capitalist development; thus, milestones in the history of capitalist development should be understood as political attempts to reestablish capital's power in response to workers' insubordination (see, for example, Tronti 1980, 31–32). Dalla Costa and James's fidelity to this methodological reflex is exhibited in their interpretation of Marx: "For Marx," James writes, "history was a process of struggle of the exploited, who continually provoke over long periods and in sudden revolutionary leaps changes in the basic social relations of production and in all the institutions which are an expression of these relations" (Dalla Costa and James 1973, 5). What might be functional constituents of capitalist production have the potential to be, and at various moments in history have in fact become, its active and potentially subversive antagonists.

The demand for wages for housework seems to have intrigued Dalla Costa and James, initially at least, as a mechanism for the development of feminist subjectivity. Far from being a seamless system, the social factory is rife with tensions and contradictions that open spaces for critical perspectives and political action. But unless women make demands, they argue, the family will continue to be functional for capital (43). The task is to identify and cultivate feminist dysfunctionality, and the demand for wages was one way they hoped this could be accomplished.

A DEMAND FOR WAGES

There is an interesting ambiguity in much of the wages for housework literature: Should the demand for wages be read literally or figuratively? Was it presented as a concrete policy objective or a critical ploy? Was it intended to be an end in itself or a means to other ends? Indeed, "it is still not clear," writes Ellen Malos in 1980, "whether campaigners for wages for housework really want what they are asking for" (1995a, 21). Dalla Costa and James offer some interesting responses to such questions. Although it is usually recalled in the secondary literature in feminism as a pivotal text in the wages for housework movement, Dalla Costa and James's *The Power of Women and the Subversion of the Community* addresses the demand for wages only very briefly and dismisses it on the ground that it would only further entrench the gender division of labor in the home (Dalla Costa and James 1973, 34). In two footnotes to the text, the demand for wages receives a still rather tentative, but certainly more positive endorsement. It should be read, Dalla Costa suggests in these notes, not only as a demand, but also as a perspective. In the discussion that follows, I want to begin with this formulation, one that other movement texts echo, and develop it further into what I see as the most compelling reading of the demand. The discussion will be divided into two parts, the first elaborating the demand as a perspective and the second focusing on it as a provocation. The limitations of the content of this specific demand will be addressed later; for now, I want to explore what a demand is and what it can do, drawing out some of its multiple valences as a theoretical focus and practical strategy.

THE DEMAND AS PERSPECTIVE

As its advocates consistently argued, wages for housework is not just a demand, it is a perspective (see, for example, Dalla Costa and James 1973, 53, n. 16; Federici 1995, 187). As a perspective, it is not only a matter of the content of the demand, but of what it is that "we are saying" when "we demand to be paid" (Edmond and Fleming 1975, 7), a matter of the critical analyses that inform and might be elicited by the demand. More specifically, the demand for wages was conceived not only as a concrete reform, but as an opportunity to make visible, and encourage critical reflection on, the position of women in the work society—both in the waged labor system and in its satellite, the family. Toward this end, its promoters suggested that wages for housework could function as a force of demystification, an instrument of denaturalization, and a tool of cognitive mapping.

First, as a force of demystification, the demand for wages aimed to produce some critical distance from the dominant discourses of work and family. In particular, the demand aimed to trouble that conception of the family sustained by its sharp contrast to the world of work. By naming part of what happens in the family as work, the demand for wages confounds the division between work as a site of coercion and regimentation and the family as a freely invented site of authentic and purely voluntary relations. The demand "makes clear this is a job like any other, that must be paid like any other, and that *we can refuse like any other*" (Power of Women Collective 1975, 87). It calls into question the ideology of separate spheres that subtends the idealization of the family as haven in a heartless world by obscuring the role that economic imperatives, gender norms, and compulsory heterosexuality play in shaping familial relationships. In the words of one advocate, "we want to call work what is work so that eventually we might rediscover what is love and create what will be our sexuality which we have never known" (Federici 1995, 192). As a perspective, then, the demand was an attempt to demystify and deromanticize domestic labor, while simultaneously insisting on its necessity and value. Not only can it demystify the relationship between work and family, but the wages for housework perspective also sheds critical light on the wage system. From this angle, one benefit of the wages for housework perspective is similar to a benefit that some proponents of comparable worth claim for that demand. Besides the concrete gains that many women would realize from comparable worth legislation, its radical potential lies in its ability to open up the wage relation to new kinds of scrutiny by politicizing estimations of skill and determinations of value (Blum 1991, 16–17). The wages for housework perspective has a similar potential to demystify the wage system insofar as it can draw attention to the arbitrariness by which contributions to social production are or are not assigned a wage.

Clearly one of the primary attractions of the wages for housework perspective was its denaturalizing effect. To insist that a woman receive payment for what is supposed to be a spontaneous desire rooted in women's nature produces a certain cognitive dissonance. One advocate underscored the value of the demand in these terms: "*It is the demand by which our nature ends and our struggle begins because just to want wages for housework means to refuse that work as the expression of our nature*, and therefore to refuse precisely the female role that capital has invented for us" (Federici 1995, 190). To demand a wage for a practice "so identified with being female" is to begin a process of disidentification: "Even to ask for a wage is already to say that *we are not that work*" (Edmond and Fleming 1975, 6). Thus, "to the degree that through struggle we gain the power to break our capitalist identification," women can, Cox and Federici claim, at least determine who it is that "we are *not*" (1976, 8; emphasis added).

Finally, advocates saw the wages for housework perspective as a means by which to chart the relationship between production and reproduction within the social factory. The demand for wages was in this sense a tool for what Fredric Jameson calls cognitive mapping—that is, an attempt to construct "a situational representation on the part of the individual subject to that vaster and properly unrepresentable totality which is the ensemble of society's structures as a whole" (1991, 51). The demand did not offer a ready-made guide, but rather compelled its audience to participate in its development. "The practical, continuous translation of this perspective" is, Dalla Costa claims, feminist work (Dalla Costa and James 1973, 53, n. 16), a form of analytical labor that the demand as a form requires of its addressees. To make sense of the slogan "wages for housework," one has to fill in the blanks of the broader analysis that supplies the demand's warrant and rationale. The perspective that both informs and emerges from the demand conceives the household as an economic unit with complex linkages to the waged-labor economy—a structural component of, rather than a haven from, the world of work. Insofar as the demand operates as a condensed form of analysis of the household and its relationship to larger economic forces and logics, it disturbs the model of separate spheres, demanding that we map across the borders of the public and the private, between the realms of work and family. In particular, the perspective suggests an alternative map of the working day, one that challenges the typical conception of the day as it is defined by wages. "Up to now," the demand's supporters explain, "the working class, male and female, had its working day defined by capital—from punching in to punching out. That defined the time we belonged to capital and the time we belonged to ourselves." "But," they continue, "we have never belonged to ourselves, we have always belonged to capital every moment of our lives. And it is time that we made capital pay for every moment of it" (Cox and Federici 1976, 12).[15]

THE DEMAND AS PROVOCATION

As was the case with the demand for wages for housework as a perspective, the demand as a provocation had utility beyond the merely practical. What is often overlooked in assessments of the demand is its performative dimension: as a perspective, it functioned to produce the feminist knowledge and consciousness that it appears to presuppose; as a provocation, it served also to elicit the subversive commitments, collective formations, and political hopes that it appears only to reflect. The collective practice of demanding thus has its own epistemological and ontological productivity. As not only a perspective but a provocation, the demand for wages should be understood as an attempted claim and incitement of antagonism, collective power, and desire.[16]

As a way to gain some purchase on the demand as a provocation, let us first take a step back and reflect on what it means to make a demand. There are several ways to conceive the demand for wages. One could describe it as a proposal for reform—specifically, a policy or program designed to rationalize the wage system by making up for some of its deficiencies. Although this description is accurate to a degree, to get a sense of what is missing from it, consider the difference between a demand on the one hand and a request or plea—a first step in an effort to seek compromise or accommodation—on the other hand. Neither the policy proposal, with its aura of neutrality, nor the plea, with its solicitousness, manages to capture the style and tone of the demand for wages for housework; none of them conveys the belligerence with which this demand was routinely presented, or the antagonism it was intended thereby to provoke. Although the demand for wages may have been, at least in part, a serious bid for reform, there seems to have been little effort on the part of its proponents to be seen as reasonable or to meet others halfway, and little interest in working within the logic of the existing system and playing by its rules. Consider the response by two of the demand's advocates to the charge that the demand for wages was economically unfeasible:

> As for the financial aspects of Wages for Housework, they are "highly problematical" . . . only if we take the viewpoint of capital—the viewpoint of the Treasury Department—which always claims poverty when it is replying to the working class. Since we are not the Treasury Department *and have no aspiration to be,* we cannot see with their eyes, and we did not even conceive of planning for them systems of payment, wage differentials, productivity deals. It is not for us to put limits on our power, it is not for us to measure our value. It is only for us to organize a struggle to get all of what we want, for us all, and on our terms. For our aim is to be priceless, to price ourselves out of the market, for housework and factory work and office work to be "uneconomic." (Cox and Federici 1976, 14)

There are two points to note about this passage, one about style and another about content. First, refusing to adjust their arguments so as to appeal to their various interlocutors, the demand was typically delivered insistently, without the possibility of compromise. In the words of another proponent, "We want our wages, and we're not waiting!" (Fortunati 1975, 19). They were not opening an exchange of ideas so much as they were "serving notice" (Campaign for Wages for Housework 2000, 258). Second, although securing wages may have been their immediate goal, the statement makes it clear that this was not the only goal, a point to which we will return a little later.

Still less does the demand for wages resemble an effort to persuade, let alone to coax, entice, or seduce. For example, those who demanded wages were not looking for recognition for women's sacrifices or selflessness. "Our power," explain two of the demand's advocates, "does not come from anyone's recognition of our place in the cycle of production, but from our capacity to struggle against it" (Cox and Federici 1976, 6). Rather than inhabit the subordinate position of housewife and try to use it to their advantage as moral high ground and a way to evoke either sympathy or guilt, they were more interested in announcing their power. As James explains in regard to their relationship to other Left groups and trade unions, "we're neither debating with them nor moralizing at them"—rather, James and her colleagues will speak to them in the shared vocabulary of material class interest (1976, 27). Instead of assuming the position of injured party, these feminists present themselves as a force to be reckoned with. In this sense the demand is a "rejection of defense as a strategy" (James 1976, 26).

The demand was thus not only a declaration of revolutionary antagonism, but a demand for power in at least two senses. First, in making a "demand for autonomy" (James 1976, 26), the proponents of wages for housework sought the conditions—in this case, the income—that could secure for women a measure of independence from men, from capital, and from the state. This is why proponents of the demand were critical of those feminists who focused not on less work and more money for women, but only on achieving the "socialization of housework" through the provision of state services like child-care centers or collective kitchens: "In one case we regain some control over our lives, in the other we extend the state's control over us" (Federici 1995, 193).

But the demand for wages was not only a demand for autonomous power, it was also an occasion to acquire and nurture that power; it is about "the autonomy that the wage *and the struggle for the wage* can bring" (James 1975, 18). Here we see more clearly the demand's status as a means rather than an end. Indeed, Dalla Costa argues that we need a better understanding of what a demand is:

It is a goal which is not only a thing but, like capital at any moment, essentially a stage of antagonism of a social relation. Whether the canteen or the wages we win will be a victory or a defeat depends on the force of our struggle. On that force depends whether the goal is an occasion for capital to more rationally command our labor or an occasion for us to weaken their hold on that command. What form the goal takes when we achieve it, whether it is wages or canteens or free birth control, emerges and is in fact created in the struggle, and registers the degree of power that we reached in that struggle. (Dalla Costa and James 1973, 53, n. 17)

By this reckoning, wages for housework was not primarily or immediately about wages but about power; the demand was a provocation to collective action, what James describes as an "organiser of power" (1976, 28). It was not just a goal but also a movement, a process of becoming the kind of people who—or, rather, the kind of collectivities that—needed, wanted, and felt entitled to a wage for their contributions. In this respect, it was a demand for the power to make further demands—for more money, more time, better jobs, and better services (see, for example, Dalla Costa 1975, 126). A demand is in this sense always a risk, a gamble, the success of which depends on the power that the struggle for it can generate. We get a clear sense from the passage quoted above that for Dalla Costa and James, the content of the demand—whether, for example, it was for wages or free birth control—was less important than the political act of demanding itself. To the extent that the demand could provoke the collective power to pursue something different, something more, it was worth pursuing.

By this reading, then, the demand for wages was a provocation of antagonism, power, and, finally, desire. Although sometimes predicated on a sense of what housewives need or what they deserve, what is more striking is how often the demand was articulated in terms of what its advocates want. "We don't *want* the jobs," declares one tract, "we want the money" (Los Angeles Wages for Housework Committee 1975, 124). Here it might be instructive to return to the terminological terrain on which we began this discussion to consider the differences between a demand as something someone wants and a claim of need or a rights claim. Rather than finding the demand's foundation in the more impartial register of a real, demonstrable need or in a rights claim in the guise of which it could be cast as a "legitimated demand,"[17] the proponents of wages for housework were more often content to present the demand as a statement of desire: "We are going to make them give us what we want" (Fleming 1975, 91).[18] In comparison to needs and rights—both of which allege some measure of objectivity, the former because of its resonance with the biological, and the latter through its association with the juridical—demands register more clearly the subjective dimensions of the assertions. To put it in different terms, whereas needs and rights can be imputed to subjects or advanced on their behalf, demands are asserted by them. Indeed, the act of demanding connotes a kind of personal investment and passionate attachment, the presence of a desiring subject behind the demand. In contrast to a demand, a claim—in this case, a rights claim or a claim about needs—assumes a kind of impersonal distance from those who would assert it: "one" might advance a claim, but it is "we" or "I" who makes a demand. Whereas a claim operates more legibly on a register of rational exchange, a demand packs more of an affective charge. To return to an earlier point, demands presume a field of conflict and relations of antagonism that the language of needs, rights, and claims more often serve to circumvent, forestall, or deny.

Again, the performative dimension is crucial: the demand for wages was less about meeting existing needs than expanding them, less about the satisfaction of desire than its cultivation. What campaigners for wages for housework wanted was, as they often repeated, more time and more money. As a provocation of political desire for more, the demand for wages clearly set itself apart from familiar modes of Left asceticism, a point its proponents were acutely aware of: "The left is horrified by the fact that workers—male and female, waged and unwaged—want more money, more time for themselves, more power, instead of being concerned with figuring out how to rationalise production" (Cox and Federici 1976, 18). Rather than demand only what they think they are likely to be conceded, as other practitioners of Left politics might advise, advocates of wages for housework aimed for what they wanted. Indeed, the demand for wages for housework was sometimes asserted with a kind of joyful excessiveness, as exemplified in one tract billed as a "notice to all governments," which concludes its announcement of the demand for wages with a final declaration that reads rather like a ransom demand: "WE WANT IT IN CASH, RETROACTIVE AND IMMEDIATELY, AND WE WANT ALL OF IT" (Campaign for Wages for Housework 2000, 258). Whereas, the tract announces, "we have brought up our children to be good citizens and to respect your laws," now, the writers warn, "we will bring them up to EXPECT more." Self-sacrifice is rejected as both strategy and ideal. "Our problem," Dalla Costa argues, "is that we never have enough, not that we have too much" (Dalla Costa and James 1973, 43).

This brings us back to the beginning of this discussion, and the question of whether the demand for wages for housework was something its proponents wanted to achieve. The answer would seem to be equally yes and no. On the one hand, the demand for wages was conceived and pursued as a concrete goal. It was not, they explain, that securing wages is in itself "the revolution," but rather that it is "a revolutionary strategy," one that might effect a shift in the economy of power in a way that could create possibilities for new struggles and further successes (see Cox and Federici 1976, 14). On the other hand, although it may have been an objective, it was also—and more important—a means to other ends. Its proponents describe it as a demand for money, but also as a demand for power and an occasion to cultivate it. That was what James means when she describes wages for housework as "the perspective of winning" as opposed to a program of merely gradualist change (1976, 27). It was a means by which to constitute a feminist and anticapitalist political collectivity whose ultimate aim was the radical transformation of the institutions of work and family. To recall a passage quoted earlier, the advocates' aim was to be "priceless," to extricate a portion of their lives from capital's logics and purposes, to make housework—together with other forms of work—"uneconomic," to render them unproductive. The demand for wages for housework thus possessed a dual character: it was a reformist project with revolutionary aspirations.

It is important to remember that in her foundational essay, Dalla Costa only endorses the demand for wages in a footnote added after the essay was first drafted in June 1971, after the demand had gained a certain currency within feminist movements in Italy and elsewhere. It was only once the demand began to be advanced with increasing "strength and confidence" that it could be imagined as a viable locus of feminist and anticapitalist organizing (Dalla Costa and James 1973, 52, n. 16). Unfortunately, what Dalla Costa, James, and others support in these texts as a tactic was sometimes conceived, as Malos observes, as a total strategy (1995a, 20); and the movement for wages for housework continued long after it ceased to garner support from and inspire the imagination of feminists beyond those who had already enlisted. It is important to recognize that as tactics of movements, demands will come and go. To borrow the words of Barbara Taylor in the epigraph to this chapter, "they appear—and are lost again" (1983, ix). Demands that function as perspectives, and especially those that serve as provocations, will always be ephemeral achievements: bound by circumstance, they build on the energies and resistances of specific moments. One can imagine, for example, how the demanding assertion of feminist antagonism and power in particular might have appealed to feminists in the early 1970s as they contended with popular notions of feminine competition, weakness, and self-sacrifice. Today there are some new possibilities for, and obstacles to, change. In the present context, rather than try to preserve or resurrect the content of demands from the past, we should consider demands with the content, rhetorical style, and intended effects that could render them more adequate to this moment.

Alisa Del Re expresses what is arguably one of the key problematics of Marxist feminism in these terms: "Confronted by a system founded on the concealment of the actual costs of reproduction—which women have paid for until now, and calculable in terms of money and labor, but also in terms of quality of individual and social life—women must find a way to present their bill" (1996, 110). As the proponents of wages for housework so vigorously insisted, simply moving into the waged-labor force does not, in and of itself, present the bill. They wanted to confront collectively the present systems of social production and reproduction rather than merely individually escape them. Exposing the productivity of reproductive labor might, they hoped, transform it into a potential source of power, a kind of lever. The demand for wages for housework was one way to publicize and politicize this labor, one way to present the bill.

Despite its promise as a perspective and provocation, however, there are at least two fundamental problems with the content of the demand for wages for housework that make it untenable today. First, as its critics have long argued, the gender division of labor would be further entrenched by the payment of this wage to housewives.[19] Some of its supporters contest this claim, arguing that the denaturalization of domestic work is the first step in empowering women to refuse it (see, for example, Federici 1995, 191; Cox and Federici 1976, 11). But this response remains unpersuasive: certainly there are other ways to make this labor visible and contestable that neither name a gendered subject nor offer the means to perpetuate the division of labor that is its material foundation. Second, rewarding more forms of work with wages would do more to preserve than to challenge the integrity of the wage system. A possible reply is that by drawing attention to the arbitrariness with which contributions to social production are and are not rewarded with wages, the demand for wages for housework carries the potential to demystify the wage system. Be that as it may, wages for housework nonetheless demands an expansion of the wage relation rather than a transformation of its terms. In this final part of the chapter, I want to consider a different way to present the bill, with another demand long familiar to the autonomist tradition: the demand for a basic guaranteed income.

We can begin with a description. Basic income is an income paid unconditionally to individuals regardless of their family or household relationships, regardless of other incomes, and regardless of their past, present, or future employment status (van Parijs 1992, 3). Designed to establish a floor below which income would not fall, basic income would enable many to be perhaps not independent of the wage system, but certainly less dependent on its present terms and conditions. The idea is not new to US politics. In the 1960s, various proposals along these lines were debated within the Nixon administration and received extensive consideration in the media (Aronowitz et al. 1998, 67; Theobald 1966, 16–17). As noted in the previous chapter, from the mid-1960s through the mid-1970s, the National Welfare Rights Organization supported basic income as an alternative to the precariousness and invasiveness of—as well as the social hierarchies created by—the welfare system. And the group was not alone: as Brian Steensland observes, "guaranteed annual income plans were *the* welfare reform strategy of the late 1960s and 1970s" (2008, ix). Since the 1980s, it has been the subject of growing interest on the part of both academics and activists across Europe and North America, as well as in many other locations.[20] Proponents argue that it can be paid for by a variety of measures, most important by a streamlined, more progressive, and more effective system of individual and corporate taxation (McKay and Vanevery 2000, 270; Chancer 1998, 120–22).

Several details of the demand for basic income are debated by its advocates, including the amount of the income, what if any conditions should be imposed on it, and the timing of its distribution. As I will explain, to be both a worthy alternative to wages for housework and a substantive contribution to a postwork political project, the income demanded should be sufficient, unconditional, and continuous. The level of income considered "basic" is the first and perhaps most significant point of contention, as the amount determines whether the income would merely subsidize low-wage jobs or would give individuals the freedom to opt out of waged work (Pateman 2003, 141; Gorz 1999, 81–84). To be relevant to the politics of work refusal, as was the demand for wages for housework, the income provided should be large enough to ensure that waged work would be less a necessity than a choice (see McKay 2001, 99). An income sufficient to meet basic needs would make it possible either to refuse waged work entirely, or, for the majority who would probably want the supplementary wage, to provide a better position from which to negotiate more favorable terms of employment. If the income were merely a small addition to wages, it would risk supporting precarious employment and rationalizing the present wage system. At a level adequate to live on—as a basic *livable* income—it would represent a more substantial rupture with the current terms of the work society.

The second point of debate is whether or not conditions would be placed on receiving the income. What some advocates call a participation income would, for example, require the recipient to make some kind of socially useful contribution, like performing volunteer or caring work, or studying (Robeyns 2001, 85). The problem with this approach is that it maintains the commitment to an ideal of social reciprocity centered on work, even if it allows a more expansive notion of what would count as a productive contribution. As an alternative possibility, a citizen's income or social wage that is paid unconditionally is preferable to a participation income because of the way it more thoroughly separates income from work (Pateman 2003; McKay 2001). Finally, some proponents prefer a one-time payment in the form of a stakeholder grant, and others a regular payment over a lifetime.[21] One way to think of this is in terms of the difference between an inheritance and an income: as a capital grant, the former might serve to redistribute some wealth, but the latter more clearly offers itself as either a supplement to or a substitute for a wage. The primary target of a stakeholder grant is economic inequality; in the form of a regular payment over time, the payment also offers at least some degree of freedom from the times, spaces, activities, and relations of paid work. To summarize, the specific demand for basic income that I want to consider as a successor to the demand for wages for housework and a tactic of a contemporary postwork politics is a basic income rather than a wage support, an unconditional income instead of a participation income, and a social wage as opposed to a capital grant.

FROM WAGES TO INCOME: THE DEMAND AS PERSPECTIVE

To explore the possibilities and limits of the demand for basic income, I want to apply the conceptual scheme gleaned from our earlier examination of the demand for wages for housework and consider it in this section as a perspective, and in the next as a provocation. To recall the previous discussion, the demand for wages for housework was predicated upon a critical perspective on the nature of both work and family and a mapping of their relationship across the times and spaces of the social factory. In order to appreciate how the demand for basic income as a perspective might build on and improve upon the perspective of wages for housework, we need to return the latter's analysis of the social factory and update some of its terms.

The wages for housework analyses were grounded in an essentially Fordist model of the social factory, with production and reproduction parceled out into separate spheres represented by the iconic figures of the male proletarian and the housewife. The advocates' insistence on the productivity of reproductive labor was a bid to subvert this model of separate systems. Indeed, the focus on housewives and the claim about the productivity of their work, together with the assertion of the political character of relations in the supposedly private sphere of the family, were at once the product of this Fordist order's own imaginary and perhaps one of the more trenchant expressions of its refusal: a refusal of the privatization and depoliticization of the personal, a refusal of the naturalization of allegedly nonproductive domestic practices, and a refusal of the gendering of the division between production and reproduction. But in the move from an industrial to a postindustrial economy, from Keynesian to neoliberal regimes of governance, from Taylorist to post-Taylorist labor processes and management strategies, and from a Fordist wage relation predicated on mass production for mass consumption to a more heterogeneous model of the wage relation based on flexibility, the relation between production and reproduction that the wages for housework perspective attempted to map becomes even more complex and the borders between them more difficult to discern. In the context of what I will summarize as post-Fordism, the distinction on which both the analysis and political project rested becomes even less tenable.

Consider the relation between waged production and domestic reproduction. First, wages for housework's insights into the productivity of reproductive labor and their analysis of unwaged housework and caring labor as part of the process of value production must now be developed further. The interpenetration of production and reproduction has deepened as domestically produced goods and services continue to be replaced with commodified forms, and as many modes of service and caring labor are transformed into waged forms of employment. Production and reproduction thus come to resemble one another more closely, in terms of both their respective labor processes and their outcomes. Second, not only is reproductive labor more clearly productive today, as evidenced by its many waged forms, but productive labor is increasingly reproductive in the sense that it often creates not only strictly economic goods and services but also social landscapes, communicative contexts, and cultural forms. Indeed, social practices and cultural codes are both inducted into the production and circulation of commodities and generated from it. "In effect," Antonio Negri argues, "productive labor is no longer 'that which directly produces capital,' but that which reproduces society" (1996, 157).

Not only do productive and reproductive labor increasingly overlap, with the distinction between what each creates—whether commodities or socialities—more difficult to see, but the borders around each activity and the list of those engaged in them are also harder to discern. For example, in an economy that draws on the accumulated knowledges—scientific, technological, informational, and communicative—of what Marx once called the general intellect (1973, 706), the circuits of value production can more clearly be seen to extend both across social space and over historical time. As Paolo Virno explains it, "the productive co-operation in which labor-power participates is always larger and richer than the one put into play by the labor process" (2004, 103). The work of reproducing the labor power required for this system of production is equally dispersed. Even when reproductive labor is conceived narrowly as the work of parenting, it is difficult to limit to the site of the household. Although we may imagine as private the relation between parents and children in the context of a family model where parents raise "their" children, it is clear that, to the extent that such children are eventually expected to assume their place as producers and consumers, they are also "public goods."[22] Today it is arguably even more difficult to imagine restricting to individual parents the work of producing workers and consumers with the attitudinal orientations, affective capacities, and communicative skills required by postindustrial production and consumption. Productive subjects are reproduced both within and outside the wage relation, both within and beyond the family. When the notion of reproduction is expanded to cover the reproduction of the socialities necessary for production, the distinction between production and reproduction becomes even more amorphous. What Dalla Costa calls "the community"—the outside of the factory that includes the household—is, in an economy increasingly based on service and communication, even more clearly essential to the reproduction of labor power.[23] The point is that in today's economy, both the labor of production and the labor of reproduction are difficult to limit to an identifiable set of workers, let alone to identities as specific as proletarian and housewife.

As the wages for housework movement's analysis of the social factory indicates, the time of production continues well beyond the formal working day, the space of production reaches beyond the discrete workplace, and the relations of production extend beyond the specific employment relation. The point I want to emphasize here is that in the shift from Fordism to post-Fordism, these tendencies have been multiplied and amplified—or, at the very least, have been made more obvious. As a consequence, although the present terms of the work society still require work, the difference between production and reproduction and between work and nonwork becomes increasingly obscure, as the same task could be either a waged or an unwaged activity. As Virno aptly puts it, the difference between work and nonwork comes to resemble the more arbitrary distinction between "remunerated life and non-remunerated life" (2004, 103).

The wages for housework perspective on the social factory demystified both work and family by engaging some of the political-economic, ethical, and gendered discourses that undergird both spheres and promoted the cognitive mapping of the relations among work's various sectors. The demand for basic income has the potential to accomplish something comparable, although shifting the focus of its analyses from the Fordist to the post-Fordist social factory. Although its pedagogy is less clearly inscribed in the very language of the demand than the slogan "wages for housework," the demand for basic income nonetheless presumes an analysis of the political economy of the contemporary wage system, and to engage with the demand requires a reconsideration of its standard rationale. Rather than register the fact that some workers— namely, those performing unwaged domestic work—are not now adequately included in the wage system, the demand for basic income points toward an even less reliable determination of who is and who is not included. The demand for basic income extends the insight of the wages for housework perspective that an individual's income depends on a network of social labor and cooperation broader than the individual wage relation (see Robeyns 2001, 84–85). Whereas the demand for wages for housework intended to expose the dependence of waged work on household-based relations of reproduction, the demand for basic income entails, as Ailsa McKay and Jo Vanevery observe, "an implicit recognition that all citizens contribute to society in a variety of ways," including contributions "that may or may not have monetary value or even be measurable" (2000, 281). The demand for wages for housework sought to expose some of the inadequacies of the relationship between work and income by imagining what it might take to repair the wage system; the demand for basic income's proposal to break the link between work and income highlights the arbitrariness of which practices are waged and which are not.[24]

A major difference between the two demands is that whereas the demand for wages for housework served better as a critical perspective on the wage system than as a concrete proposal for reform, the demand for basic income offers both a critique and a constructive response. As a reform, basic income could help address several key problems of the post-Fordist US political economy that renders its wage system unable to function adequately as a mechanism of social distribution. These include the increasingly inadequate quantity and quality of waged labor manifest in high levels of unemployment, underemployment, and temporary and contingent employment, as well as the problem—noted in chapter 1—of measuring individual contributions to increasingly collective and immaterial labor processes. The demand for basic income poses a critique but also provides a remedy: reducing our dependence on work.

The demand for basic income presumes and evokes a critical perspective not only on the relationship between income and work, but also on the relationship between income and family membership. To recall our earlier discussion of wages for housework, as a perspective that demand tried to make visible the interdependence between the wage system and the institution of the family. The family is not a separate sphere, but part of society's economic apparatus. The family and its ideology help to obscure the costs of productive labor by privatizing, feminizing, and naturalizing much of the work involved in its reproduction. The problem is that neither the wage system nor the institution of the family is able to meet the needs of those individuals whose forms of productivity and intimacy do not line up with such restrictive institutions of social cooperation and economic distribution. One of the advantages of basic income is that, as McKay and Vanevery point out, it would be distributed to individuals irrespective of family membership or household form

(2000, 281). In this way, the demand refuses to privilege either work or family as institutions on which an individual must depend if he or she is to secure the necessary means to support a life. Once again, the advantage of basic income is that it can both generate critical perspectives and offer an effective policy change. Whereas the wages for housework perspective sought to expose the link between the wage system and the family, as many have observed, its achievement risked preserving the relationship. As a perspective, the demand for basic income raises questions about whether narrow definitions of either work or family can or should suffice as principles governing the allocation of income (see McKay and Vanevery 2000, 268); as a concrete reform, it could ease the economic strain that can compel individuals to participate in both waged work and family membership. As Carole Pateman notes, "a basic income has the potential both to encourage critical reassessment of the mutually reinforcing structures of marriage, employment and citizenship, and to open the possibility that these institutions could be re-made in a new, more democratic form" (2006, 110).

The demand for basic income thus recalls and amplifies both the antiproductivism and the antifamilialism of the wages for housework perspective. As a means to challenge at once the work ethic and the family-values discourse with which it is linked, this demand is reminiscent of an earlier demand for basic income that was advanced within a movement often cited in the wages for housework literature as a source of inspiration. The welfare rights movement, in both the United States and England, was another "revolt of the wageless" that the wages for housework authors found instructive (see, for example, Edmond and Fleming 1975, 9; Cox and Federici 1976, 12). The demand for a basic income was in fact a key tenet of the US National Welfare Rights Organization in the 1960s and 1970s. Like advocates of wages for housework, the organization attempted to gain recognition for the labor of parenting while at the same time refusing the work ethic's praise for and privileging of work. Eileen Boris explains that the organization "recognized the necessity of not merely expanding the definition of work to embrace the unpaid labor of care giving or motherwork, but of refocusing the debate from work to income" (1999, 37). These activists were, Felicia Kornbluh (1997) argues, animated less by the notion of a right to work than by a right to consumption predicated upon an adequate level of income. As an effort to secure an income independent of wages, the demand for basic income registers the refusal of an ethics that enforces dependency either on marriage or the wage relation; indeed, the demand calls into question the adequacy of any ideal of social reciprocity that is reduced to a series of individual contracts.

BASIC INCOME AS PROVOCATION

As a perspective, a demand encourages critical reflection on the present order of things: what are the problems the demand seeks to address, and what is the rationale for the solution it puts forward? As a provocation, a demand points toward the future: what would be different if, for example, wages were paid for housework, or income were provided irrespective of work or family membership? As a mode of provocation, the collective practice of demanding should be understood also as a constitutive event, the performative force of which inevitably exceeds the scope of the specific reform.

There are a number of different ways to approach basic income as a provocation to something new. I want to touch, very briefly, on two that bear interesting resemblances to the earlier discussion of the demand for wages for housework: basic income as a provocation to freedom and as a provocation of desire. As for the first of these, although the demand for basic income can certainly be seen as a means to reduce inequality, it can also be understood as an invocation of the possibility of freedom. By "freedom" I mean neither individual self-sovereignty nor libertarian license,[25] but rather what the wages for housework tradition envisioned as a condition of collective autonomy: freedom as the time and space for invention. Basic income can be demanded as a way to gain some measure of distance and separation from the wage relation, and that distance might in turn create the possibility of a life no longer so thoroughly and relentlessly dependent upon work for its qualities. Therefore, we might demand a basic income not so that we can have, do, or be what we already want, do, or are, but because it might allow us to consider and experiment with different kinds of lives, with wanting, doing, and being otherwise. The demand for basic income could also be an occasion to contemplate the shape of a life beyond work, the kind of freedom that, as Marx speculates, "begins only when labour determined by necessity and external expediency ends," in a sphere of existence that lies "beyond the sphere of material production proper" (1981, 959). The demand can serve thus as a provocation to imagine the possibilities of a postwork alternative in which the structures, relations, values, experiences, and meaning of work might be substantially refigured.

But perhaps the most provocative aspect of the demand for basic income today is its anti-asceticism. Indeed, it is worth noting that in debates about basic income, cost is not necessarily the primary point of contention.[26] Rather, it is the ethics of the demand that often seems to generate the most discomfort—specifically, over the way the demand is seen to denigrate the work ethic and challenge ideals of social reciprocity that have been so firmly attached to the ideal of the labor contract.[27] Here too the demand for basic income echoes the demand for wages for housework: both speak to the possibilities of subjects rich in desires and needs. As a provocation of desire—for more money, more time, more freedom—the demand for basic income, like the demand for wages for housework, sets itself apart from so many other approaches to political claims making. Rather than preach the ethics of thrift and savings, the politics of concession, or the economics of sacrifice, the demand for basic income invites the expansion of our needs and desires. In contrast to the more familiar styles of political analysis and strategy that revere work and decry consumerism, it rejects the usual prescription that we should work harder and want less. On the contrary, the demand is excessive, defying what are proclaimed to be reasonable limits on what we should want and demand. By challenging the link between individual production and consumption, by refusing the notion that waged work is the only legitimate means of access to even a minimal standard of living, the demand for basic income points in the direction of a life no longer subordinate to work. On the one hand, this refusal of asceticism may render the demand more difficult to achieve and, in that sense, limit certain aspects of its power as a perspective and provocation. On the other hand, to anticipate an argument I will pursue in chapter 5, the demand is also compelling because it departs from those strictly productivist values that link the worth of individuals to their commitment to work and that tether access to income to its performance. Precisely where the demand fails to pass muster with a model of political calculation sutured to the present may be where it can succeed in sparking the political imagination of, and desire for, a different future.

Using our earlier reading of the wages for housework literature as a model for our consideration of the demand for basic income allows us to recognize the latter demand as not merely a policy proposal but a perspective and a provocation, a pedagogical practice that entails a critical analysis of the present and an imagination of a different future. What makes this demand a worthy successor to the 1970s demand for wages for housework has to do with its advantages as a perspective and provocation, but also as a reform. Indeed, it is arguably a better vehicle by which to advance some of the key goals of the earlier movement: as a perspective, it can challenge both productivist ethics and family values and provoke the possibility of a social form that no longer privileges these now-dominant regimes of economic production, social cooperation, and political order. The potential of the demand to be both epistemologically and ontologically generative ensures the value of advancing it despite the fact that its success in the short term is a long shot. What increases its worth as a successor project is that as a practical reform, basic income offers tangible benefits to a broader constituency than the housewives who were the focus of the earlier demand. In terms of the two critiques of the demand for wages for housework discussed above—namely, that the gender division of labor would be further entrenched by the payment of this wage to housewives, and that the integrity of the wage system would be upheld rather than contested by rewarding more forms of work with wages—the demand for basic income is a more viable alternative. By proposing to award the income universally to individuals and thus lessening the dependence of income on work, basic income not only recognizes but offers a response to the inability of both the wage system and the institution of the family to serve as reliable mechanisms of income distribution.

Reading the demand for basic income in conjunction with the wages for housework literature can also reveal one potential weakness of the demand: its gender neutrality. This raises questions about the capacities of basic income as both a feminist perspective and a feminist reform. Can it promote the kind of critical reflection on the organization of social reproduction and the gender division of its labor that even the slogan "wages for housework" could so often elicit? And would the provision of a basic income reinforce the gender division of domestic labor because, as some opponents argue, fewer men than women would leave paid employment (Gheaus 2008) or challenge that division, as some supporters claim, by giving more men the opportunity to contribute to unpaid caring work (Pateman 2003, 141)?

In sorting through these questions, it might be useful to return again to wages for housework and consider the advantages and disadvantages of the feminist contents of that demand. As I noted above, one way to understand the wages for housework project is as part of a larger effort to publicize and politicize the contradiction between social reproduction and capital accumulation. After all, as James argues, "Marx's analysis of capitalist production was not a meditation on how the society 'ticked.' It was a tool to find the way to overthrow it, to find the social forces who, exploited by capital, were subversive to it" (Dalla Costa and James 1973, 6). The point was not to present a theoretical replication of capitalist logics, but to stimulate the autonomous needs and desires of those on whom capitalism depends for its reproduction. Despite what was often presented in terms of a broad conception of social production that extended across the social factory and an expansive notion of who might be included in the political projects that would contest its organization, housework was their focus and the housewife their privileged political subject. Why focus on housework as the specific site of antagonism? Because, they argued, that is what all women have in common; all women are housewives (19). This was, needless to say, a contentious claim. What did they intend by it? They did not mean that all women were unwaged wives and mothers; rather, they seemed to mean that the gender division of domestic labor, exemplified in the figure of the housewife, was fundamental to the production of gender difference and hierarchy; it was more like a shared condition or context that touched all women's lives directly or indirectly. Given that, they assumed that the housewife could be imagined as a site of identification for women, on the basis of which they could be hailed into militancy as feminists.

This model of identity politics proved to be something of a double-edged sword: certainly one can appreciate the effort to locate a common ground within a terrain of struggle around which people might organize; yet, like other forms of identity politics that seek to draft people into political collectives on the basis of a shared identity, the approach both alienated women who were for any number of reasons not willing to be included in the category of housewife and risked further entrenching an identity that the advocates were invested in consigning to the dustbin of history. Whereas the demand for wages may have had a denaturalizing effect, the demand by housewives for wages for housework threatened to resolidify this labor as women's work performed in the family.

Precisely because it does not address its potential recipients as gendered members of families, the demand for basic income is arguably better able to serve as a feminist perspective and provocation. Not only does it avoid reproducing reified gender categories, but its benefits are not exclusive to a particular group. For this reason, the demand can speak to the concerns of a number of differently situated subjects—including, but not limited to, a broader constituency of women than the demand for wages for housework was able to reach. However, given the demand's gender neutrality, to ensure that the organization of social reproduction and the gender division of its labors are taken up as part of the perspective generated by the demand's explication and circulation, the discursive agenda will need to include both that organization and its gender division. In any case, it is not clear that the gender division of unwaged household and caring labor can be engineered out of existence, that the struggle against it can be won through legislative means or on the terrain of public policy. As the example of wages for housework suggests, the explicit feminist substance of the demand for basic income may be less significant than the political process of its proposition as part of a larger feminist project. By this measure, it is not the content of the demand but the collective practice of demanding that will determine whether what we win "will be a victory or a defeat" (Dalla Costa and James 1973, 53, n. 17).

CONCLUSION

Although I have stressed the more visionary dimensions of the demand for basic income, I want to conclude with a reiteration of its practicality —to insist, borrowing language from the chapter's epigraph, that as a goal it is not only "visionary and utopian," but also "necessary and realistic" (Taylor 1983, ix). First, it offers tangible assistance to a variety of differently positioned workers. Its benefits include much-needed support for the unemployed, underemployed, and precariously employed; a stronger position from which to negotiate better working terms and conditions; a measure of relief from the economic forces that can constrict choices about family membership and household formation; and support for the unwaged domestic and caring labor that has long been central to feminist political agendas. Second, the demand for basic income recognizes and attempts to address economic trends that render the present system of income distribution increasingly inadequate. When the productive and reproductive sectors of the economy are not just interdependent but interpenetrated; when the productivity of our practices so often exceeds the scope of what is included in the wage relation that what one does or does not get paid for appears ever more random; and when the model of full-time, lifelong, secure employment is less and less plausible as a social norm and work-based benefits are harder to come by, a guaranteed basic level of revenue offers a more rational way to allocate income. The authors of "The Post-Work Manifesto" argue that "what has been called utopian in the past must now be recognized as "a practical necessity" (Aronowitz et al. 1998, 69). By pursuing a more substantial alteration of the wage relation, the demand for basic income attempts to address—rather than continuing to ignore or deny—the realities of post-Fordist work, to offer a measure of security in an economy of precariousness.

CHAPTER 4

"Hours for What We Will"

Work, Family, and the Demand for Shorter Hours

> A woman is handicapped by her sex, and handicaps society, either by slavishly copying the pattern of man's advance in the professions, or by refusing to compete with man at all. But with the vision to make a new life plan of her own, she can fulfill a commitment to profession and politics, and to marriage and motherhood with equal seriousness.
>
> BETTY FRIEDAN, *THE FEMININE MYSTIQUE*

> I'm just like any modern woman, trying to have it all: loving husband, a family. It's just I wish I had more time to seek out the dark forces and join their hellish crusade, that's all.
>
> MORTICIA ADDAMS, IN THE 1993 FILM *ADDAMS FAMILY VALUES*

Many of the shortcomings of early second-wave liberal feminism are by now familiar. Take, for example, Betty Friedan's 1963 prescription for careers for women (which she distinguished from mere "jobs") as an alternative to culturally mandated domesticity. As her feminist critics have since pointed out, most women's experience with waged work was not then and is not now what Friedan had in mind when she waxed eloquent about the many rewards of a serious, disciplined, lifelong professional commitment. Most women in the United States worry less about being able to break through the glass ceiling than they do about falling through a structurally unstable floor. Focused as she was on a very specific population of white, middle-class American women, Friedan largely ignored the realities of a dual-wage labor market, constituted in part by the racial and gender divisions of labor, the poles of which have continued to move apart since 1963. Add to women's often rather grim prospects for wage labor the challenges of single parenthood or the stubbornly persistent gender division of labor in the heterosexual family, and the result is an increasingly strict economy of time, with women putting in longer working hours and enjoying less free time than men (see Sirianni and Negrey 2000, 62–63).

One aspect of this legacy that has not been adequately confronted, however, is its valorization of work. Friedan's celebration of waged work as a means to social status and self-development and as a haven from cultural assumptions about feminine domesticity continue to inform feminist analytical frames and political agendas. By and large, feminists who address questions of work today focus on the struggle for more and better work and tend to neglect the possibility of struggling also for less work. As we saw in the previous chapter, the wages for housework tradition—with its signature demands for more money and less work— offers an important alternative to this pro-work tendency. The demand for money in the form of a basic income was the focus of the last chapter; here I want to address more directly the demand for shorter working hours as a locus of antiwork politics and postwork imaginaries. Toward this end, a second aspect of the legacy of wages for housework will be important as well: the recognition of the links between work and family, and insistence that the struggle against the one must include a struggle against the other. Once again, the inclusion of unwaged domestic labor poses a considerable challenge—in this case, to the politics of work time. As we will see, an analysis of the relationship between waged work and family will be crucial in thinking about what counts both as work and as its reduction. That analysis will also help to expose the shortcomings of the most popular defense of shorter hours, one that Friedan herself later came to embrace—namely, as a way to expand family time and thereby counter what she called "the real economic threat to family values" (1997, 13).

Following the model of wages for housework in yet another respect, the demand for shorter hours will be conceived here not only as a call for reform but as a perspective and provocation. On the one hand, it is a demand for a reduction in working hours to improve the quality of life. The demand for a six-hour day with no decrease in pay is the formula that I will take up here. I want to emphasize that my focus is not on efforts to reorganize work schedules (through, for example, flextime options) but rather on attempts to reduce the number of hours people work—a reduction, moreover, that would not entail a cut in wages (unlike most forms of part-time work). On the other hand, as we have seen, a demand is more than a simple policy proposal: it includes as well the perspectives and provocations that both inform and emerge from the texts and practices by which it is promoted. Besides presenting a useful reform, the demand for shorter hours is also based on and potentially generative of a critical perspective on—and the imagination of alternatives to—the current organization of work and the dominant discourses that surround it. Thus, in addition to identifying a specific concrete goal, the movement for shorter hours can also serve to provoke an interrogation of the basic structure of work and the needs, desires, and expectations that are attached to it.

The struggle over time has been central to the history of capitalist development. Marx recounts part of this history in his chapter on the working day in *Capital*. According to his account, worker militancy over the length of the working day was critical to the process of industrialization; indeed, it was the successes of the proletarian struggle for shorter hours that provoked capital to mechanize production and thus shift the focus from absolute surplus value to relative surplus value (Marx 1976, 340–416; see also Cleaver 2000, 89). The increase in productivity that ensued helped to set the stage for what Marx imagined as a new kind of freedom, a basic prerequisite of which would be the continued reduction of the working day (1981, 959). In the United States, the struggle for the shorter day and the shorter week was the focal point of the labor movement up until the end of the Great Depression. The insistence on shorter hours was seen as an important source of solidarity, a demand that could hold together a coalition of different types of workers. As Samuel Gompers put it during the fight for the eight-hour day, "however much they may differ upon other matters . . . all men of labor . . . can unite upon this" (quoted in Rodgers 1978, 156). Women workers tended to be particularly interested in such demands (Roediger and Foner 1989, 164). Support for shorter hours peaked in the early 1930s, when the idea was hailed by its various proponents as a way to—depending on the proponent—increase productivity, reduce unemployment, drive up wages, strengthen the family, make time for domestic duties, or increase leisure time. In 1933 the Senate even passed Senator Hugo Black's

Depression-era bill limiting the work week to thirty hours, which was shortly thereafter abandoned in favor of the Roosevelt administration's preference for creating jobs instead of reducing work. As Benjamin Kline Hunnicutt notes, in the same period that government support for the "right to work" a full-time job grew, the movement for shorter hours lost momentum. Job creation, once derided by union activists as "make work," emerged as a centerpiece of US economic ideology (1996, 34). The demand for shorter hours, increasingly associated with a constituency of women workers, was sidelined, leaving postwar labor feminists, as Dorothy Sue Cobble puts it, "with a politics of time designed primarily with men in mind" (2004, 140–41). Although efforts to achieve a shorter work year and work life continued in the postwar period (through, for example, vacation days and retirement benefits), unlike in Europe, there has been no substantial progress in the United States toward a reduction of the work day and work week since 1939 (139–40; Roediger and Foner 1989, 257–59).[1]

However, the issue of shorter hours is now making its way back onto the broader US intellectual and political agenda. This resurgence revives and reinvents various elements of the idea's historical legacy. Some of the current approaches, however, hold more potential for feminists than others. One of the problems, as we shall see, is that some of the strategies by which the demand can be promoted as a policy can limit it as a perspective and provocation. As an example, one of the arguably most successful strategies employed in previous movements was to demand limits on the working day for women on the ground that long hours threatened their health. Once achieved, the precedent could then be used to secure the reduction of men's hours. One can well imagine how the deployment of the trope of feminine frailty, the narrative of rescue, and the ideal of masculine protection might have enhanced the demand's legibility and appeal. But although this might have improved the prospects of the reform's success, to the extent that this affirmation of gender difference relied on and reproduced traditional gender stereotypes, it proved more limited in its capacity to generate a broader critical perspective on and framework for public dialogue about the quality and quantity of work in women's and men's lives. What may render a demand more appealing does not necessarily enhance it as a perspective on the present, or a provocation toward a different future.

So what might we want when we demand shorter hours, and what might we want to do in those hours? The way the proposal is framed has consequences for its eventual success as both a persuasive demand and a provocative perspective. As a demand, it should be broadly appealing—that is, it should be relevant to more than a small minority of workers—and potentially effective as a way to better their lives. Moreover, a feminist demand for shorter hours should include a broader accounting of what is recognized as work and feminist analyses of its value. Beyond the assertion of a specific policy proposal, to demand is also, as we have seen, to assert a particular discursive agenda. Considering the demand for shorter hours also in these terms, I want to take into account the ways in which it could provide a vocabulary and conceptual framework for new ways of thinking about the nature, value, and meaning of work relative to other practices. With this in mind, in the pages that follow I will build an argument about what a contemporary feminist movement for shorter hours in the United States could accomplish, and how it might most fruitfully be conceived. The discussion will be organized around three different cases for shorter hours that have recently been advanced: one that demands shorter hours as a means of securing more time for family, and two others that de-emphasize—albeit in different ways—the family as the primary rationale for reducing work. For each of these three approaches, a representative text will serve to illustrate some of their advantages and disadvantages.

LESS WORK AND MORE FAMILY

The most common rationale for shorter hours—and hence the first argument I want to address—is that it would make more time for family. This approach is particularly powerful because the emphasis on family resonates comfortably with mainstream political priorities on both the Left and the Right. After all, commentators across the ideological spectrum frequently assume that the family is the source of popular political motivation and the basis for political judgment. Furthermore, tapping into this familiar discourse frames the demand for shorter hours in terms of the easily articulated issue of work-family balance. Yet despite these advantages, I find this the least compelling rationale for work reduction. There are, as we will see, significant pitfalls to organizing a critical discourse about work and a struggle for shorter hours around the idea of the family.

Arlie Russell Hochschild presents a particularly rich and insightful version of this family-centered approach in *The Time Bind: When Work Becomes Home and Home Becomes Work* (1997). In that book, Hochschild attempts to confront what is for her an important puzzle: why do so few of the employees of a "family friendly" Fortune 500 company (which she calls Amerco) take advantage of its various programs offering shorter hours for working parents, even though they report feeling strained to the limit by the long hours they put in between work and home? Hochschild's answer, based on a study of company policies and interviews with employees, is that because work is becoming more like home and home more like work, the people she interviewed tend to prefer to spend more time at work and less at home.[2] She claims that Americans live in a culture that increasingly devalues the unpaid work of parenting while overvaluing paid work, thus reinforcing the relative attractions of work over family. This time bind imposes many obvious stresses and strains on parents but is, she argues, particularly harmful to children. What is needed, Hochschild concludes, is a time movement that centers on shorter and more flexible hours at work to create more time for family.[3]

Hochschild writes eloquently and sympathetically about people's struggles to reconcile the pleasures and demands of work and of life outside work and offers an astute and timely case for a movement that urges us to rethink the assumptions and values of this work-obsessed culture. In effect, she deploys the familiar discourse of "work-family balance"—a version of which shaped the family-friendly policies she investigated at Amerco—to mount a far more substantial challenge to the present organization of work than one finds circulating in human-resource departments. The problem with this rationale for shorter hours is that ultimately it cannot avoid invoking and reinforcing the conservative or neoliberal family values that have figured so prominently in recent public debates and legislative initiatives. There are a number of points at which these normative discourses of the family gain entry to or are enabled by Hochschild's analysis. The discussion that follows will focus on five ways in which this text reproduces a restrictive and prescriptive conception of the family. Rather than being specific to this particular argument, the problems are typical and, I would argue, to some degree inevitable limitations of an analysis that privileges the family as the ground for work reduction. Indeed, one of the reasons this particular text is so interesting is that, in contrast to the classic works of early liberal feminism, this more contemporary contribution is attentive to the diversity of household practices and yet still fails in the last analysis to distance itself from traditional family discourse.

Hochschild is clearly sensitive to the dangers from a feminist perspective of privileging a traditional model of the family, and yet she mines that model for standards against which she can formulate her critique of the organization of waged work. For example, fundamental to her analysis is what emerges in the account as a standard of a "child's time"— a value that the working parents she interviewed continually ignored. Faced with time pressures, parents, as she describes it, "stole" time from their children (1997, 192). Even when one couple reported that their children were not suffering from a lack of time with their parents, she disagrees, claiming that "in truth, the children were on an elaborate Rube Goldberg assembly line of childcare, continually sent from one 'workstation' to the next" (189–90). Different estimates of how much time children need with their parents are characterized as a form of denial: "Responding to overwhelming demands on their time, some Amerco parents decided that everything seemed fine at home, that families simply did not need as much time or attention as had once been imagined" (221). Refusing to recognize "a need as a need" is one line of "defense against having to acknowledge the human costs of lost time at home" (229). Parents were thus, we may presume, in denial about their children's true needs when they thought that a hot meal at night was not always required or when they thought that daily baths were unnecessary (228). This notion of the amount of time that children need from parents, presented as uncontested and without a history of its own, functions in Hochschild's argument as a seemingly neutral standpoint from which to critique contemporary work schedules and work values. But of course the model of intensive parenting she poses as a norm is not natural, nor is it uncontested—a conclusion to which many of her interviewees' rejection or "denial" of the model can perhaps attest. The problem is that the standard of "children's time"—what they need, when, and from whom—is linked to and made possible by a family model that features a full-time, unwaged woman at home, a model that was always only available to some families and is increasingly available only to a few. As Sharon Hays points out: "One cannot simply *extract* the gendered division of labor from this portrait, since the isolation and protection of that home absolutely depended upon having one person who was fully dedicated to its maintenance" (1998, 31). While apparently either neutral or broadly inclusive of different household formations in some respects, Hochschild's argument implicitly privileges certain family forms and practices over others.

In addition to privileging a specific family model, her analysis also tends to naturalize the family in a way that serves to establish its fundamental difference from and superiority to work. This naturalization of the institution of the family appears, for example, as a consequence of the way it is contrasted to a particular understanding of the world of work. At Amerco, managers encouraged employees to feel part of "the Amerco family" and reinforced family-like ties among co-workers. As Hochschild describes it, "layer after layer of thin culture was thus poured on from the top" (1997, 18). In her interviews, she "heard little about festive reunions of extended families, while throughout the year, employees flocked to the many company-sponsored ritual gatherings" (44). These work relationships, she suggests, are less substantial and less authentic because they are not natural or voluntary. Of course, one need only recall the frequency with which the language of family values figures in political discourse or to consult the Defense of Marriage Act to recognize that the institution of the family has its own management discourses that are designed to manufacture consent and adjust individuals to preconceived roles. Yet Hochschild expresses concern about the "surprising" amount of family life that "has become a matter of efficiently assembling people into prefabricated activity slots" (212), as if that is not precisely what the institution of the family already was, as if to suggest that someone's position, responsibilities, and behavior in the family had once been a matter of a unique and purely organic individual choice. Whereas work relationships are manufactured from above, family relations, she suggests, arise spontaneously from below; to the extent that she characterizes work relations as thin and inauthentic, family relations, we are left to surmise, are—or should be (there is some tension here)—substantial and elemental.

Hochschild further resorts on occasion to a nostalgic vision of the family. This nostalgia is registered in an appeal to the historical ideal of separate spheres in her critical account of the present relationship between work and family. One can see this in her references to the ways in which what had been a haven—in this case, of unalienated labor—is now contaminated by work: the family is taking on an "industrial" tone, a

"Taylorized" feel; parents are subject to "deskilling," with children forced onto a "childcare conveyor belt"; domestic tasks are increasingly "out-sourced," and "family-generated entertainment" is now replaced by television and other commodities (Hochschild 1997, 45, 49, 209, 190, 232, 209–10). Hochschild's allusions to the degradation of preindustrial craft labor and her suggestion that the current penetration of work into family is something new help to augment her claim that it is both desirable and possible to reseparate the two once we revalue the home and have more time to resume our efforts there. One can appreciate the ways in which this nostalgic image of the family could serve to entice and inspire some to rally to its defense and challenge the dominance of work that threatens it.

The attempt to contest the overvaluation of waged work that traditional ideas of work promote by revaluing unwaged work in the household further predisposes Hochschild to a moralization of the family. What we need, in her view, is a greater " 'emotional investment' in family life in an era of familial divesture and deregulation" (249). Indeed, Hochschild's strategy seems to be to demoralize waged work, to challenge the hold of traditional work values on the individual and social imaginaries, by remoralizing work in the family, calling for renewed vows of commitment there and contending that this is where we ought to spend more time and energy. Not only does this strategy risk a kind of sanctification of domestic work that continues to resonate problematically with conventional assumptions about women's natural or socially necessary domesticity, but the effort to revalue unwaged household and caring labor replicates the very ideas about the moral virtues of work that it intended to call into question. Rather than challenge the traditional work values that are linked to waged labor, it risks simply expanding their scope. The problem, it seems to me, is that using the moralization of nonwaged work to argue for a reduction of waged work precludes a broader or more insistent interrogation of dominant work values.

Finally, despite Hochschild's commitment to and talent for demystifying the family, using it as the standard against which to critique work leads her nonetheless to idealize the family. Reporting the harms that long hours now inflict on families is one thing, but it is something else to acknowledge more fundamental problems with the institution of the family that could threaten its appeal as an alternative to working time and a reason to demand its reduction. Here I find it interesting that

Hochschild does not comment more on the gender division of domestic labor in this text, despite both her fine previous work on the issue (1989) and the frequency with which it was raised as a problem in the interviews she recounts. It is not that she is inattentive to the distribution of household and caring labor, but when she does comment on rather than simply describe the division and the conflicts it generates, she presents the issue as more incidental than essential to the family form she defends. Yet the frequency with which the gender division of labor in the home was both practiced and identified as a source of women's pressures in and dissatisfaction with family life in her interviews suggests the need for a more direct critique of the family. Perhaps, to pursue an alternative explanation, the problem is not that work is that good, that attractive, and that satisfying to the people she interviewed, but rather that family life is really that bad, that there are more fundamental problems with the institution. But to the extent that these problems could render the family less an alternative to work than an equally deserving target of reform, paying attention to them risks undercutting the family-centered line of argument.

These elements of the argument—the tendency to privilege one family form over others, and to naturalize, moralize, wax nostalgic about, and idealize the family—serve to lend authority both to Hochschild's critique of current working practices and to her vision of a specific alternative to them. But these aspects of her argument also enable and perpetuate a normative model of the family, an ideal of family life that is deeply problematic from a feminist perspective, one that has been used as a standard from which to condemn a wide variety of relationship practices and household patterns. Her argument also tends to overlook the gender division of labor in the traditional family. Of course none of these depictions of the institution are required for the argument; indeed, one could, and often Hochschild does, make the case for work reduction without evoking a narrow and prescriptive model of the family. My claim is not that this version of the family is necessary to the perspective, but rather that it is a rhetorical temptation built into the line of argument. This is the trap that the argument sets, for both authors and readers, by relying so centrally on the trope of the family in the current context. For example, while it is true that "one need not compare" the childhoods of those whose parents work long hours "to a perfect childhood in a mythical past to conclude that our society needs to face up to an important problem," one would also expect that it might be tempting to try (248). For some, this strategy might make the demand for shorter hours more intelligible and appealing. But this seems a high price to pay; essentially the force of the demand is bought at the cost of its capacities as a critical feminist perspective. Rather than appropriate this discourse of the family for feminist ends, there are other, more promising ways to define the demand for and shape the perspective on shorter hours.

LESS WORK FOR "WHAT WE WILL": DECENTERING THE FAMILY

The solution would seem to be to displace the family from the rationale for reduced hours, and the second approach I want to consider does that, emphasizing instead a broader and more open-ended set of justifications for and benefits of shorter hours. An inspired example of this approach can be found in "The Post-Work Manifesto" by Stanley Aronowitz et al. (1998). Their call for a thirty-hour week of six-hour days without a reduction in pay is part of a broader postwork vision and agenda that the authors propose as a response to current economic conditions and trends in the United States. Citing what they describe as an increase in working hours—whether through more overtime, the colonization of nonwork time by work, or piecing together multiple temporary or part-time jobs—they argue that "it is time for a discourse that imagines alternatives, that accounts for human dignity beyond the conditions of work. It is time to demand and get a thirty-hour workweek" (64). Economic restructuring, technological change, and work reorganization increasingly erodes job security, while at the same time, "the virtues of work are ironically and ever more insistently being glorified" (40). Arguing that we must think critically about the work ethic and imaginatively about possibilities for the future, the authors attempt to outline a post-work political agenda animated by a vision of "shorter working hours, higher wages, and best of all, our ability to control much more of our own time" (33). With the decline of well-paid, secure, and full-time work, what may in the past have been deemed an unaffordable luxury is, they suggest, increasingly an economic necessity (64, 69).

The movement for shorter hours is linked in this formulation to a social vision that is very different from that of the family-centered approach. In contrast to the vision of nonwork time devoted to family, the authors of "The Post-Work Manifesto" present a far more expansive set of possibilities, including time for family, community, and polity (70). I will discuss the specific advantages of this broader conception of the goals of work reduction below. Here I want to highlight one further possibility that the authors present: more time for "what most pleases us" (76). In their insistence on this, they reinvoke an important goal—some scholars have argued it is the most important goal—of earlier movements for shorter hours: time for leisure (Hunnicutt 1996, 52). Recalling the slogan for the eight-hour movement—"eight hours labor, eight hours rest, and eight hours for what we will"—this approach acknowledges that an important part of "what we will" is the enjoyment of leisure time. Rather than, for example, appealing primarily to norms of family responsibility, this formulation suggests that a movement for shorter hours should be animated not only by the call of duty but also by the prospect of pleasure. Departing from more familiar models of political asceticism, the approach offers the expansion of this kind of unbounded time as another goal that can enrich the demand for shorter hours and broaden its perspective on the possibilities of nonwork time.

Despite the many advantages of this approach (others of which will be discussed below), it is limited in one respect: the analysis does not attend adequately to the entire working day. As a result, shorter hours of waged work may lead to a reduction in total working hours for men, but not always for women. If in the period of the eight-hour movement, "what we will" for male workers did not often include doing their share of unwaged reproductive labor, studies of the domestic division of labor do not give much reason to be more hopeful today. Given the current privatization of social reproduction and the gender division of unwaged domestic labor, even if an employed woman's time on the job decreases, her work in the household—housework, consumption work, child care, and elder care—could easily expand to fill the extra time. To the extent that the present organization of domestic labor is not contested and employers can continue to make distinctions between workers on the basis of their assumed responsibility or lack of responsibility for the work of social reproduction, we are more likely to be offered what are alleged to be solutions for the problem of long working hours—more part-time, flextime, and overtime work, and multiple jobs—than we are to win shorter hours for all workers. The point is that any account of working time must include an account of socially necessary unwaged labor, and any movement for reduced working time must include a challenge to its present organization and distribution.[4] Where earlier movements for shorter hours took for granted the gender division of privatized reproductive labor at the heart of the modern family ideal, it seems to me that a feminist movement for shorter hours today must confront and actively contest both the dearth of social support for and the gender division of that labor. This inattention to the whole of the working day also hampers the effort to contest not just work schedules but work ethics. As was the case with the family-centered approach, this effort to challenge the moralization of waged work will be at best constrained and at worst undercut if it does not extend the critique of productivist values to nonwaged household work, because the moralization of this work—defining it as that to which we should devote our lives—remains uncontested.

The family is not privileged in this rationale for and vision of shorter hours. The problem is, rather, that it is more or less ignored. The demand for shorter hours will be limited to the extent that it does not adequately account for the mutually constitutive linkages between work and family—or rather, to switch vocabularies here, between the present organization of waged work and unwaged household labor. The wage system, work processes, work ethics, and modes of worker subjectivity are intimately bound up with kinship forms, household practices, family ethics, and modes of gendered subjectivity. Attempts to challenge or reform any one of these—like the schedules of and dominant values attached to waged work—must take into account the complexity of the entanglements here.

Not only wages—I am thinking here of the "female wage" and the "family wage"—but hours too were historically constructed with reference to the family. That is to say, when the eight-hour day and five-day week became the standard for full-time work shortly after the Second World War, the worker, typically imagined to be a man, was presumed to be supported by a woman in the home. (Although this was of course a predominantly white and middle-class arrangement, it need not be accurate in fact to function effectively as a social norm and political tool.) If instead the male worker had been held responsible for unwaged domestic labor, it is difficult to imagine that he could credibly have been expected to work a minimum of eight hours a day. As Juliet Schor has argued, this system of hours could never have evolved without the gender division of labor and the high rates of full-time, household-based reproductive work among women at that point in history (1997, 49–50). This gender division of labor as a normative ideal was supported in turn, in some cases, by waged domestic labor, which itself was marked not only by gender but also by racial divisions (see, for example, Glenn 1999, 17–18). These gender and racial divisions of labor are also what enabled the postwar labor movement to focus on the issues of overtime and wages rather than on work-time reduction. Even today, assumptions about family form and the gender division of reproductive labor continue to underwrite and be in turn underwritten by new developments in work schedules. Thus, for example, some studies suggest that where the labor force is primarily made up of women, employers are more likely to use part-time workers to maintain flexibility; indeed, certain jobs are constructed to be part time because they are generally filled by women (Beechey and Perkins 1987, 145). Thus part-time work for women—which is often low-paid and has few or no benefits and few opportunities for advancement—continues to be rationalized by reference to women's assumed position as secondary wage earners and primary unwaged reproductive laborers. Men, in contrast, are more likely to provide flexibility by working overtime (Fagan 1996, 101; Williams 2000, 2). Both full-time and overtime are better able to pass as reasonable options insofar as it can still be assumed that someone else can take primary responsibility for domestic labor. My point is that work time—including full-time, part-time, and overtime—is a gendered construct, established and maintained through recourse to a heteronormative family ideal centered on a traditional gender division of labor. Attempts to challenge the legitimacy of the eight-hour day would do well to make visible and contest these aspects of the organization of social reproduction on which work schedules have been based.

Similarly, any attempt to challenge contemporary formulations of the work ethic should also take aim at those aspects of the discourse of the family that help to sustain them. One can detect, for instance, a mutually reinforcing asceticism that animates both the work ethic and the family ideal. One of the most persistent elements of the work ethic over the course of US history is its valorization of self-control in the face of the temptations and what Daniel Rodgers characterizes as a faith in the "sanitizing effects of constant labor" (1978, 123, 12). This same productivist asceticism, which was designed to encourage work discipline and thrift, has also served to animate the ideal of heterosexual marital monogamy. In the nineteenth century, for instance, the white, middle-class family was idealized as the form that could redirect sexual appetites and desires toward productive ends (see, for example, D'Emilio and Freedman 1988, 57). One can see this assumption at work in the efforts by early-twentieth-century social reformers to impose both bourgeois work discipline and bourgeois family forms on immigrant households (Lehr 1999, 57; Gordon 1992). Indeed, the alliance between the work ethic and this family ideal is nowhere more visible than in the history of social welfare policy in the United States. According to Mimi Abramovitz's historical account, social welfare policy has been shaped by two fundamental commitments, one to the work ethic and the other to what she calls the family ethic—a set of norms prescribing proper family forms and roles that "articulates and rationalizes the terms of the gender division of labor" (1988, 1–2, 37). Perhaps one of the clearest distillations of these two systems of norms can be found in the overt efforts of the 1996 welfare reform to promote both the work ethic and heterosexual marriage—for example, by means of work requirements and the enforcement of paternal responsibility. Improbable as it may seem, waged work and marriage are the two socially recognized and politically approved paths from what has been called social dependency to what the Personal Responsibility and Work Opportunity Reconciliation Act heralds as "personal responsibility." The broader media and policy debates about social welfare, relying on narrow models of both what counts as work and what counts as family, frequently focus on the poor single mother, often deployed as a racialized figure, for her imagined failure to conform simultaneously to the dominant family model and hegemonic work values.[5]

The partnership between the work ethic and the family ethic is sustained in and through a variety of cultural forms. One can see this interconnection operating behind the interesting coincidence of labels marking the male and female version of the tramp. The figure of the male tramp, seen as a threat to social order and values, figured prominently in public discourse from the late nineteenth century until the early twentieth century, when the word also came to designate a negative moral judgment on modes of female sexuality (Rodgers 1978, 226–27; J. Mills 1989, 239). What interests me here is how the tramp functions as a disavowed figure in both work and family discourse, how a similar controlling image marks in comparable terms the boundary between the normative and the abject.[6] Contrary to the central tenets of both the work ethic and the family ethic, the tramp is in each usage a figure of indulgence and indiscipline. Both male and female tramps are wanderers who refuse to be securely housed within and contained by the dominant institutional sites of work and family (see Broder 2002). Both are promiscuous in their unwillingness to commit to a stable patriarch, as shown in their lack of loyalty to an employer or to an actual or potential husband. The tramp is thus situated against legible models of both productive masculinity and reproductive femininity. Given that the accumulation of property was supposed to be one of the central benefits of a disciplined life of wage labor, and respect for property a cornerstone of the sanctity of marriage, both male and female tramps violate yet another set of fundamental social values. Each is a potentially dangerous figure that could, unless successfully othered, call into question the supposedly indisputable benefits of work or family and challenge the assumed naturalness of their appeal (see Higbie 1997, 572, 562). Just as male tramps, these "villains on a stage of toilers and savers," threatened to inspire otherwise compliant workers by their "shameless rebellion against all work," the figure of the female tramp threatened the ideals of sexual propriety and women's roles at the heart of the bourgeois family model (Rodgers 1978, 227). Though the language of the tramp may have fallen out of use, the basic offenses that the label identified continue to be registered under and regulated by means of more contemporary controlling images. The racialized figure of the welfare queen, in which the supposed violations of both work ethic and normative family form are distilled, is one of its most injurious reiterations.[7]

My point is that the work ethic and the family ethic remain joined together by a host of historical, economic, political, and cultural threads. This renders shortsighted any claim to challenge the schedules of waged work without addressing the organization and distribution of unwaged reproductive work, and makes problematic any effort to demote prevailing work values while either promoting or leaving uncontested prevailing family ethics. What might be the terms of a time movement that cannot be subsumed into the discourse of family values or serve to augment the power of traditional work values and that—by taking into account the whole of our working hours, both waged and unwaged— could be a feminist movement too?

A contemporary time movement must certainly focus on the linkage between waged work time and domestic life, but a challenge to long hours must also include a challenge to the contemporary ideology of the family. To recall the wages for housework perspective explored in the previous chapter, if, as Selma James argues, work and family are each integral to capitalist valorization, then "the struggle against one is inter-dependent with the struggle against the other" (Dalla Costa and James 1973, 12). A third text, Valerie Lehr's *Queer Family Values: Debunking the Myth of the Nuclear Family* (1999), recognizes the relevance of the house-hold to the topic of work hours but seeks to avoid advancing a normative discourse of the family.

Lehr ends her critical analysis of and proposed agenda for US gay and lesbian family politics with a very brief discussion of the demand for shorter hours. Although this may seem on the surface to be a rather odd conclusion to a book about the family that is centered at least initially on an examination of the struggle for gay and lesbian marriage, it is actually a logical outcome of the author's efforts to situate evolving discourses of the family in the context of some of the changing exigencies of capitalist production and accumulation. Lehr argues that rather than continuing to allow capital and the state to define and constitute what counts as an acceptable family, we should pursue strategies that give people more freedom in determining their intimate and social relationships (1999, 171–72). Reducing the workweek is offered as one significant way to provide the material basis for enlarging this freedom. Lehr poses two basic approaches to securing the resources that can enable choice: either expand the state's welfare provisions and, with it, the state's potential to shape and control our lives, or, as she prefers, attempt to formulate demands that have the potential to allow greater autonomy from the structures and institutions, including the state, that now presume to dictate so many of our choices (172). As an example of the latter ap-proach, the demand for shorter hours is "intended not to bring the state into people's lives, but to use state power to enable citizens to have the resources that they need to make real choices" (13).

Both "The Post-Work Manifesto" and *Queer Family Values* suggest how the demand for shorter hours could be made not in the name of the family but in the name of freedom and autonomy. I refer here not to the solipsistic notion of freedom as individual sovereignty, but to a different conception that can best be described as the capacity to represent and recreate oneself and one's relationships, the freedom to design, within obvious bounds, our own lives.[8] This account links freedom not to pure voluntarism or to autonomy vis-à-vis others, but to the possibility of gaining a measure of separation or detachment from capitalist control, imposed norms of gender and sexuality, and traditional standards of family form and roles. It is thus not only a matter of securing individual freedom of choice, but—as the autonomist Marxist tradition might have it—of making some space for the collective autonomy that might alter some of the terms of such choices. In this way, shorter work hours can be seen as a means of securing the time and space to forge alternatives to the present ideals and conditions of work and family life. This conception of the value of shorter hours is also an important element in "The Post-Work Manifesto." Its authors refer to the prospects of a "self-managed life" and time away from "the impositions of external authority," envisioning what it would be like to "finally have the time to imagine alternatives to the present and the possibility of a better future" (Aronowitz et al. 1998, 76). Like Lehr, they offer a more expansive conception of potential alternatives than is found in the family-centered approach, highlighting, for example, the importance of citizens' time and the possibility of a heightened politicization. Indeed, beyond improving the standard of living, these authors hope that additional nonwork time could enable higher levels and new forms of collective projects and political participation (74; see also Lehr 1999, 174–75).

What Lehr adds to this is a focus on the prospect of nonwork time as relationship time, time to recreate and reinvent relations of sociality, care, and intimacy. From this perspective, the goal is not to liberate the family from the encroachments of work. The institution of the family should be recognized as an integral part of the larger political economy, not a separate haven; the normative discourse of the family is intimately linked to and implicated in the work values that should be challenged. The goal is rather to claim the time to reinvent our lives, to reimagine and redefine the spaces, practices, and relationships of nonwork time. The demand could thus be imagined also in relationship to the possibilities of what Judith Halberstam calls "queer time": temporalities that are, among other things, "about the potentiality of a life unscripted by the conventions of family, inheritance, and child rearing" (2005, 2). By these means, the movement against work becomes linked to a transfigurative politics—not just an opportunity to advance preexisting demands, but also a process of creating new subjectivities with new capacities and desires, and, eventually, new demands.

To return once again to that famous slogan from the eight-hour movement—"eight hours labor, eight hours rest, and eight hours for what we will"—we may now more clearly see an interesting ambiguity in the phrasing of the demand. Does time "for what we will" refer to time for what we want, or time for what we will to be? In other words, is it more about getting what we wish for or about getting to exercise our will? Is it a matter of being able to choose among available pleasures and practices, or being able to constitute new ones? Both, I think, are crucial goals that the demand for shorter hours should articulate and advance: more time to partake of existing possibilities for meaning and fulfillment, and time to invent new ones. It is thus not only about more time for leisure as the term is traditionally conceived. It could instead be articulated as time to explore and expand what Rosemary Hennessy describes as "the human capacity for sensation and affect" that has been corralled within and reified by the logics of commodity production, consumer culture, and identity formation in late capitalism (2000, 217). Contrary to those critics of consumer society who fear that shorter working hours would create only more time for mindless consumption, thereby ensuring our further descent into commodity fetishism, there is reason to expect that if given more time, people will find ways to be creative—even if those ways do not necessarily conform to traditional notions of productive activity. Rather than simply a state of passivity, it is important to recognize the potential social productivity of nonwork. By this measure, the problem posed by an expansion of nonwork time is not, as E. P. Thompson notes, " 'how are people going to be able to *consume* all these additional time-units of leisure?' but 'what will be the capacity of experience of the people who have this undirected time to live?' " Perhaps if what Thompson calls the Puritan time-valuation were to relax, we could, as he speculated, "re-learn some of the arts of living" (1991, 401). Again, one of the things this conception of the demand for shorter hours should help us to think about is the value of nonwork time as a resource for social, cultural, and political projects of transvaluation.

But perhaps rather than highlight the social productivity of nonwork —remaining thereby within the terms of productivism's own logic—we should reflect for a moment on why it is that the prospect of nonproductive time is so disturbing, why it is that, as Aronowitz observes, "we may be terrified of free time" (1985, 39). Many objections to the demand for basic income center not on its expense but on its ethics, and the possibility of shorter hours raises comparable concerns—in this case, threatening the model of productive subjectivity and the prohibition on idleness that remains fundamental to its elaboration. Indeed, the possibility of more time for consumption may be less threatening than the prospect of idle time, not only because of what we might do with more nonwork time, but of what we might become. Productivist ethics assume that productivity is what defines and refines us, so that when human capacities for speech, intellect, thought, and fabrication are not directed to productive ends, they are reduced to mere idle talk, idle curiosity, idle thoughts, and idle hands, their noninstrumentality a shameful corruption of these human qualities. Even pleasures are described as less worthy when they are judged to be idle. And what might be cause for ethical distaste in the case of the individual can, when compounded into a generalized indiscipline, become a threat to social order. This fear of free time, whether manifested as idleness or indiscipline, should not be underestimated. If nothing else, it can testify to the ways in which models of both the individual and the collective have been shaped by the mandate to work, and continue to be haunted by what Rodgers describes as the "immense, nervous power" of the contrast between work and laziness (1978, 241).[9]

Beyond creating time for people to fulfill their duties to the family as it is presently conceived, a feminist time movement should also enable them to imagine and explore alternatives to the dominant ideals of family form, function, and division of labor. The demand for shorter hours should not only speak in the name of existing commitments but also spark the imagination and pursuit of new ones. The point is to frame it not in terms of the relentless choice between either work or family, but to conceive it also as a movement to expand the range of possibilities, to secure the time and space to imagine and practice the personal relations and household configurations that we might desire. Shorter hours could thus be about having time for housework, consumption work, and caring work; time for rest and leisure; time to construct and enjoy a multitude of inter- and intragenerational relations of intimacy and sociality; and time for pleasure, politics, and the creation of new ways of living and new modes of subjectivity. It could be imagined in these terms as a movement for the time to imagine, experiment with, and participate in the kinds of practices and relationships—private and public, intimate and social—that "we will."

TOWARD A FEMINIST TIME MOVEMENT

As I stated at the beginning of this chapter, an argument for shorter hours should be assessed as a demand, but also as a perspective and a provocation, an opportunity to think differently and a call to act collectively. The task, then, is to consider how to articulate the demand—its content and rationale—to ensure that the reform could be effectively advanced and, at the same time, that it could serve as an occasion to raise new questions and spark fresh deliberation about the possibilities and limits of the present organization and ethics of work.

It is important to underscore the potential value in the present moment of the critical perspective that the demand could generate. At its best, the demand for shorter hours could open up a public debate about the present and future status of work and provide an avenue for developing a critical discourse on work values. The continued cultural authority of the work ethic today is both disturbing and puzzling: "Just what is the reason for public and private silencing around discussions of the work ethic? What is the 'secret' that has the force of a social 'fact'— that paid work is a condition of human nature and that 'one must work till one drops'?" (Aronowitz et al. 1998, 72). Again, the point is not to deny the present necessity of work or to dismiss its many potential utilities and gratifications, but rather to create some space for subjecting its present ideals and realities to more critical scrutiny. A feminist perspective on work-time reduction in the United States could enable a change in some of the ways we think about work by denaturalizing both the eight-hour day—the seemingly obvious, unquestioned standard for full-time work—and the even more insistently naturalized privatization and gendering of reproductive labor. It should provide an opportunity to raise questions about those aspects of life that are too often accepted as unalterable. Of course the terms of such a public discussion about work values and routines would have to be made more complex. While the term "work" succeeds in registering the social dimensions of certain practices and thereby rendering them subject to political debate, what counts as work—particularly with regard to unwaged caring practices like parenting—would need to be continually reevaluated. Perhaps we need a new vocabulary to better account for the range of people's productive or creative practices and experiences, and to enable us to confront most effectively the structures and discourses that organize them. At the very least, we need to replace the category of nonwork with a range of distinctions.

Let me conclude with a few observations about how best to conceive a feminist movement for shorter hours and what it might accomplish. It is important to emphasize that the goal is the reduction rather than the mere rearrangement of paid work time. While the problem of work-family balance may be widely recognized, the strategy most popular with employers—the flexible work schedule—neither reduces the hours of work nor challenges the assumption that social reproduction should be a private, and largely female, responsibility (Christopherson 1991, 182–83). The demand for a six-hour day is crucial; however, it can only be a beginning or a part of the struggle. A feminist demand for work reduction should attend to the whole of the working day by, for example, insisting that estimates of the socially necessary domestic labor time of individuals be included in both calculations of working time and proposals for its reduction (Luxton 1987, 176). The demand must link this critical analysis of waged work to an interrogation of the organization of both waged and unwaged reproductive work. In terms of waged domestic labor, this requires challenging the gender and racial divisions of waged domestic labor and the low value placed on this work. On the unwaged front, it might mean demanding the reduction of this work time as well as by struggling to make visible and contest the gender division of unwaged household and caring labor, as well as the lack of adequate publicly funded services to support this socially necessary labor. Up to this point, feminists have had relatively little success in degendering and socializing responsibility for social reproduction. But making time for more women and men to remake their lives requires demands for services like high-quality, affordable child care, education, and elder care, and for adequate levels of income for unwaged and underwaged parents.

There are myriad possible benefits of reduced work hours. For instance, an important goal of the shorter-hours movement historically, and one that is certainly relevant today, was to alleviate unemployment by expanding the number of employees necessary to cover the shorter shifts. In addition, a shorter work week could reduce underemployment by raising some part-time employment to the status of full-time. Besides flextime, the second most prominent existing remedy to the problem of time is the part-time schedule, which most workers cannot afford. Key to this proposal for shorter hours is that it does not entail a reduction of income. This would ensure that it would be relevant not only to more-privileged workers but to workers at all pay levels.[10] A third solution to the problem of time, hiring domestic workers, is similarly unavailable to most people. To return for a moment to the epigraphs at the beginning of this chapter, it should be noted that both Betty Friedan's and Morticia Addams's solution to the time bind involved the long-standing practice by which some women hire other women as domestic service workers (Friedan recommended that women hire housekeepers, and Morticia hired a nanny) as a way to create the time to pursue other projects. As with the other two strategies, flextime and part-time, hiring domestic workers constitutes a partial solution to a general problem, a private strategy for the relatively privileged to deal with what is and will remain a collective predicament.[11] Because they avoid challenging the existing organization of production and reproduction, such individual solutions only perpetuate the larger problem. In contrast, the demand for shorter hours—particularly when it is linked to struggles to gain recognition for, and to restructure the social organization of, domestic labor—could appeal to a broader constituency and make it possible for new political alliances to form across race, class, and gender lines.

Indeed, the politics of time in general and the demand for shorter hours in particular seem relevant to the feminist politics surrounding waged domestic work. Feminists recognize that buying more services is not the simple remedy for working more hours that the popular media often assume. The titles of recent articles in feminist journals like "Is it Wrong to Pay for Housework?" (Meagher 2002) and "Do Working Mothers Oppress Other Women?" (Bowman and Cole 2009) suggest some of the problems that this option poses for some feminists, even if these particular authors answer their questions with a qualified "no." Although discussions of such questions elicit a variety of positions, there is broad consensus among feminists involved in such debates that it is important to improve the conditions of domestic employment, that the work deserves more respect and should be better compensated, that the employment regulations governing it need to be both enforced and en-hanced, and that the organizing initiatives of workers must be supported. Interestingly, however, the question of hours is seldom raised; the debate tends to focus more on whether there are feminist reasons to accept or reject domestic work's commodification than on the long working hours that arguably produce a significant measure of the demand for these services. Although these struggles for better work are vitally important, so too, I want to suggest, is the demand for less work.

Reducing work hours has always been an issue around which different groups could find common cause. As David Roediger and Philip Foner observe in their history of US labor and the working day, "reduction of hours became an explosive demand partly because of its unique capacity to unify workers across the lines of craft, race, sex, skill, age, and ethnicity" (1989, vii). Today it has the potential to bring together a broad coalition of feminists, gay and lesbian activists, welfare rights advocates, union organizations, and campaigners for economic justice. Hochschild claims that a focus on expanding family time in order to meet children's needs could serve as a cause around which to organize a broad coalition of time activists; certainly, she suggests, we can agree on the importance of that (1997, 258). But such a demand can easily slide into and reinforce the kinds of traditional norms and assumptions about the nature of family life that still dominate discussions about and representations of intimacy and sociality. My concern is that tapping into this discursive reservoir and these wells of social meaning to fuel the demand for reform risks compromising the demand's promise as a perspective and a provocation. Therefore, rather than fighting for shorter hours in the name of the family, I believe that a more compelling, broadly appealing demand and a richer, more generative perspective and provocation can be fashioned around the goals of freedom and autonomy. Conceived in these terms, time is a resource to use however we might wish. The demand would be for more time not only to inhabit the spaces where we now find a life outside of waged work, but also to create spaces in which to constitute new subjectivities, new work and nonwork ethics, and new practices of care and sociality. By framing the demand for shorter hours in terms of this more open-ended and expansive set of goals, by demanding more time for "what we will"—and resisting the impulse to dictate what that is or should be—we can create a more progressive coalition and sustain a more democratic discourse.

CHAPTER 5

The Future Is Now

Utopian Demands and the Temporalities of Hope

> Be realistic, demand the impossible.
>
> GRAFFITI

> Only thinking directed towards changing the world and informing the desire to change it does not confront the future (the unclosed space for new development in front of us) as embarrassment and the past as spell.
>
> ERNST BLOCH, *THE PRINCIPLE OF HOPE*

In the current political climate, the demands for basic income and shorter hours could of course be dismissed as "merely utopian." Rather than waste time on impractical and untimely demands, so the argument goes, feminists and others should conserve their meager energies and set their sights on more politically feasible goals. This familiar logic makes it easy to write such demands off as unrealistic, and therefore as potentially dangerous distractions from the necessarily modest and small-scale parameters of political reform. That is, the supposed utopianism of these demands is often considered a fatal flaw. One could perhaps contest the claim that these demands are aptly designated utopian in this time and place, and certainly I have tried to point out their practicality in relation to current economic trends. But there is another way to respond to the critique. What if the utopianism of these demands is not a liability but an asset? What if we were to respond to the charge of utopianism not with embarrassment or defensive denial but with recognition and affirmation? And what might such a utopianism without apology look like?

Rather than deny the applicability of the appellation "utopian" to escape its pejorative connotations, in this chapter I want to accept the label, reconsider utopianism as a distinctive mode of thought and practice, and explore what a utopian demand is and what it can do.

Of course, part of what is in dispute here is the status of the term. The definition of "utopia" in this chapter is broadly conceived, including not just the more traditional list of literary and philosophical blueprints of the good society, but also, as I will describe, a variety of partial glimpses of and incitements toward the imagination and construction of alternatives. One of these more fractional forms, the "utopian demand"—as I use the phrase—is a political demand that takes the form not of a narrowly pragmatic reform but of a more substantial transformation of the present configuration of social relations; it is a demand that raises eyebrows, one for which we would probably not expect immediate success. These are demands that would be difficult—though not impossible—to realize in the present institutional and ideological context; to be considered feasible, a number of shifts in the terrain of political discourse must be effected. In this sense, a utopian demand prefigures—again in fragmentary form—a different world, a world in which the program or policy that the demand promotes would be considered as a matter of course both practical and reasonable. It is not, however, just the status of the program or policy that is at stake; as the proponents of wages for housework recognized, the political practice of demanding is of crucial importance as well.

Since my claim is that the power of these demands can be better grasped once their utopian dimensions are more fully understood, I will begin with a more general exploration of the territory of utopianism. In preparation for this analysis of the utopian demand, I divide the chapter into three sections. The first reviews the case against utopia. The analysis in this section is historical, focusing on how utopianism came to be marginalized in the period after the Second World War, and on what grounds it has most often been discredited since. By drawing on a few examples from the Right and Left, we can collect many of the most significant obstacles and objections to utopian thinking and activism. In response to these critiques, the second section presents a philosophical defense drawn primarily from the work of Ernst Bloch. The discussion centers on the ontology and epistemology of utopian speculation and finishes with an exploration of the concept of hope and the cognitive and affective challenges it poses to those who would take it on as a project. In the third section, the analysis shifts registers yet again, moving from the historical focus of the first section and the philosophical territory of the second to the formal terrain of the utopian archive. The brief exploration of the forms and functions of utopian expression considers the possibilities and limitations of a range of genres, from the traditional literary and philosophical utopia, to the manifesto, and, finally, to the utopian demand. My supposition is that setting the utopian demand in relation to these other, more familiar artifacts can bring into sharper focus both its general qualifications and its specific merits as a utopian form.

UTOPIA'S CRITICS

In this section, I want to gather some of the standard objections to utopian thought and practice. We can begin with what might be called an anti-utopianism of the Right—to match the genealogy of Left anti-utopianism that follows—but it is really drawn from a tradition of liberal discourse, and the specific examples I consider have been prominently represented in mainstream political discourse. We might think of this, then, as an official anti-utopianism. Although Marxism harbors its own anti-utopian tendencies, a point I will touch upon below, liberalism has long been home to some of utopianism's most vociferous and— particularly in the Anglophone context—influential critics. Disowning its own utopian origins and impulses once it attained the comfortable status of a dominant ideology dedicated to the conservation of existing regimes, liberalism endorses piecemeal reformism as the only acceptable political course. Socialism, broadly conceived, is liberal anti-utopianism's most enduring target; thus anti-utopianism was, for a substantial part of the twentieth century in the United States, intimately linked to anticommunism. Consequently, the specific contents of liberal anti-utopianism in the United States shifted significantly with the fall of state socialism at the end of the Cold War. To understand the current case against utopianism, it is useful to review briefly its evolution in relation to some of these various instantiations, including liberal, neoliberal, and neoconservative versions, as they continue to provide a repertoire for official anti-utopianism.

To trace the lineages of contemporary anti-utopian discourse in the United States, I want to focus on two key texts produced at very different moments in the evolution of official US anti-utopianism, each of which was celebrated for both its persuasiveness and its prescience. The first of these, Karl Popper's *The Open Society and Its Enemies,* first published in 1945, anticipated the Cold War threat to liberalism's ideological ascendance and confidence; the second, Francis Fukuyama's 1989 "The End of History?," declared the end of that threat. Each text announces the dawn of a new political era and marks a specific moment of anti-utopian revival, when liberalism's general distrust of utopianism reasserts itself in reaction to new events. Fascism was one of these threats, but the two authors agree that at least by 1950 the more pressing challenge was posed by communism (Fukuyama 1989, 9; Popper 1950, vii).[1] As bookends to the Cold War, one mode of anti-utopianism expresses the anxieties of liberalism under siege while the other emerges from the confidence in liberalism's triumph.

Popper's book, together with an article that amplifies some of its central themes, offers an unusually clear and forceful example of a nonetheless rather typical brand of Cold War anti-utopianism. The struggle between reason and passion is the stage upon which this critique is staged. We must understand, Popper argues, that proposals for radical change threaten reason and hence civilization. He distinguishes rationalists like himself—whose ideals are discovered by and propagated through reasoned argument and held with what he describes as "the rational attitude of the impartial judge" (1947–48, 115)—from "Utopianists" whose ideals are spread by appeal to the emotions and adhered to with passionate attachment. The former evinces a "sane attitude towards our own existence and its limitations," while the latter interjects a "hysterical" element (116). Whereas reason is linked in his account with the promise of human community and harmony, utopianism—with its "irrational" appeals to inherently divisive affects and emotions—leads ineluctably, according to this Hobbesian logic, to violence (1950, 419). Such dreams of a substantially different and better world are dangerous; they threaten to "intoxicate" and then seduce us, upsetting the apparently hard-won and always tenuous rule of reason. Rejecting the approach to political activism and reform he labels "Utopian engineering" in favor of "piecemeal engineering," Popper strives to convince us that small-scale alterations of the existing system—"searching for, and fighting against, the greatest and most urgent evils of society, rather than searching for, and fighting for, its ultimate greatest good" (155)—is the only rational course of political action. There is, according to this analysis, no reasonable alternative to liberalism.

Fukuyama agrees with Popper that the small-scale reform of liberal democracies is the only reasonable approach to social change, but for rather different reasons.[2] Whereas Popper wrote on the eve of the Cold War, Fukuyama wrote when the two major challengers to liberalism targeted by Popper's critique—fascism and communism—had been declared defeated. Trying to come to terms with the sense that "something very fundamental has happened in world history" (1989, 3), Fukuyama advances the thesis that what the end of the Cold War signals is nothing less than "the end point of mankind's ideological evolution and the universalization of Western liberal democracy as the final form of human government" (4). It is not just that the Cold War is over, history itself has come to an end. This "triumph of the West," together with the "total exhaustion of viable systematic alternatives to Western liberalism," obviates ideological pretensions to and struggles for a different and higher form of human society (3, 13).[3] Fukuyama's brand of liberal anti-utopianism is thus no longer presented as prescriptive but as descriptive: it purports to explain a political reality that we need to acknowledge, rather than to advance an ideal we should strive to achieve and rally to defend. The mighty and subversive passions that loom so large in Popper's account are cut down to size in Fukuyama's, reduced to no more than the easily resisted and relatively mundane lures of nostalgic longing. For better or worse, utopian dreams have been drained of their affective charge. To the utopian belief that a new and better world is possible, an earlier generation of anti-utopians responded with the argument that there *should* be no alternative. These anti-utopians declare—in this new ideological moment in Anglo-American liberalism, a moment that marks the ascendance of neoliberalism—that there *is* no alternative. What Popper defends in the name of rationalism is now proclaimed under the banner of realism. Utopia is no longer dangerous, just irrelevant.

What Popper advocates, the unrivaled ascendance of liberal ideology, Fukuyama declares achieved. Yet both authors admit to some regrets, as if in these moments of political transition—poised, as each felt himself to be, on the brink of a new political era—they are close enough to the epochs now supplanted to contemplate some remorse. Although Popper defends pragmatism and empiricism against irrational dreams of a different society, he acknowledges as indeed all "too attractive" the pull of utopianism (1947–48, 112), gesturing in this way to the boredom of sobriety, the tedium of always standing on the side of reason against the passions and the wearisome vigilance required to resist their appeal.[4] Fukuyama's regret—perhaps because it assumes the form of a relatively harmless nostalgia for that which has been decisively defeated—is more pronounced, more explicitly thematized. In contrast to Popper's Hobbesian mode of argument, which incites the passions in order to convince us of the threat they can pose, Fukuyama exhibits something closer to a Weberian resignation to a disenchanted world, a perspective inflected by a profound ambivalence about what has been sacrificed on the altar of progress. Confronted with such loss, Fukuyama pines for earlier eras not yet devoid of daring and creativity, before political innovation, courage, and idealism gave way to instrumental reason, cost-benefit analysis, technocratic problem solving, and shopping (1989, 118).[5] It is no wonder that their two brands of anti-utopianism breed remorse: what the accounts disavow—Popper's enemy and Fukuyama's casualty of war—is the very possibility of political imagination and aspiration, nothing less than hope itself.

Fukuyama declares liberalism the winner, but not with the kind of confidence that accompanied declarations in the 1990s of liberalism's unrivaled and world-historic ascendancy. In the transition from the Cold War era of superpower competition to the emergence of triumphant neoliberalism in the age of empire, Fukuyama's then rather speculative claims (the title of the essay was a question: "The End of History?") ossify into official common sense. The end of the Cold War and the threat to liberal politics that Popper so feared cleared the way for the rise of neoliberalism in its fundamentalist mode, a discourse that in many ways dominated the 1990s. Centered on the strident insistence that, in Margaret Thatcher's famous formulation, there is no alternative, the neoliberal anti-utopianism of the 1990s seemed to be absolved of Popper's regrets and relieved of Fukuyama's nostalgia. This acquiescence cast as realism was compounded by what Pierre Bourdieu characterizes as a new kind of economic fatalism "that wants us to believe the world cannot be any different from the way it is" (1998, 128). Neoliberalism's renewed "romance of the capitalist market" as the site of freedom's security is coupled with a revived romance of the privatized family as the necessary locus of social reproduction and a haven in a heartless world (Brenner 2000, 137). The parameters of what is accepted as reality and representations of it that are deemed realistic narrow to coincide with whatever is judged to be consistent with the exigencies of global capital accumulation.

This late 1990s consensus was at least interrupted, if not thrown into crisis, in the early years of the next decade. Fukuyama's prediction of a boring harmony, as Samuel Huntington notes, soon revealed itself to be an "illusion" (1996, 31). Financial crises, global rebellions against neoliberalism, and terrorism and the ongoing war on terror posed challenges to older Cold War and post–Cold War mappings of the world order, giving rise to a political climate in some ways even less hospitable to ideas that challenged the legitimacy of the status quo and political demands or cultural practices that attempted to weaken attachments to what Huntington calls our "civilizational identity." There are, according to this neoconservative discourse, new threats to liberal reason that demand our sacrifice and vigilance, the defeat of which will require the affirmation of shared assumptions and values. Thus the United States in the era of George W. Bush was cast back into an environment more conducive to Popper's anti-utopianism of crisis than to Fukuyama's anti-utopianism of triumph.

What I am calling official anti-utopianism alternates between these basic options, an anti-utopianism fueled by a sense of liberalism under threat and one born of a sense of its dominance. While liberalism continues to mutate into new forms, its case against utopia continues to revolve around a fairly stable set of indictments—between something akin to Popper's approach and Fukuyama's diagnosis, between the rationalist and realist rebukes, between the claim that there should be no alternative and the assurance that there is no alternative. Liberalism continues to consider small-scale reformism the only rational and realistic political option. Speculation about alternative futures is, from the perspective of this classic anti-utopian ontology and epistemology, at best naive and at worst dangerous.

Echoes of these two modes of critique, summarized in the insistence that there *should* be no alternative and the conclusion that there *is* no alternative, can also be found in Left brands of anti-utopianism. But there are further objections to consider as well. A brief exploration of the decline of and retreat from utopianism within second-wave feminism might illustrate the logics and styles of some of the recent anti- or post-utopianisms of the Left and provide an opportunity to add to the list of rejections of and resistances to utopian expressions and commitments.

Feminism is an interesting representative case because feminist projects have long been linked with utopianism. If political realism tends to be associated with a mode of hard-nosed, hard-ball politics, utopianism can be understood—building on this traditional gender logic—as both softhearted and softheaded, or, more precisely, softheaded because softhearted. This traditional feminization of utopianism is reinforced by its link to feminism's historical investment in denaturalization as a mode of theoretical practice and political intervention. When social relations are stabilized by recourse to claims about their natural basis, analyses that question their value and propose alternatives can easily be dismissed as unrealistic. One of Anglo-American feminism's early architects, Mary Wollstonecraft, was thus forced to acknowledge—as a way to inoculate herself from the penalties of the charge—that even her relatively moderate visions of gender equality could, despite her own conviction of their reasonableness, "be termed Utopian dreams" (1996, 35).

Feminists themselves have, at different times and to different degrees, embraced and actively pursued utopian thinking or sought to distance themselves from it. The 1970s witnessed a resurgence of Left utopian projects in the United States, and perhaps nowhere were they pursued with more energy and creativity than within feminism. Radical and socialist feminists in particular cultivated utopian themes with their insistence that everyday life could and should be wholly transformed. This was the period in which Shulamith Firestone's infamous call to seize control over the means of reproduction (1970, 11) was received with no little interest; in which radical feminist groups like the Feminists audaciously demanded not just equal treatment but the elimination of the institutions of heterosexual sex, love, marriage, and the family (1973, 370); in which alternative communities were founded and abandoned in a flurry of experimentation; and in which the feminist literary utopia flourished, imagining a dizzying variety of worlds in which existing gender formations were variously destroyed, reversed, or revolutionized.[6]

However, this interest in feminist utopian thought and activism soon waned. The early 1980s witnessed a decline of feminist utopian literature, matched by a comparable retreat from the utopian in feminist theory (Fitting 1990; Benhabib 1991, 146–47; Goodwin 1990, 3–4). This diminution of utopian energies in US feminism in the 1980s and 1990s must be understood in the context of the same processes of economic and political restructuring that were linked to the resurgence of official brands of anti-utopianism. Economic developments that eroded the traditional bases of working-class power and rendered workers increasingly vulnerable to employers and welfare reform that sought to make mothers more dependent on either waged work or marriage were hardly conducive to utopian hopes about alternatives to work and family. The pressures of getting by in hard times tend not, as Robin Kelley notes, to be generative of the political imagination; instead, "we are constantly putting out fires, responding to emergencies, finding temporary refuge, all of which make it difficult to see anything other than the present" (2002, 11). Consumed by the here and now, the possibilities of alternatives to the ever more reified structures of late capitalism come to seem more distant in such periods. "The leaner and meaner world of the 1980s and 1990s was," as Tom Moylan describes it, "marked by anti-utopian deprivation rather than utopian achievement" (2000, 103).

These same developments fueled an assault on many of the bases of political movements in the 1960s and 1970s, including feminism. The 1980s backlash against the more robust and radical forms of identity-based politics, including feminism, and the 1990s restoration of some of their elements within tamer affirmations of diversity or multicultural difference raised new questions about the viability of the more utopian elements of these theoretical projects and political movements. In such a context, utopian forms of speculation and activism were often reconceived as inadequate to the realities of a hostile political environment and the skepticism of less sympathetic imagined publics. In this new climate, utopian forms of thinking and demanding were understood to be not only naive, but—insofar as they threatened to compromise feminism's already shrinking credibility with more mainstream audiences—even dangerous. The message taken to heart by many feminists in the 1980s was that, as Sarah Goodwin laments, "we must, apparently, become skeptical, practical, and realistic, and outgrow utopia" (1990, 4).

In response to these challenges, some feminists scaled back the scope of their political demands, their commitment to revolutionary change giving way to an absorption in struggles to hold the ground already won. As one socialist feminist complained in the mid-1980s, "in the face of the right, we have to pedal hard to stay in the same place, or fight for demands initiated by mainstream feminists" (English et al. 1985, 101). Feminists had once entertained the possibilities of a future beyond gender, family, and work, but in this new environment, political horizons seemed to narrow. Thus, the aspiration to move beyond gender as we know it was supplanted by efforts to secure the recognition and equal treatment of a wider variety of the genders we now inhabit; the project of "smashing the family" and seeking alternatives was largely abandoned in favor of achieving a more inclusive version of the still privatized model; postwork militancy was eclipsed by the defense of the equal right to work balanced with family; and anticapitalist agendas were overshadowed by the urgency of rear-guard actions and more purely defensive efforts to mitigate the impact of structural adjustment policies, including feminist efforts to design less odious approaches to welfare reform.

That there should be no alternative was not only a consequence of neoliberal triumph and Left retreat. It was also a result of the increasing dominance of a model of academic critique that disavowed the element of proposition. Whereas the 1980s witnessed a retreat from feminist utopianism, feminist critique continued to flourish. Indeed, although the prescriptive dimensions and radical political imaginaries of feminist theory may have been eclipsed, they were replaced by a reinvigorated concentration on and tremendous achievements in more purely diagnostic work. Abandoning a more explicit normative project was one way to avoid those forms of critique—totalizing, foundationalist, moralizing, and essentialist—that poststructuralism in the 1980s and 1990s in particular taught us to recognize and interrogate. Although feminists in this period often decried the passive subjects of overly determinist analyses and routinely affirmed the possibility of political agency, there was a tendency to stop short of imagining alternative futures or mapping out paths toward which feminists might commit their collective energies, presumably because they did not wish to risk having such claims about better worlds and prescriptions for change exclude, marginalize, or render invisible those who would nourish different dreams and pursue alternative programs. Thus the disavowal of the project of normative theory was a way to refuse one's implication in the normative claim's impositions and exclusions. There should be no alternative not because this world is the best possible but because, to cite an oft-quoted passage from Foucault, "to imagine another system is to extend our participation in the present system" (1977, 230). Wendy Brown paraphrases the logic of this feminist Left in these terms: "If there is always a governing political truth, at least let *us* not be the fundamentalists; if every regime is an Occupation, at least let us not be the occupying force" (2005, 101). Jane Bennett's description of Foucault's general strategy—to leave his own normative commitments tacit in order to minimize their moralizing effects (2002, 19)—is what emerged within feminism as perhaps the dominant approach to critique. Rather than develop ways, as Bennett describes an alternative approach, to "render one's affirmative theory more invitational than insistent" (20), affirmation was, and in many ways still is, more often rejected as an integral component of critique and abandoned as a way to avoid the risks of political proposition.[7]

In at least some quarters of the Left, the investment in critique became bound up as well with a set of affective states, including both *ressentiment* and melancholy, that are more attached to the past and its present than to the possibility of and desire for different futures. Brown has charted some of this territory with analyses of both certain modes of politicized identity constituted by wounded attachments and the specter of what she names Left melancholy. As Brown describes it, identity politics fueled by *ressentiment* "becomes deeply invested in its own impotence, even while it seeks to assuage the pain of its powerlessness through its vengeful moralizing, through its wide distribution of suffering, through its reproach to power as such" (1995, 70). In this way critique can be misdirected and visions of change limited by the preoccupation with the preservation and vindication of existing identities. As for Left melancholy, in one iteration of this analysis, the Left mourns its own (often idealized) past, its now-superseded forms of organizing and modes of political experience. In some accounts, this mourning can turn into melancholy. As Brown describes the melancholic mode of Left affect, a description that pertains to *ressentiment* as well, it is characterized by a structure of desire that is more backward-looking than anticipatory; melancholic subjects are more attached to their marginalized Left critique than to the continuing possibility of social change (1999, 26, 21), while the subject of *ressentiment* becomes more attentive to and invested in his or her injury than in the possibility of its overcoming (1995, 74). These modes of political being, characterized by the affects of loss and sometimes despair, and by a preoccupation with the past and the injuries left in its wake, can harbor their own mode of anti-utopianism. Certain kinds of preoccupations with and attachments to history can overwhelm capacities for creating different futures. Whereas the tactical retreat from radical demands and the embrace of a model of critique shorn of its affirmative dimensions echoes, albeit for very different reasons, Popper's warnings about the dangers of utopianism in a hostile world and insistence that there should be no alternative, these brands of Left *ressentiment* and melancholy resonate with Fukuyama's insistence that, whether we like it or not, there simply is no alternative.

We have by this point collected a number of principled objections, historical obstacles, and affective resistances to utopian thought and practice. Utopia has been criticized in the name of the real and its correlates, reason and realism; it has been disavowed by a model of critique that conceives the normative claim only as a target and not also one of its elements; and it has been overshadowed by a host of temporally inflected affects, from Popper's fear and Fukuyama's nostalgia to modes of Left *ressentiment* and melancholy that tend, in some instances at least, to deflate desires for different and better futures. Yet, despite the oft-cited declarations of its demise, political utopianism survives, a persistence that suggests there are other arguments to consider about its attractions and effects. To find some responses to the challenges posed by its critics, I will revert to a strategy that I have followed in previous chapters and return to one of the lesser-known alternatives within the Marxist tradition—in this case, the work of Ernst Bloch—for insight and inspiration. With Bloch, we will revisit the practice of utopianism and briefly reconsider its ontological and epistemological warrants. Then drawing on both Bloch and Nietzsche, I will explore hope as a mode of temporality, a cognitive and affective relation to time and a way to approach the relationships among historicity, presentism, and futurity. What follows is thus a philosophic interlude of sorts, one that begins and ends with Bloch and learns from Nietzsche in the meantime.

IN DEFENSE OF UTOPIA:
ERNST BLOCH'S ONTOLOGY OF THE NOT YET

Once again Marxism is both an obvious and an unlikely resource—in this case, for a defense of utopianism: obvious because it has so often served as the target of the anti-utopians, including Popper and Fukuyama; unlikely because historically Marxists have so often repudiated the label. Indeed, there is no little irony in the charge of utopianism being leveled at Marxism given that tradition's general hostility to the category.

The pejorative use of the term "utopia," already present in the writings of Marx and Engels, was given further sanction by those tendencies invested in establishing Marxism's scientific credentials.[8] But just as there are countertraditions within Marxism that refuse the productivist glorification of work, there are also Marxisms that embrace rather than disavow utopian desire, speculation, and demands. Ernst Bloch is certainly the most notable example, with his sustained effort to, as he describes it, "bring philosophy to hope" (1995, 1: 6).

Bloch's very distinctive style seeks to provoke the political and philosophical imagination as much as the faculty of critical judgment, and the arguments are conducted in the register of affect as much as that of analysis. At its best, his writing is philosophically rich, conceptually innovative, and heuristically evocative. At its worst, it can be frustratingly obscure and self-indulgent.[9] But there are reasons for reading Bloch critically and selectively that extend beyond the vagaries of style: he is at once one of the most inventive of Marxists and a staunch proponent of the Soviet regime, and the contradiction between his affirmation of the creative imagination and his tendencies toward orthodoxy significantly limits the force of many of his claims. Thus, on the one hand, Bloch conceives the world as "unenclosed" (1: 246) and the future as open; on the other hand, he sometimes sets aside his principled objections to teleological guarantees and determinist narratives because of his certainty that Marx has successfully charted our course.[10]

Approached critically and employed selectively, however, Bloch's major work in three volumes, The Principle of Hope, can serve as a rich resource for an alternative conception and assessment of utopian thought and practice—one that is dedicated to the assertion that it is both reasonable and realistic, not to mention an everyday occurrence, to act as if another world were possible. In response to the narrowness of reason, reality, and realism as these categories are deployed in anti-utopian thought, in each case as the measures of utopia's failure, Bloch fashions an alternative ontology and epistemology. If reality encompasses not only what has come to be but also its potential to become other, then utopian thinking, a mode of thought in which reason is allied with the imagination, can count as a particular brand of realism. To draw out the most relevant elements of his thought, I will focus on his categories of the "not-yet-become," the "not-yet-conscious," and, finally, the central category of his opus, "hope." But first, a brief account of Bloch's notion of utopian reason offers a response to the notion of reason that anchors the model of critique that Popper posed.

Utopian Reason

The irrationalism of utopian thinking is perhaps the easiest of the anti-utopian charges to address. Indeed, the refusal of the narrow concept of reason that sustains Popper's critique of utopianism spans a rich history, from the romantic revolt against the Enlightenment to second-wave feminists' critiques of the gendered binary of reason and emotion and more-recent work on the philosophy and science of affect, to name just a few of its highlights. Bloch's contributions to this critique emerge out of long-standing conflicts in Marxism about the scientific and revolutionary adequacy of the tradition's analytical apparatuses. Along with many other subtraditions within Marxism, Bloch stands opposed to those objectivist Marxisms that deem utopian thinking devoid of analytical viability and conceive historical materialism as a scientistic project deprived of vision. In contrast, Bloch considers his project as a reconciliation of two tendencies within Marxism, what he calls the "cold stream," with its dedication to the demystifying powers of empirical analysis and analytical reason, and the "warm stream," with its desire, imagination, and hopefulness. In keeping with Marx's famous eleventh thesis, knowledge practices are evaluated as much for their potential political effects as for their empirical accuracy and critical acuity. Politically effective knowledge requires not contemplative reason, "which takes things as they are and as they stand," but participating reason, "which takes them as they go, and therefore also as they could go better" (Bloch 1995, 1: 4).

More specifically, Bloch's critique of a notion of reason that would exclude utopian thinking turns on two maneuvers. First, he challenges any definition that would deny the intellectual productivity of the imagination. In refusing the sharp division between analytical and creative reason, Bloch troubles as well simple oppositions between discovery and invention and between interpretation and creation. Second, he refuses the opposition between cognition and affect that also informs the conception of reason at the heart of Popper's anti-utopianism. For Bloch, utopian hope—a category we will explore in more detail below—not only requires both reason and imagination, but is characterized by the presence of two different affects, the "warm" affect of enthusiasm and the "cold" affect of sobriety (3: 1368). Hope as a category rejects both the opposition between reason and passion and the neglect of the faculty of imagination upon which Popper secured the irrationality of utopianism.

The Not-Yet-Become

Whether or not utopianism as a type of speculative practice or mode of political aspiration is necessarily unrealistic, as its critics charge, depends on what counts as real. Both Popper and Fukuyama presume a rather attenuated—or, to borrow Bloch's description, "narrowing and diminishing" —notion of reality, one that counts as real only what can be isolated as fact from a process of becoming (1: 197). Bloch's alternative, a process model of ontology, which traces complex processes of historical emergence, is not uncommon in the philosophical tradition; what makes his contribution to the project of ontology's historicization rather less familiar is his insistence that it attend as well to the forward movement of that which has become.[11] The ontology of what Bloch calls the "Not-Yet-Become" affirms reality as a process that not only extends backward but also stretches forward: "The Real is process," the "widely ramified mediation between present, unfinished past, and above all: possible future" (1: 196). According to Bloch's more expansive notion of reality, a notion that lies at the heart of the "Not-Yet-Become" and anchors his defense of utopianism, "anticipating elements are a component of reality itself" (1: 197). In order to grasp the present, Bloch suggests that we must not only understand its emergences from and attachments to the past, but also attempt to grasp its leading edges and open possibilities; everything real has not only a history, but also a horizon.

Bloch challenges not only the conception of the real that informs such objections to utopianism but also what, as realism, might constitute its adequate representation. After all, the assumption that reality is static, that the future will not be different from the present, is hardly realistic. Realism demands the recognition that there is a future born in every present, and that what it will become is not yet decided. Reality is a process in which we can intervene.[12] Bloch's alternative brand of realism considers the present in relationship to both the lingering past that constitutes its denizens and their expected, imagined, desired, feared, dreaded, or longed-for futures. "Real realism," as Bloch describes it, seeks to grasp the present in relationship to both its genealogies and its fronts.

There is one more assumption underlying both Popper's prescription for utopia's defeat and Fukuyama's proclamation of its demise that Bloch contests: the claim that utopianism is extraordinary enough to be judged incompatible with the pragmatism demanded of ordinary existence and, consequently, tenuous enough that one could imagine it overcome. Indeed, to its critics, utopianism is something anomalous, a rarified pursuit and peculiar indulgence, something distant from the normal routines and practical concerns of everyday life. It is because utopian desire is deemed exotic that Popper can expect not only that it should, but that it could, be conquered, and Fukuyama can claim that it has dried up, its wellsprings exhausted. Here again Bloch offers a counterargument that can better account for the persistence of the capacity for and will to utopia.

The "Not-Yet-Conscious" is the term Bloch uses to designate what enables us to anticipate the Not-Yet-Become as an open possibility. He develops this concept through a comparison, or series of comparisons, to the Freudian conception of the unconscious. The Not-Yet-Conscious is another side of the unconscious, one that taps a reservoir of social and political desire comparable to the individuated desire of the Freudian libido. Whereas the Freudian unconscious is backward-looking, a storehouse of the forgotten and repressed, the Not-Yet-Conscious is oriented toward the future. Bloch complains that whereas *"there is nothing new in the Freudian unconscious"* (1: 56), the Not-Yet-Conscious is conceived as a source of creativity and site of intellectual productivity (1: 116).

The Not-Yet-Conscious—this capacity for thinking and wanting the future—can be discovered in a wide variety of practices and artifacts. One place where Bloch locates it, although only in incipient form, is in the act of daydreaming. Although many examples of mundane proto-utopianism could be used to illustrate the argument about the ubiquity of utopian desires and imagination, the daydream seems a particularly appropriate instance to consider because, like utopia itself, it is so often doubly discredited as at once wasteful and trivial: a notoriously unproductive use of time—indeed, perhaps the epitome of an "idle indulgence"—and, compared to the night dream, a superficial phenomenon without the same psychological heft and depth. Bloch means to question these judgments, responding to the productivist critique with the suggestion that the daydream night be something to cultivate rather than outgrow, and challenging the psychological critique's assumption that the night dream unlocks doors to our deepest drives and motives, whereas the daydream can be dismissed as pointless and inconsequential. This indictment of the daydream extends beyond its supposed uselessness and triviality. Daydreaming is often treated as an embarrassment, not only for the lack it represents—a lapse in concentration, a waste of time, an interruption of productive activity—but for what it reveals of our immoderate desires to be and have more, an excess of social desire comparable to the libidinal excesses that can fuel the sleeping dream. And it is not just that these desires for undeserved pleasures are seen as irredeemably self-indulgent; these experiments with the social and political imagination are also considered dangerous—risky violations of that strategy of social adjustment by which we allow ourselves to want only what we are likely to have. In this familiar estimation, daydreams are without value, neither sufficiently productive nor functionally reproductive to merit indulgence or warrant exploration.

Here Bloch again poses a rather polemical contrast to the Freudian night dream. Speaking of polemics, it is worth noting that the daydream that emerges from Bloch's analysis is something of an ideal type: he highlights certain tendencies and minimizes others, magnifying those he wants us to notice so that we might learn to recognize something different in a phenomenon that is so familiar and yet, oddly, so philosophically unattended. Bloch invites us to recognize in these wishful escapes and individual fantasies the traces of a rather different kind of desire and mode of speculation, another form of cognitive and affective practice, and he deploys the distinction between the daydream and the night dream as a way in. According to Bloch, each kind of dream "enters and unlocks a very different region" (1: 87); as we will see, both the modes of dreaming and the contents of the dreams tend to differ.

More specifically, there are four points that distinguish daydreams from night dreams. First, unlike a night dream, a daydream is more typically characterized by what Bloch calls a "clear road." In contrast to both hallucinations and night dreams, a daydream may mute or even distort reality, but does not generally alter it wholesale; the basic tenets of the physical and social setting of the action tend to remain more or less familiar. Moreover, daydreams are more subject to the dreamer's guidance than are sleeping dreams; the dreamer "is not abducted or overpowered by his images, they are not independent enough for this" (1: 88). Daydreams are directed constructions; dreamers can make choices about their contents. Second—and closely related to the first point—daydreams are more likely to be characterized by a "preserved ego": "The daydreaming 'I' persists throughout, consciously, privately, envisaging the circumstances and images of a desired, better life" (Bloch 1970, 86). The dreamer is typically recognizable as the self, even if transformed into a self that the dreamer might wish to become. Another sign of the ego's relative strength is that this daytime imagination tends to be less subject to censorship. Whereas the dream work serves to disguise the wishes that animate nighttime journeys, such wishes are revealed more clearly as the wellsprings of daydreams. In the process of daydreaming, dreamers are less likely to feel ashamed of their wishes or as inclined to atone for the pleasures found in entertaining them. Indeed, in this arena in which the daydream ego—a "utopistically intensified ego," an ego "with the will to extend itself" (1995, 1: 91)—imagines a better life, desires are given a freer rein; here we allow ourselves the private exploration of our desire for more, with less of the usual self-recrimination and moralizing that can hobble the utopian imagination of different worlds.

Bloch presents the third and fourth characteristics of the daydream under the headings of "world-improving" and "journey to the end." As world-improving exercises, daydreams, or at least those that Bloch wants to recognize and consider, typically involve a social component. That is, the daydreamer is less likely to imagine being alone on a deserted island than to envision herself or himself as part of a social world (1995, 1: 92). Night dreams tend to be intensely private, even solipsistic, with their contents disguised and therefore difficult to communicate. (Here one has only to recall the tedium of listening to a friend struggle to recount the details of a recent night's dream.) The wishful images of daydreams, on the other hand, being both grounded in a recognizable reality and more intersubjectively oriented, are more readily communicated (1: 93–94). (One suspects it would be far more interesting to hear a friend recount a recent daydream, but since daydreams are less subject to self-censorship and in them our desires are so directly exposed and indulged, they are also less likely to be shared.) But daydreams are not just worldly rather than otherworldly, they tend toward world-improvement. As world-improving exercises, daydreams differ from night dreams in that they typically invoke a reformed intersubjective situation, one compatible with the strengthened—stronger, happier, more admired, better loved, and so forth—version of the self that is dreamt. They are forward dreams in that sense, less wholly backward-looking than "forerunners and anticipations" (1: 87). Bloch reminds us to pay attention to the collective element, the world-improving aspect that may be part of even the most narcissistic of these musings. And finally, as journeys to the end, daytime fantasies are more committed to the fulfillment of their wishes. Daydreamers practice imagining the outlines of a situation in which their wishes could be satisfied. Unlike the night dream, then, the daydream "has a goal and makes progress towards it" (1: 99).

Daydreams in this sense indulge desires for different futures, experiment with ways to fulfill them, and enjoy their imagined satisfaction. Daydreams are not utopias, but in them we might nonetheless catch a glimpse of the same Not-Yet-Conscious that animates utopian thinking: nascent expressions of political reason and imagination inspired by the desire for and will to new and better forms of life, even if only in this limited and—in Bloch's estimation—unambitious form. One reason Bloch's treatment of these dreams is so interesting is that it can help us to appreciate the omnipresence of the speculative social imagination and begin to take charge of its practice. In contrast to people like Fukuyama who conceive of utopianism as a relatively isolated phenomenon that could be subdued, the example of daydreaming suggests that there may be something far more persistent and durable that fuels the imagination of better worlds.

As we have seen, Bloch defends utopia on the very epistemological and ontological grounds the critics use to attack it. Bloch seeks to shift our conception of utopian thought and desire from the merely illusory to something with an ontological grounding in and claim to the real; from an unrealistic pursuit to a practical endeavor with the epistemological authority of a mode of realism; from the most exotic of indulgences to the most mundane of practices. But there is one more challenge that we need to address: the affective obstacles to the type of imagination of and investment in the future on which utopian thinking and action depends.

The Project of Hope

Arguments about what counts as reason, realism, and reality are familiar philosophical territory. The final impediment is more difficult to address. Rather than presume to argue why we should be less fearful, resentful, or melancholic, which would be both pointless and presumptuous, I want to suggest instead only that another approach to time could be encouraged as well. The following discussion explores both the possibilities and the challenges of hope conceived as a project that cultivates and is cultivated by a different affective economy of time. Bloch insists on the importance of fostering the modes of reason, imagination, and desire that contribute to wishful images like daydreams and channeling them into a "polished utopian consciousness" (1995, 1: 12). Whereas part of these daydreams might be nothing more than mere escapism, "the other part has hoping at its core" and is, he insists, "teachable" (1: 3). The process of bringing this material to consciousness and developing it leads us to the territory of what Bloch calls conscious-known hope (1: 147)—or hope as a project. I will begin with Bloch's very useful two-part definition of hope and then turn to Nietzsche to develop the understanding further. Although he is not typically approached as a utopian theorist, we will see that Nietzsche offers some important supplements to Bloch's analysis. My readings of each of the two theorists focuses on a pair of concepts: two that are key to Bloch's notion of the concrete utopia, the real-possible and the novum, and two that are central to Nietzsche's proposed cure for *ressentiment* and nihilism, the eternal return and the overman. My claim is that through an encounter with these dual teachings of Bloch and Nietzsche, we can better understand the paradoxes at the heart of utopian hope and some of the challenges—at once cognitive and affective—of its intellectual and political projects. Hope is, by this measure, not something one either has or does not, but rather something that can be fostered and practiced by degrees—although, as our two instructors suggest, not easily or without risk.

Hope is, for Bloch, an expansive category. But to provide an initial point of entry, he divides it into two analytically separable, though empirically intertwined, elements: hope, as he explains it, is both a cognitive faculty and an emotion. As a cognitive faculty, hope is a mode of thinking through time that works, as noted above, through the media of both imagination and reason, the counterpart of which is memory (1995, 1: 12, 112). But hope is also an emotion—or, perhaps more accurately, an affect.[13] Whereas hope as a cognitive capacity is analogous to the faculty of memory, and what we might call "hoping" is a practice comparable to remembering or historicizing, hope as an affect—or what I will call "hopefulness"—can best be grasped, Bloch claims, in contrast to fear and anxiety (1: 12).[14] Hope as a political project requires both a honing of the cognitive capacity and the production of the affect; in both forms, Bloch insists, it is something that can be trained and cultivated. Although Bloch offers a useful starting point with this two-part definition, I find that his discussion of utopian hope functions better as a guide to the cognitive practice of thinking the future than as an insight into the affect. So I am going to impose a division of philosophical labor, relying on Bloch for an analysis of the project of knowing a different and better future and turning to Nietzsche—read here, perhaps somewhat against his inclination, as a theorist of utopian hope—for additional insights into what it might take to want and will such a future.

The greatest challenge facing hope as a cognitive practice is our difficulty thinking beyond the bounds of the past and present. Bloch insists that both modes of temporal reasoning—thinking backward and thinking forward—are necessary for thinking the fullness of any one moment in time. In this sense, Bloch speaks of fusing memory and hope rather than ceding any portion of the temporal frame to the purview of only one or the other. Yet, whereas historicity is a familiar philosophical territory, futurity remains relatively neglected. Hence, part of the project of "learning hope" involves developing the cognitive capacity to think through time in both directions.

Bloch's distinction between abstract and concrete utopias is one of the lessons he offers toward this end. Unlike those who accuse utopians of having their heads in the clouds, the utopian Bloch insists on the importance of keeping our feet firmly on the ground. In order to be both a useful intellectual exercise and a politically effective force, utopian hope must be based in analyses of the present conjuncture and in relation to existing tendencies and credible possibilities. The contrast between abstract and concrete utopias is designed to express precisely this point. Abstract utopias are conjured up without sufficient regard to present trends and conditions that could render them possible, as opposed to impossible, futures.[15] Their contents are fantastic and their function compensatory (Levitas 1997, 67). Concrete utopias are, in contrast, developed in relation to what Bloch calls the "Real-Possible." A concrete utopia, as "a dream which lies in the historical trend itself . . . is," as Bloch explains it, "concerned to deliver the forms and contents which have already developed in the womb of present society" (1995, 2: 623). As utopias "mediated with process" (2: 623), their function is more anticipatory than compensatory (Levitas 1997, 67). In this way, the distinction between abstract and concrete utopias turns on the future's relationship to the past and present. Hoping as an exercise of concrete utopianism does not ignore the present as it has come to be; it is not inattentive to history. On the contrary, it must be cognizant of the historical forces and present potentials that might or might not produce different futures; the present is a fulcrum of latencies and tendencies.[16]

But of course, although utopian hope as a cognitive practice must begin with the present, it cannot end there. The epistemological challenge of utopian thinking stems from the fact that the hopeful subject affirms not only a possible as opposed to an impossible future, but also a radically different future, one that is both grounded in the real-possible and ventures far beyond it. This brings us to the second feature of the concrete utopia: whereas concrete utopianism is grounded in present possibilities, it should not be confused with either idealism or futurism. In terms of what we might think of as the idealisms of the status quo, any number of dreams of change without rupture come to mind: from neo-conservativism's ideal of national solidarity anchored by the work, family, and religious values of its citizens, to neoliberalism's postpolitical vision of the world made free and fair by the unhindered reign of market logics or the post-neoliberal vision of a postracial city on the hill that was often attached to the Obama campaign's signifiers of hope and change. Although such dreams of national destiny fulfilled or redemption achieved may tap into utopian longings, they remain for the most part better versions of the present rather than visions of radically different worlds. Similarly, concrete utopian thinking should also be distinguished from futurism. Contrary to that practical "science" of prediction, concrete utopianism in Bloch's estimation is not a slave to the objectively possible (1995, 2: 580). The category of the novum is one of a number of his concepts that serves to disrupt mechanistic or predictive models of time's passing in order to attend to the unexpected and transformative "leap into the New" (3: 1373). The novum in this sense affirms "a world of *qualitative reversibility, changeability itself*," rather than one beholden to "the mechanical Time and Time Again" (1: 286). According to this account, to succumb in thinking the relationship between the present and the future to the seductive simplicity of determinism or the comforts of teleology is to betray the novum. Rather than imagine the future in terms of a predictable evolution from the present, as is the case with both the idealism of the status quo and futurism, concrete utopian thinking must approach it as a more contingent development, with possibilities for significant ruptures and unexpected developments.

The cognitive task of utopian hope is to think these two elements of the concrete utopia together: the commitment both to the real-possible and to the novum, to the new that is familiar insofar as it is sown from the seeds of the present and—as Jameson describes the novum—"the utterly and unexpectedly new, the new which astonishes by its absolute and intrinsic unpredictability" (1971, 126). And herein lies the challenge: to think the relationship between present and future both as tendency and as rupture. The future is at once that which we must map cognitively and that which necessarily exceeds our efforts at representation. Within the narrowly delimited terms of this cognitive field, the gap between the present and the future that the novum opens would seem to signal the failure of thought to be adequate to its object. I will have more to say about this familiar dilemma when we explore different utopian forms and their approaches to what remains a key conundrum of utopian studies. Here I will just note that the power of utopian visions stems in part from the fact that knowing the future on the one hand and wanting it and willing it on the other hand, though certainly linked, are not the same thing and are not necessarily achieved by the same means. More specifically, wanting a different future and making it may not hinge on knowing what it might be. Bloch recognizes that the emotional or affective dimension of utopian hope is the necessary link between utopia as a knowledge project and utopia as a political project. Utopian thought and practice depend on our capacities for affect as much as they do on the exercise of judgmental and creative reason. "The work of this emotion," he insists, "requires people who throw themselves actively into what is becoming, to which they themselves belong" (1995, 1: 3). For hope to be a political force, it must be more than a matter of thinking: it must also be a matter of desire and will. The affective dimension of hope must be added to our understanding of the category if we are to grasp it as a political, rather than a merely epistemological, force.

Before we turn to Nietzsche to develop Bloch's account of the affective project of utopian hope and to grasp the challenges it poses, I want to return once again to Bloch's suggestive description of hope as an affect that he contrasts to fear and anxiety. What seems to be fundamental to

fear and anxiety for Bloch, and what distinguishes them from hopefulness as an affective orientation, is their impact on the subject. There is
something about fear and anxiety that is diminishing and disempower-
ing: "Indeed, something of the extinction of self announces itself in
them" (1995, 1: 75). Fear in particular, as Bloch describes it, drawing on
Sartre, is a state that "cancels out the person" (3: 1366). Fear tends to be a
consuming force, one that once it takes hold can claim precedence over
other dimensions or commitments of the person. Building on this insight and extending it to the field of social relations, we can recognize
that fear can be similarly disabling, rendering its subjects at once exposed
to others through their vulnerability and yet disconnected as a consequence of their protective response. Not surprisingly, fear is an affect
with an important and, for our purposes here, illustrative political pedigree and history.[17] Thomas Hobbes offers what may be the classic analysis of the political effectiveness of fear, the passion he honors for leading
subjects in the state of nature to consent to give up their power and
submit to the will of the sovereign. What renders fear such an important
affect for Hobbes is that, as Corey Robin points out, the subject of fear is
not paralyzed by it; rather, fear functions as a spur to action, specifically
to action that would preserve the self (2004, 41). That is, fear serves to
clarify and accentuate a subject's commitment to self-preservation. By
prompting us to act while diminishing our individual and collective
capacities, fear is at once animating and undermining. In Hobbes's account, fear functions—usefully in his view—as a politically disabling
affect: the subject fearful of death chooses preservation at the expense
of freedom.

Whereas the fearful subject contracts around its will to self-
preservation, the hopeful subject—the basic contours of which we can
glean from Bloch's account—represents a more open and expansive
model of subjectivity. Not reduced to defending the self as such, hopefulness enables a more extensive range of connections and purposes. As
Bloch describes it, "the emotion of hope goes out of itself, makes people
broad instead of confining them" (1995, 1: 3). What seems crucial to this
contrast between the fearful subject and the hopeful one is that the latter
seeks not just to survive but to become more, so that, in Bloch's terms,
"self-preservation becomes self-extension" (1: 76).

Although Nietzsche is not typically read as a utopian theorist, and
hope is not the category through which he articulates his analyses, his

teachings of the eternal return and the overman can be used to develop further this initial figuration of the hopeful subject. In comparing these various models, like the subjects of fear and hope, I am drawing on a philosophical trope that poses arguments in relation to representative types—in this case, subjects characterized in terms of an affective relationship to time—trusting that what might be merely reductive as psychological portraits can prove instructive as figures of political allegory. Nietzsche's model of what I am proposing as a hopeful subject emerges out of a contrast to yet another type, the "man of *ressentiment*," a subject model through which Nietzsche develops his critical diagnosis of the illnesses to which he thought us to be particularly susceptible.[18]

As with Bloch's conception of hope, Nietzsche describes *ressentiment* in terms of both an affective state and a cognitive practice, the latter as an overdeveloped memory in relation to the power of forgetting. Nietzsche sees the "man of *ressentiment*" as lingering over old wounds; his obsession with the past prevents him from the joyful experience of a full present (1967, 127). This subject is characterized as well by a quality of will that is fundamentally reactive, a subject overwhelmed by rancor, regret, and an accusatory stance toward that which emerges from the past and bears its marks. The subject of *ressentiment* experiences an affective relation to time that results in self-punishment and self-diminution and is unable to affirm what he or she has become.

An obvious problem from the perspective of utopian hope is the quality of this subject's relationship to futurity. Haunted by a past that overwhelms the present, the forces of *ressentiment* also hollow out the subject's visions of the future, reducing them to either more of the same or visions that could avenge the past. The past looms large, overshadowing the possibility of a new and different future. But the trouble with the affective temporality encapsulated in Nietzsche's portrait is not so much that such a subject looks backward and not forward. Even more important is the subject's relationship to the present, a mode of being in the moment that is disabling, an affective temporality that generates apathy and resignation.

The first step toward a new, more hopeful temporality thus requires that we can first wrestle a viable present from the past, that we can alter our relationship to a past that threatens to render us not the authors of the present but merely its artifacts. The doctrine of the eternal return or recurrence of all things—quite simply, the idea that the past recurs to

keep producing the present—was Nietzsche's cure for a poisoned relationship to the past and what it has deposited in the present. The eternal
return is posed as a doctrine that would have us believe that the present
will return eternally, that "the complex of causes in which I am entangled
will recur—it will create me again!" (Nietzsche 1969, 237). The idea is
meant to challenge our capacities to affirm the present, to become a
being "who wants to have *what was and is* repeated into all eternity"
(Nietzsche 1966, 68). "How well disposed," Nietzsche asks, "would you
have to become to yourself and to life *to crave nothing more fervently* than
this ultimate eternal confirmation and seal?" (1974, 274). The task is not
to forget the past or to ignore the constitutive force of history—the
reality of pain and suffering, for example, must be acknowledged, not
denied—but to achieve a relationship to the past that could be more
enabling of a different future.

There are two aspects of the teaching of the eternal return that should
be noted here. First, it is important to recognize that for Nietzsche, the
doctrine is less an epistemological proposition than an ontological intervention. As Kathleen Higgins observes, "It is our acceptance of the doctrine, and not the *truth* of the doctrine's propositional content, that has
practical implications for our lives" (1987, 164). In other words, it is not
really a matter of our belief in the eternal return, not really a question of
whether we could think the passing of time in this way; it is instead a
matter of the affective impact of "this great *cultivating* idea" (Nietzsche
1968, 544), of what would happen "if this thought gained possession of
you" (1974, 274). What would it mean to feel this way, who would you be
if you were to experience this orientation to time?

The second point to note is that the affective temporality that Nietzsche prescribes with the eternal return—the particular relationship between historicity and futurity the affective registers of which he struggles
to map—hinges on the notion of affirmation that he deploys. The eternal
return acknowledges the lingering impact of the past on the present and
future, and attempts to disallow a particular mode of that lingering that
results in *ressentiment* and even nihilism. The solution is to "redeem the
past" by willing it, or, as Nietzsche describes it, by transforming every "It
was" into " 'But I willed it thus! So shall I will it' " (1969, 216). But here is
the point I want to emphasize: this will that wills the past must be
understood as a creative will (see 163); the affirmation of the present that
the doctrine teaches is not a simple endorsement or ratification of every-

thing the past has produced, but an active intervention into our ways of inhabiting the past. The practice of affirmation is a willful intervention, an active appropriation of its object; in Gilles Deleuze's formulation, affirmation is not acquiescence (1983, 181). To will the past in this way is not to accept or be reconciled with it, but to affirm what we have become through its passing—not as a source of rancor and resignation, but as a basis for making the future. As an antidote to *ressentiment*, willing the past is an effort to conjure up our power against the determinative force of a history we cannot control and against our animosity toward the present it has produced.[19] Affirmation in this sense requires that we not refuse what we have now become after measuring ourselves against the standard of what we once were or what we wish we had become, but affirm what we are and will it, because it is also the constitutive basis from which we can struggle to become otherwise.

Self-affirmation is the first step toward this new affective temporality that Nietzsche prescribes. If the affirmation of a present no longer under the spell of the resented past, of a life relieved of our reproach, is the first step, the second step concerns that other side of time, the relationship between the present and the future. Nietzsche's prescription for the subject of *ressentiment* depends not only on the capacity to live in the present and affirm selectively what one has become; this subject of the present, this model of "man," must be at once affirmed and overcome: "Man is a bridge," Nietzsche insists, "not a goal" (1969, 215). Although a future alternative to "man" may be the goal, the present will be the site of its construction; "only a buffoon," Nietzsche declares, "thinks: 'Man can also be *jumped over*'" (216). The goal is not to preserve the present and what we have become—to settle on the bridge, as it were—but to affirm them so as to enable the subjects who could then will a better future. After all, for Nietzsche, the animating force in life is not the will to self-preservation but the will to power; the goal is not—to switch now to Bloch's terminology—self-preservation but self-extension.

The overman marks yet another subject type. But this figure of "man" overcome is less a vision of a new model of the human subject than it is a way to mark the place of another side of self-overcoming and the subject type who would take it on as a goal. The overman stands in contrast to those "masters of the present" committed to their self-preservation who would "sacrifice the future *to themselves*" (Nietzsche 1969, 298, 230). The eternal return tests us with the question: could we bear the eternal recurrence of everything that now exists, including ourselves? The figure of the overman challenges us from another point in the temporal frame: could we bear to will our own transformation, are we willing to "create beyond" ourselves (145)? Can we want, and are we willing to create, a new world that would no longer be "our" world, a social form that would not produce subjects like us? "Loving and perishing," Nietzsche notes, "have gone together from eternity," not only as a consequence of the sacrifices that we might make out of love but also in the changes that inevitably occur in the affective relationship to the outside. To affirm oneself as an agent—or, as Nietzsche would have it, to love as a creator—is to be willing to perish too, as the other side of creation is destruction. What would it mean to respond to the prospect of our own "perishing" in a different future, a future in which neither we nor our children—to note that common trope by which we still might imagine a place for ourselves, or people bearing family resemblances to ourselves—would exist, and to respond, moreover, not with fear and anxiety but with joy and hope? Adding this second element threatens to render this Nietzschean alternative temporality paradoxical indeed: on the one hand, we are asked to confront the past in order to carve out a present that we can inhabit and to affirm ourselves as we have become; on the other hand, we are asked to take on the project of creating a different future, and with it our self-transformation. This is what makes Nietzsche's vision so difficult: its mandate to embrace the present and affirm the self and, at the same time, to will their overcoming; its prescription for self-affirmation but not self-preservation or self-aggrandizement. The affective temporality Nietzsche prescribes is one that can create some distance between the present and the sometimes crushing determinative power of the past in order to be strong enough to will a new future, in which the self we affirm would no longer exist.

There are two points I want to draw from this bringing together of Bloch's and Nietzsche's theories of utopian hope. The first lesson of both accounts is that utopian hope hinges at least as much on the quality of our relationship to the past and present as it depends on our orientation to the future. Our tendency to be trapped, both cognitively and affectively, in the past and present is the problem facing hope as a project. But the solution is by no means to ignore or disavow the past and present. Both Bloch's insistence that a concrete utopia must pass through the real-possible and Nietzsche's teaching of the eternal return claim the present as the site of utopian becoming. Bloch thus insists that not only the artifacts of the past but the seeds of the possible future lie in the present, and, for that reason, it cannot—to borrow a Nietzschean formula—"be jumped over" as it is in abstract, fantastic utopias. As the reading of Nietzsche also emphasizes, it is not only a matter of attending cognitively to the present to locate the seeds of possible futures; it is also a matter of affirming the present as the site from which political agents—focused not only on their injuries and armed not only with a critique of the present but fortified as well by the affirmation of their collective power to resist and create—could act collectively to change the world. The faculty of hope is tethered not only cognitively but affectively to the present, although for both theorists, it is a present with tendencies, edges, fronts, and agents.

Second, their dual teachings convey the challenges, at once cognitive and affective, at the heart of the project of utopian hope. But Nietzsche's paradoxical conception seems to pose the greater challenge. Hoping as a cognitive practice may require us to think in terms of both tendency and rupture, to reconcile the future as emerging from and linked to the present, yet radically unrecognizable. But hopefulness as an affective disposition requires a great deal more: to will both (self-)affirmation and (self-)overcoming; to affirm what we have become as the ground from which we can become otherwise. The difficulties of the affective temporality—this particular relationship to the past, present, and future that Nietzsche challenges us to cultivate—should not be underestimated. Loving and perishing may indeed, as Nietzsche claims, always go together, but when what is to be destroyed is the world that makes us possible, the world in which we can exist as legible subjects, the task of creating a new world can be a frightening, even dystopian, prospect. The fear of utopia, as Jameson has astutely captured it, is ultimately bound up with the fear of becoming different: "a thoroughgoing anxiety in the face of everything we stand to lose in the course of so momentous a transformation that—even in the imagination—it can be thought to leave little intact of current passions, habits, practices, and values" (1994, 60).[20] Cultivating utopian hope as a political project of remaking the world is a struggle to become not just able to think a different future but to become willing to become otherwise. "What," Brown asks, "sustains a willingness to risk becoming different kinds of beings, a desire to alter the architecture of the social world from the perspective of being disenfranchised in it, a conviction that the goods of the current order are worth less than the making of a different one?" (2005, 107). The project of hope as conceived here requires the affirmation of what we have become as the constitutive ground from which we can become otherwise. The hopeful subject in this view is less an already constituted subject seeking revenge or restitution, recognition or vindication, than a constitutive subject armed not only with the desire to become stronger but, more provocatively, with the willingness to become different. Thus the project of hope must struggle against both the resentment of what has come to be and the fear of what might replace it, not because the future is settled—on the contrary, it could be a catastrophe—but because a different and better world remains a possibility.

UTOPIAN FORMS AND FUNCTIONS

At this point I want to take the analysis in a somewhat different direction, descending from the virtual heights of philosophical speculation to the investigation of actual utopian artifacts—projects of hope, to be sure, but once instantiated in concrete forms, ones that will inevitably constrain, to one degree or another, the utopian impulses and possibilities explored above. Although we could find utopian desires embedded in and enabled by a wide variety of cultural forms and political practices, the discussion that follows will focus on those forms of utopian expression most recognizable to political theory, from the traditional literary and theoretical utopias that offer detailed visions of alternative worlds, to the utopian manifesto, and finally, to the utopian demand. By situating the utopian demand in relationship to these more familiar and legibly utopian genres, we may be better able to grasp its qualifications as a utopian form and recognize more clearly some of its relative advantages or disadvantages.

The comparative analysis will center on the functions of these forms of utopian speculation.[21] Adapting for this discussion the dual focus on a demand as perspective and provocation that we acquired from the analysis of wages for housework, and drawing on the rich utopian studies literature, I single out two generally conceived functions: as a force of negation, utopian forms can promote critical perspectives on and disinvestment in the status quo; as a mode of affirmation, they can function as provocations toward alternatives. One function is to alter our connection to the present, while the other is to shift our relationship to the future; one is productive of estrangement, the other of hope. I will begin with a brief review of each of these functions and then consider how they might be served well or poorly by the various utopian forms.

The first function of a utopian form is the broadly deconstructive one of neutralizing or negating the hold of the present. Part of the specific, though by no means unique, power of utopian forms stems from their capacity for what Darko Suvin (1972) characterizes as estrangement—that is, their ability to render unfamiliar the all-too-recognizable contours of the present configuration of social relations and the experiences and meanings to which we have become habituated.[22] It is an estrangement that can undercut the present social order's ascribed status as a natural artifact, necessary development, and inevitable future. The utopia serves in this sense as a dereifying technique that enables, as Zygmunt Bauman describes it, a relativizing of the present, to mark it as a contingent product of human history and, thereby, to open the possibility of a different future (1976, 13). Not only can the utopia provide an opportunity for this distancing from the present order, but it can also serve to suspend or momentarily disable those epistemologies and habits of thinking that—whether in the form of common sense, practicality, or an appeal to "just the facts"—bind us to the present, keeping us locked within its narrow orbit of social options and political possibilities.[23] Finally the utopian form can also provide moments of disidentification and desubjectivization: depictions of the inhabitants of other worlds that can serve as figurations of future models of being might present us with the means to make ourselves strange as well. In this respect, as Vincent Geoghegan argues, the utopia's "unabashed and flagrant otherness gives it a power which is lacking in other analytical devices" (1987, 2), an otherness that not even the genealogist's use of the historical past can often match. Beyond providing opportunities for dereification and disinvestment that can encourage openness to possibilities of new and different futures, this first broadly deconstructive function of the utopia also serves to incite and enhance our more specifically critical capacities. By estranging us from the engrossing familiarity of the everyday, the utopian form can provide us with a standpoint in the new from which to assess the present critically.[24] In some instances, for example, one might be able to see the presence of social problems and the extent of their impact more clearly by imagining their absence. The utopia's critical force comes not from some simple opposition to the ideological supports of the present, but rather from its efforts to push against at least some forms of ideological containment from within (see Moylan 1986, 18–19).

Whereas the first function of the utopian form is to look backward from a virtual social situation to reorient our perceptions of the actual present, the second is to redirect our attention and energies toward an open future. Estrangement is central to the extractive or neutralizing operations described above; in contrast, hope is crucial to what I will call the provocation function. By providing a vision or glimmer of a better world, particularly one grounded in the real-possible, the utopia can serve to animate political desire, to engage our aspirations to new and more gratifying forms of collectivity. Beyond provoking desire, utopias can also inspire the political imagination, encourage us to stretch that neglected faculty and expand our sense of what might be possible in our social and political relations. In this sense, the utopia—to borrow Jean Pfaelzer's formulation—"tempts us as an evocation of political desire" (1990, 199). Finally, as part of this provocation function, utopias can serve as inspirational models; they can help to activate political will, to mobilize and organize movements for social change.

There are two points to add to these initial descriptions. First, it is important to underscore the performative dimensions of these two functions. In terms of the estrangement function, one of the qualities that distinguish the utopian project of critique from other modes is the way that it directs, but does not typically provide, the analysis. In contrast to the more familiar modes of political theory that present explicit evaluations of specific institutions or social regimes, which the reader is then expected to accept or reject, utopian forms tend to invite the reader to engage in the practice of comparative analysis and participate in the process of critical reflection. In this sense, the reader is hailed less as recipient than as participant in the process of critical reflection on the present (see also Fitting 1987, 31). The performative quality of the provocation function is both more pronounced than it is in some other genres, and also more important to recognize in that it allows us to see the utopia in a new light, "to grasp it"—I am drawing here on Jameson's reading of Louis Marin—"as a process, as *energeia*, enunciation, productivity, and implicitly or explicitly to repudiate that more traditional and conventional view of Utopia as sheer representation, as the 'realized' vision of this or that ideal society or social ideal" (Jameson 1977, 6).

Because a utopian alternative is proposed not as an empirical reality but as an intellectual possibility, it might be better able to engage us in the process of the construction and elaboration of that possibility— suggesting, once again, a certain advantage in what some see as the fundamental weakness of this nonempirical mode of theoretical inquiry. According to this reading, the value of a utopian form lies less in its prescription for *what* to want, imagine, or will than in its insistence *that* we want, imagine, and will. Miguel Abensour argues that the role of utopias should be understood in terms of the education of desire—not as moral education but, as E. P. Thompson explains Abensour's view, to "teach desire to desire, to desire better, to desire more, and above all to desire in a different way" (Thompson 1976, 97). In this sense, the utopian form's power lies in its capacity to provoke more than prescribe, to animate more than to prefigure. Jameson too affirms utopias less as artifact than as praxis, less for their content than their form; the utopian form, as he describes it, "is not the representation of radical alternatives; it is rather simply the imperative to imagine them" (2001, 231). By this account, a utopia offers not so much the content of a political alternative as an incitement of political will.

The second point I want to emphasize is that, although they are presented here as two separate functions, one deconstructive and the other reconstructive, their simultaneous presence transforms each of them.[25] For example, to the extent that it is coupled with an affirmative dimension, the distancing and critical perspective that may be enabled as part of the estrangement function is not best captured either on the model of Nietzschean forgetting or Marx's ruthless criticism of every-thing existing. The "no" to the present not only opens up the possibility of a "yes" to a different future, it is altered by its relationship to that "yes"; the affective distancing from the status quo that might be enabled is different when it is paired with an affective attachment either to a potential alternative or to the potential of an alternative. Marin's term "neutralization" might better describe the results of the estrangement function than a term like "critique": the object of critique retains a kind of power and presence, holding the critic in its spell in a way that the object of neutralization does not.[26] As a source of provocation as well as estrangement, the utopian form can potentially animate the desire for the possible, as opposed to simply the vindication or restoration of what has been lost; stimulate the imagination of what might become rather than nostalgia for what once was; and also mobilize on the basis of hope for a different future, rather than only on outrage and resentment over past and present injustices.

To summarize, then, we have explored two general utopian functions. One function is to generate distance from the present; the other is to provoke desire for, imagination of, and movement toward a different future. Again, although we can for expository purposes separate these two functions, it is the combination of estrangement and provocation, critique and vision, negation and affirmation that packs the punch. Although the utopian project is most often associated with traditional literary or philosophical utopias, there are a wide variety of forms—even within the field of political theory—in which utopian aspirations or modes of thinking have found expression.[27] Each form performs these functions differently; each has its own possibilities and limitations as a project of hope. The following analysis begins with the form most commonly associated with the term—namely, the traditional and critical literary and philosophical utopia—then moves to the manifesto and, finally, to the utopian demand. Proceeding as if along a continuum, the discussion ranges from those forms, like the traditional and critical utopias, that place more emphasis on generating critical estrangement, to other forms, like the manifesto and especially the utopian demand, that accentuate the provocation function; and from visions that are more fully elaborated to those that are more partial and fragmentary, mere glimpses of other worlds.

Traditional and Critical Utopias: The Literature of Estrangement

The traditional utopia, the detailed outline of an imagined better society, is the utopian form most closely identified with the term. The category comprises the modern literary utopias—beginning with the text that introduced the term, Thomas More's *Utopia*—and includes as well most of the canonical utopias in political theory, from the ideal constitutions of the ancient period to the blueprints of the social contract theorists and model communities of the utopian socialists. As we will see, a revival of this form of writing in the 1970s also transformed it; the critical utopia, as this more recent version has been called, together with the shift in reading protocols brought to bear on the genre by a new wave of utopian criticism, moved the focus from blueprint to project.

As a sustained exercise in utopian speculation, this form possesses its own distinctive capacities to spark the imagination of other worlds and enable estrangement from existing ones. Its comprehensive scope, for example, offers certain advantages. Not only can its wealth of detail serve to bring alternative worlds to life and thereby lure a reader out to the edges of the present, but by modeling for and demanding of readers that they think about the social systematically, such a vision of a social totality helps train the sociopolitical imagination. Mapping the interrelationships among economic, social, political, and cultural institutions, and—particularly in the literary utopias—exploring the imbrication of structures and subjects at the level of everyday life, utopias in this form are indeed, as Hilary Rose puts it, "global projects" (1988, 134). But their real force lies in their capacity to produce some critical distance from the present. Consider "On Social Contract," in which Rousseau, insisting that "the limits of the possible in moral matters are less narrow than we think," unfolds for the reader a detailed blueprint of direct democracy (1988, 140). Declaring that a will cannot be represented, that "it is either the same will or it is different; there is no middle ground," Rousseau uses his own brand of utopian absolutism to prod the reader into exploring the contours of a nonrepresentative democracy and then looking at the democratic pretensions of existing political systems from a standpoint that might reveal their inconsistencies and disorders (143). Similarly, in *Herland* (1992)—her classic utopian novel published in 1915, and set in a society containing only women—Charlotte Perkins Gilman invites her audience to entertain the idea that, as it were, the limits of the possible in gender matters are less narrow than we think. Through this exercise in denaturalization, Gilman raises questions about the basis of gender, inviting her readers to consider that, to cite just one example, women's bodies—their size, shape, and capacities—are socially produced and thus, if conditions were different, could be reconstituted. Edward Bellamy's *Looking Backward* (2000) presented an opportunity to examine social, political, and economic life in the Boston of 1887 from the perspective of an alternative future. By imagining their elimination, the text throws into sharper relief the impact of the poverty, exploitation, and class antagonisms that trouble the status of the United States as the land of equality and freedom.[28]

This traditional literary and philosophical utopian form has also been the object of extensive critique. Perhaps the form's most important limitation can be characterized as a tendency to close its visions to judgment and change. To bolster their status as solutions and to keep the critical eye trained on the present, the visions are sometimes shielded from critique and, by the same token, denuded of the forces of change that might render them more heterogeneous and dynamic, but also potentially less perfect alternatives: too often the classic utopias suspend history and eliminate antagonisms. It is this particular form's tendency toward closure that is in large part responsible for the identification of utopia with a state of impossible perfection, an equation that has long served, as Lyman Tower Sargent notes, as a key weapon in the arsenal of anti-utopianism (1994, 9).[29] To the extent that the utopian vision is characterized in terms of apparently seamless cohesion and utter stability—with the range of behaviors presumed to be fully accounted for and completely contained within a system in which contingency is mastered and conflict neutralized—they do tend to resemble the boring, static, and lifeless visions of which so many readers, including Bloch, have complained. For examples of such tendencies, we can return to the texts cited above and note as well the limitations of Gilman's stifling harmony of homogeneous sisterhood and Bellamy's regimented mode of cooperation centered on his model of the industrial army. We might also detect a similar penchant for a rigid systematicity behind Rousseau's infamous additions to the social contract, including the censorship and the civil religion, that serve to contain the potential indeterminacy of the will and the radicalism of the democracy he initially defends; he may be reticent to "give the will fetters for the future" (Rousseau 1988, 99) but is often all too ready to institute checks on its present expressions and prescribe controls on its synchronic development.[30]

This tendency toward closure is precisely what the critical utopia upends. The revival of the literary utopia in the 1970s, together with a renaissance of utopian criticism beginning in the 1980s, produced a transformation of both the genre and the interpretative practices brought to bear on its representative texts. In what Moylan labels the critical utopia, one can find a more circumspect and self-reflexive approach to utopian speculation and representation, one that, while allying with the tradition of utopian literature, also stages and attempts to confront some of its limitations (1986, 10).[31] Rather than a depiction of a flawless society cleansed of all potential for disorder, the critical utopia has its own conflicts and failures, including its own resistance to change as once-utopian ideals and practices harden into various forms of orthodoxy, habit, or convention. Critical utopias from this period include Ursula Le Guin's anarchist utopia in the *Dispossessed*, characterized in the subtitle as an "ambiguous utopia," and the "ambiguous heterotopia" of Samuel Delany's *Trouble on Triton*. Rather than shielding the vision to protect it as an attractive solution, these authors call attention to its status as a construction and invite critical judgment of its possibilities and limitations. Hilary Rose concludes from her review of 1970s feminist science fiction that "whereas the old dystopia or utopia was complete, fixed and final in its gloomy inexorability or its boring perfection, the new accepts that struggle is continuous and interesting" (1988, 121). Utopia is conceived more as an ongoing process than a solution, more a project than an outcome.[32] As Peter Stillman puts it, the self-reflexive and critical elements of these utopias serve to open utopian discourse, an opening that "will involve pervasive ambiguity, ambivalence, and uncertainty, recurrent irony and satire, and a willingness to dispute representations of possible futures so as to render closure about the future almost impossible" (2001, 19). By refuting both the equation of utopia with the static and complete blueprint and the reduction of the utopian impulse to the dream of human perfection and the will to social control, the critical utopia broadens the possibilities of utopian expression and expands the understanding of utopian projects.

But there remains a tension at the heart of this, and indeed all utopian forms. The tension is endemic to attempts to straddle the present and future, a predicament of efforts to be in time this way. We encountered a version of this earlier in the relationship between tendency and rupture. On one hand, the traditional and critical utopia seeks to achieve that "unabashed and flagrant otherness" distinctive of the form (Geoghegan 1987, 2). On the other hand, its representation both enables and risks nullifying that effort. Terry Eagleton describes the problem this way: "Since we can speak of what transcends the present only in the language of the present, we risk canceling out our imaginings in the very act of articulating them" (1999, 31). The dilemma stems not only from our limitations in thinking otherwise; the problem is not only strictly epistemological but representational. Thus while the utopian vision need not serve as a blueprint or prove itself achievable to have an impact, it has to be both legible and credible enough to do the work of estrangement and provocation. The tension in this case might be best described as that between otherness and identification, or between a vision of radical difference that can produce estrangement and provocation toward the new and a vision that is recognizable enough to engage and appeal to readers. It is through this dynamic that the relationship between the present and future is negotiated. Jameson calls this part of the dialectic of difference and identity and claims that it accounts for the ambivalences of the utopian text: "for the more surely a given Utopia asserts its radical difference from what currently is, to that very degree it becomes, not merely unrealizable but, what is worse, unimaginable" (2005, xv).

There are at least two ways to respond to this central dilemma of giving form to the utopian project. The first is to accept utopia's inability to think beyond the horizon of the present so as to imagine truly different futures and recognize the value of these failures. Jameson has argued that the critical force of the utopian narrative hinges ultimately on such limitations. The "deepest vocation" of these utopias, he insists, "is to bring home, in local and determinate ways, and with a fullness of concrete detail, our constitutional inability to imagine Utopia itself, and this, not owing to any individual failure of imagination but as the result of the systemic, cultural, and ideological closure of which we are all in one way or another prisoners" (1982, 153). Such lapses of the political imagination can help us recognize our continuing affective attachments to, and ideological complicity with, the status quo. According to this account, what is most disruptive about the encounter with such visions is not the shock of the new but the shock of recognition they can provoke. Jameson's doctrine of failure has the advantage of extending our understanding of utopia's critical function beyond the perspective it can afford on existing institutions and ways of living, to the quality of the political imagination that such institutions and ways of living either enable or disable. These recognitions of failure present the reader with an opportunity to reflect on both the incapacity for and the resistance to utopian imaginings.

If the traditional model of utopia as blueprint has its own tendencies to constrain and domesticate the utopian impulse, a second response to this basic quandary of the utopian form is to recognize the potential benefits of more-partial forms. To develop this point, let us return again to Bloch's distinction between abstract and concrete utopias. Earlier we noted that the distinction hinges on the relationship between present and future: concrete utopias are grounded in present tendencies while also striving to leap beyond them, whereas abstract utopias remain unconnected to the forces and trends in the present—Bloch's "Real-Possible"—that might render them credible rather than merely fictitious. But the abstractness of a utopia is not only a consequence of an inattention to concrete trends. Abstract utopias are further characterized by a level of detail and comprehensiveness that does not allow adequate room for the unexpected development of other as yet incomprehensible and unimaginable possibilities. The very thoroughness and specificity of a vision belies their abstract character; they claim, to borrow Carl Freedman's formulation, "to know too much too soon" (2001, 95).[33] If we agree that the complete outline is less important than "the challenge to the imagination to become immersed in the same open exploration" (Thompson 1976, 97), then when it comes to utopian visions, it may be that less is more. Rather than proposing blueprints, utopias can be powerful as disruptive traces (Wegner 2002, 21), partial visions (Bammer 1991), fractional prefigurations (Freedman 2001, 83), flashes of otherness that can provoke the reader's own reflection and desire. Utopian fragments might require more of us; to borrow José Muñoz's description of what it might take to access queerness as a utopian horizon, "we may indeed need to squint, to strain our vision and force it to see otherwise, beyond the limited vista of the here and now" (2007, 454). This insight—that when it comes to utopian visions, less might be more—will figure in the analyses of the final two utopian forms: the manifesto and the demand.

Utopian Provocations: The Manifesto

With the literary utopia, which—straddling the border between literature and political theory—occupies a minor place in annals of political theory, and the philosophical prescription for the good political order, which enjoys a more central place in the canon, the manifesto is perhaps the third most recognizable utopian form of writing in political theory. Although it shares with the kinds of texts discussed earlier a commitment to utopian speculation, it is a more minimal utopian form and thus functions differently, with its own peculiar tendencies to at once enable and constrain utopian effects.

Earlier we identified two primary utopian functions: to generate estrangement from the present and to provoke the desire for, imagination of, and movement toward a different future. Both the traditional literary and theoretical utopias and the manifesto are capable of producing critical distance, but what the former tend to do more indirectly, by providing a vantage point in a different world from which the reader can critically assess the existing one, the latter does directly, typically presenting to the reader an explicit, if brief and compressed, critique of the present configuration of social relations. But the manifesto is more fundamentally a literature of provocation, a species of utopian writing that challenges its readers to think the future and—more overtly and insistently than the traditional and critical utopias—bring it into being. If all utopian writing is eager to have an effect on the world, the manifesto goes a step further. As an exemplary literature of provocation, the manifesto seeks to bridge the divide between writing and acting. "It is a genre," Martin Puchner writes, "that is impatient with itself," for "no matter how impassioned and effective, the manifesto will always remain a split second removed from the actual revolution itself" (2006, 43, 22). As a textual practice that struggles to be a political act (see Althusser 1999, 23), its evaluation as a utopian form must take into account the context in which it is circulated and the specific ways it is received, including the kinds of actions committed in its name. "No manifesto," Janet Lyon maintains, "can be understood outside the specific historical conditions of its production and reception" (1991a, 51).

Many of the manifesto's common stylistic conventions and rhetorical practices work to enhance the provocativeness of its claims. The manifesto characteristically speaks from and within the affective register of what Bloch calls militant optimism (1995, 1: 199). Rather than being limited to an appeal to reason or interest, the manifesto takes aim at the affects and the imagination; more than a set of claims and positions, it is "an exhortation to a whole way of thinking and being" (Caws 2001, xxvii). It is in this sense also a famously self-assured piece of writing, exemplifying the confidence it wants to instill and signifying the power it seeks to organize. Casting hopes for the future as immediate possibilities, *The Communist Manifesto* figured revolution "not as a necessity whose time has come but as *imminence*" (Blanchot 1986, 19). Not surprisingly, the exclamation point is one of its preferred forms of punctuation, one that serves, to borrow Jennifer Brody's characterization, as an amplifier that "pumps up the (visceral) volume" (2008, 150); after urging readers to "get ready" and "get set," the exclamation point stands in for the pistol shot. Although it thereby "mimics the act," the exclamation point is also, to return to Puchner's argument noted above, another expression of the form's impatience with itself: it "both emphasizes the urgency to act and postpones the act itself," serving as "one more seam between manifesto and revolution, one more mediation, more of an act than a text, perhaps, but not act enough" (Puchner 2006, 43). By this reading, the proliferation of exclamation points in some manifestoes may be a symptom of this fundamental insufficiency, this inability to leap out of the page and into the world. Even beyond their punctuation preferences, manifestoes are typically demanding both in tone and in content, often delivering their assertions as ultimatums: this is what we want, the texts seem to declare, and nothing less. The declarative sentence is the mainstay of the manifesto; eschewing supporting references and prudent caveats, the manifesto, as Mary Ann Caws observes, "is by nature a loud genre" (2001, xx). Like the literary utopia in this sense, the manifesto aims to seduce its reader, but in the case of the manifesto, this encouragement is less an invitation than a dare. Finally, the extravagant gesture and immoderate demand are staples of the manifesto's interventions into the present in the name of a better future. Indeed, the manifesto "makes an art of excess" (xx), setting itself against the conventions of appropriate discussion and reasonable demands on which the reproduction of the status quo depends. Thus, "to what the dominant order relies on as 'the real,' 'the natural,' 'the thinkable,' the manifesto counters with its own versions of 'the possible,' 'the imaginable,' 'the necessary'" (Lyon 1991a, 16).

But the manifesto typically sets out to do more than provoke; it also intends to organize. Whereas the traditional utopia focuses on the vision of a better world, the manifesto concentrates on the agents who could bring an alternative into being.[34] Thus the manifesto seeks to fashion its readers into a collective subject; indeed, "this is," as Lyon notes, "precisely the function of the manifesto's characteristic pronoun 'we'" (1991b, 104). *The Communist Manifesto* is exemplary in this respect, for just as Thomas More founded the genre of the literary utopia, Marx and Engels can be said to have inaugurated the genre of the manifesto; it is not that there are no precursors in each case, but rather that these works became the models on which a generic form was based.[35] Marx and Engels's *Manifesto* provides both an explicit critique of traditional utopias, specifically those of the utopian socialists, and an alternative mode of utopian expression. In contrast both to the "castles in the air" of the grand planners and social engineers who were, by Marx and Engels's estimation, unable to account for the historical agents who could make them possible, and to the "disciples" of these inventors who, when proletarian activism does materialize on the historical stage, oppose it as inconsistent with the original vision (1992, 36–37), Marx and Engels sought to generate and organize such a political subject and inspire it to revolutionary action. Yet to prescribe in detail the world that the proletariat was to make, the vision that was to govern its struggles, would have been in effect to disavow the very agency the authors hoped to incite. To recall our earlier discussions of Bloch's categorical distinction between abstract and concrete utopias, it should be noted that Bloch uses Marx's refusal to offer a vision of communism as one example of how to render utopias more concrete. In contrast to abstract utopias, the contents of which are specified in meticulous detail, Marx "teaches the work of the next step and determines little in advance about the 'realm of freedom' " (Bloch 1995, 2: 581). The lack of a blueprint should be understood—as it was in Marx's work—as "a *keeping open*" (2: 622). The novum represents that element or quality that not only belies our efforts at prediction but also resists our desires for full description. In their *Manifesto*, Marx and Engels sought to call the proletariat as a political agent into existence, to stimulate the organization of its power and to arm it with a sense of its own strength rather than to burden it with a ready-made model.

The 1960s and 1970s produced a renaissance not only of the literary utopia but also of the manifesto, which reemerged as another outlet for and vehicle of the utopian energies of the period.[36] These manifestoes reflected the heady mix of empowerment and joy that accompanied the creation of new political subjects and were designed to expand and extend the mobilization of political desire of which they were a product. For example, US feminists appropriated the manifesto from other quarters of the Left, where it had been cultivated as a traditional masculine form characterized by an aggressive bravura, a way to wage war by other means (see Pearce 1999; Lyon 1991b, 106). The genre was particularly useful to emerging radical and Marxist feminist groups that were both part of and often at odds with the broader Left. Thus, on the one hand, as Lyon notes, "to write a manifesto is to announce one's participation, however discursive, in a history of struggle against oppressive forces" (1991a, 10). On the other hand, as a form characterized by righteous anger and polemical claims, it also served as one of the vehicles through which feminists claimed separate organizations and agendas. In this sense, both the political pedigree of the form and the belligerence of its style were no doubt attractive to feminist groups eager to announce themselves as at once antagonistic subjects within the broader Left and autonomous political forces to be reckoned with.

Feminist manifestoes also aim to constitute feminist subjects. Some manifestoes announce an agent of change already in existence, whereas others seek to call such a collectivity into being. Examples of each can be found in the many organizational manifestoes drafted in the late 1960s and early 1970s to announce the formation and promulgate the programs of newly formed feminist groups. One from 1969, "The Feminists: A Political Organization to Annihilate Sex Roles," lays out the history, analysis, organizational structure, and membership requirements of a newly formed radical feminist group in New York (Feminists 1973). A second approach can be found in "The BITCH Manifesto," published in 1970. "BITCH," it begins, "is an organization which does not yet exist." Instead it is imagined as a future coming together of a new kind of woman: "The name," the author insists, "is not an acronym" (Joreen 1973, 50). A similar strategy can be found in The SCUM Manifesto, in which Valerie Solanas implores "civic-minded, responsible, thrill-seeking females," to "overthrow the government, eliminate the money system, institute complete automation and destroy the male sex" (1991, 3). Each of these actors, whether "bitches" or "civic-minded, responsible, thrill-seeking females," are called into being and urged into imagined models of political collectivity—BITCH and SCUM, respectively. In contrast to those manifestoes that declare the formation of a specific group, together with a complete analysis and programmatic vision, these texts—by sparking a vision of what their audiences both were in some sense already and, more importantly, might want to become in the future—attempt to produce that which they seem to presume (see also Lyon 1991a, 28; 1999b, 104). To borrow from Laura Winkiel's description of this performative dimension of The SCUM Manifesto, as a way to convert the reader, manifestoes preach to the converted (1999, 63).

At its best, a manifesto is a provocation of anger and power, one that takes aim at both reason and affect and seeks to inspire at once analysis and action. Given its emphatically practical agenda, however, the manifesto is also the form of utopian writing that inspires the most fear of rabble-rousing, a fear that the feminist authors cited above appear eager to call out. Even if one rejects any facile dismissal of a manifesto's popular reach and passionate politics, one can still appreciate the potential limitations of the genre. At their worst, manifestoes have been known to rely on simplistic, even conspiratorial, analyses and to favor the dramatic, no matter if imprudent, political tactic. A more important limitation from the perspective of this analysis stems from the legacy of revolutionary vanguardism that haunts the form. This can be seen in the manifesto's often well-defined and broadly conceived recipes not for alternatives but for revolutionary events. Although the manifesto undercuts the authority of authors as "grand inventors" who would offer detailed blueprints, the programmatic nature of the manifesto's revolutionary agenda can nonetheless risk closing rather than opening multiple and unexpected paths to the future. The form's traditional association with the imaginary of the revolutionary event also shows up in the tendency to name its political subjects in advance. That is, the manifesto's "we"—what Lyon refers to as "the manifesto's daunting pronoun" —is an effort to control its emergence and delimit its membership (1991a, 175). The future may not be known, but its agent—the political subject that the manifesto seeks to address and constitute—is often prefigured. To recall an earlier criticism levied against the traditional literary and philosophical utopia, the manifesto has traditionally claimed in this regard "to know too much too soon."[37]

From the Manifesto to the Utopian Demand

The utopian demand could be grasped initially as an offshoot or even subset of the manifesto, one that takes as its focus the manifesto's "practice of enumerating demands" (Lyon 1991b, 102).[38] The discussion that follows will note the demand's resemblances to the species of utopianism that we have already considered, while also trying to underscore the form's specificity. As we move from the traditional utopia to the critical utopia, and then from the manifesto to the utopian demand, the emphasis shifts from estrangement to provocation, and the focus moves from the detailed vision of other worlds to increasingly fragmentary possibilities. One could conclude that the relative incompleteness of the demand as a form is accompanied by a weakening of its utopian effectivity. Certainly the traditional and critical utopias are better equipped than the utopian demand to produce a strong estrangement effect and, in so doing, to generate a rich critical perspective on the present. The constricted range of the utopian demand renders it less able to mount a systematic critique. However, as I argued in the discussions of the other forms—each of which has its own tendencies to at once release but also to constrain and domesticate the utopian impulse—less can sometimes be more. It is precisely the demand's limited scope relative to the other forms that, I want to claim, is the source of some of its advantages.

Situating the utopian demand in relation to other utopian forms reveals continuities that may not otherwise be readily apparent. As an act rather than a text this models' relationship to the more familiar literary genre may be hard to discern; but as we have seen, utopian forms have long been deployed to generate a practical effect, to spur political critique and inspire collective action. The gap between act and text that the manifesto seeks to reduce even further is still more thoroughly breached by the utopian demand. Just as the manifesto "calls for a more complex understanding of the text as an event and of the textuality of the event" (Somigli 2003, 27), the demand should be conceived as both act and text, both an analytic perspective and a political provocation. As we move from the manifesto to the demand, we move from a form of writing intended to inspire a mobilization of political practice to a mode of political engagement in relation to which textual analyses are also generated. The demand, like the manifesto, "cannot be cut off from the public discourse that arises around and as a result of its issuing" (26).

There is, however, a fundamental tension between the terms "utopia" and "demand" that calls for attention. The former points toward the broader social horizon of a future that is always beyond our grasp; the latter directs our attention to the present, to the specific desires that can be named and the definite interests that can be advanced. In this way the paradoxical relationship between tendency and rupture, identification and otherness, and affirming and overcoming that is produced by the utopian form's efforts to negotiate the relationship between present and future also haunts the utopian demand. With the demand, the dynamic is manifest in the conflict between the speculative ideals of utopias and the pragmatism of demands. It is important to acknowledge the ways in which this fusing of utopianism and demanding could have a dampening effect on each of the practices. Harnessing the speculative imagination to a particular and limited political project risks both stifling the utopian impulse and undermining the assertion of practical political claims making. While recognizing the potential limitations of the utopian demand as a form, I want to consider the ways in which each of the practices might also serve to animate and enhance the other. To function optimally, a utopian demand must negotiate the relationship between the terms in a way that preserves as much as possible the integrity of each of these impulses, while holding them together in a constructive tension. At its best, a utopian demand is not just a hobbling together of tendency and rupture in the form of a perfectly transparent and legible demand and an expression of pure utopian otherness. Instead, the terms can be altered by their relationship.

To function adequately as a specifically utopian form, such a demand should point toward the possibility of a break, however partial, with the present. It must be capable of cognitively reorienting us far enough out of the present organization of social relations that some kind of critical distance is achieved and the political imagination of a different future is called to work. This brings us to the heart of the differences between utopian and nonutopian demands. While remaining grounded in concrete possibilities, the demand has to be enough of a game changer to be able to provide an expansive perspective. Whereas the demand's propensity to raise eyebrows—the incredulity with which it is sometimes received—might be a liability from the standpoint of a more traditional political calculus, it is fundamental to the utopian form's capacity to animate the possibility of living differently. Here it is important to note that the demands that merit the label "utopian" are necessarily larger in scope than their formulation as policy proposals would initially indicate. None of its supporters presumed that wages for housework would signal the end of either capitalism or patriarchy. But they did hope the reform would bring about a gendered system characterized by a substantially different division of labor and economy of power, one that might give women further resources for their struggles, make possible a different range of choices, and provide discursive tools for new ways of thinking and imagining. Indeed, its proponents saw a society that paid wages for housework as one in which women would have the power to refuse the waged housework that they had fought to win. Similarly, a society in which everyone is granted a basic income would not bring about the end of the capitalist wage relation, but it would entail a significant shift in the experience of work and its place in the lives of individuals. This is a demand that—as in Ben Trott's description of a "directional demand"—instead of being fully recuperated within the economy of the same, "looks for a way out." As demands rather than comprehensive visions, they suggest a direction rather than name a destination (Trott 2007, 15). In this case, by challenging productivist values, by contesting the notion that waged work is the proper source of and title to the means of consumption, the demand for basic income points in the direction of the possibility of a life no longer subordinate to work, thus opening new theoretical vistas and terrains of struggle. The point is that these utopian demands can serve to generate political effects that exceed the specific reform.

So to function effectively as a utopia, the demand must constitute a radical and potentially far-reaching change, generate critical distance, and stimulate the political imagination. To function optimally as a demand, a utopian demand should be recognizable as a possibility grounded in actually existing tendencies. This is not to say that it should be "realistic"—at least in the sense that the term is deployed in the typical anti-utopian lament about such demands. Rather, the point is that it should be concrete rather than abstract. As a demand, the utopian vision to which it is linked should be recognizable as a credible politics grounded in a plausible analysis of current trends, as opposed to a rant, an exercise in political escapism, or an expression of merely wishful thinking. A utopian demand should be capable of producing an estrangement effect and substantial change, while also registering as a credible call with immediate appeal; it must be both strange and familiar, grounded in the present and gesturing toward the future, evoking simultaneously that "nowness and newness" that has been ascribed to the manifesto (Caws 2001).

Perhaps the relationship between utopia and demand is at its most paradoxical when approached not in terms of the relation between tendency and rupture—or, in Bloch's version, between the "Real-Possible" and the novum—but in relation to the Nietzschean relation between affirming and overcoming. In some sense, the temporality of the various forms narrows as we move from the traditional utopia to the manifesto and then to the demand. Despite the generative potential of the traditional utopia's more detailed vision of a revolutionary alternative, as the map of a distant future, it can also, to borrow Baudrillard's observation, have "the effect of stifling the current situation, of exorcizing immediate subversion, of diluting (in the technical sense of the term) explosive reactions in a long term solution" (1975, 162). If the time of the manifesto is always "now" (Lyon 1991a, 206), the time of the demand is "right now."

With utopian demands, the immediate goal is not deferred as it is in the more comprehensive utopias. To make a demand is to affirm the present desires of existing subjects: this is what we want now. At the same time, the utopian demand also points in the direction of a different future and the possibility of desires and subjects yet to come. The paradox of the utopian demand is that it is at once a goal and a bridge; it seeks an end that is open-ended, one that could have a transformative effect greater than a minor policy reform. Thus, the small measures of freedom from work that the demands for basic income and shorter hours might enable could also make possible the material and imaginative resources to live differently.

As we move from the manifesto to the demand, we also continue in the direction of more fragmentary forms, both in terms of the vision offered and the agents it seeks to provoke. Like the critical utopia, the demand aims to open us cognitively and affectively to the future rather than to attach us to a ready-made vision. But whereas the manifesto remains "a document of an ideology" (Caws 2001, xix), the demand's commitments are far less extensive and systematic. The demands for basic income and shorter hours offer neither full-blown critiques of the work society or maps of a postwork alternative; they prescribe neither a vision of a revolutionary alternative nor a call for revolution, serving rather to enlist participants in the practice of inventing broader visions and methods of change.

Like the manifesto, the focus of the demand is less on the work of building a preconceived alternative than on provoking the agents who might make a different future. Indeed, the demand takes the manifesto's concentration on activating agents—rather than on providing what Marx and Engels criticized as "fantastic pictures of future society" (1992, 36)—even further. The utopian demand does not so much express the interests or desires of an already existing subject as it serves as one of the many mechanisms of its formation. It is less the argument or rhetoric of the demand than the act of demanding that constitutes a political sub-ject. The potential effects of the collective practice of demanding were something that the proponents of wages for housework understood well. A demand emerges from that tradition as simultaneously expressive and performative. Selma James's mode of presentation of the demand for wages for housework is suggestive in this respect. As she explains it, the benefits of the movement for wages depends on the practices of organizing, demanding, and winning, each of which is measured by degrees: it is not when, but only *"to the degree that"* women organize a struggle for wages, *"to the degree that"* they demand a wage, *"to the degree that"* they win a wage, that various benefits will accrue (1976, 27–28). What is important in these formulas is less the goal that one may win or lose than the process of demanding, organizing, winning; what is crucial here is the degree to which the subjects themselves are transformed.[39] In this way, the utopian demand can be seen as something more than a demand for a specific goal or set of goals. Rather, according to this account, it is a process of constituting a new subject with the desires for and the power to make further demands. Perhaps this is what James meant when she referred to the demand for wages for housework as "the perspective of winning" (27): to struggle for wages—or, to expand the insight, for basic income or shorter hours—to want them and to assert that they are one's due, is to participate in the practice of collective hope and engage thereby in a constituting act.

If the legacy of revolutionary vanguardism does indeed haunt the manifesto in its tendency to name the "we," as in Marx and Engels's proletariat or the housewives of the wages for housework movement, the demand is not something that can presume to evoke a revolutionary subject or name it in advance of its formation. Just as Marx and Engels once insisted, contra the utopian socialists, that communism was not something to prescribe but something to invent, something that would emerge in the process of political struggle, the demand could be said to allow its advocates to emerge in the collective practice of demanding. If prescriptions of alternatives close down possibilities, so too does the naming of agents. The demand is neither the "document of an ideology" nor the platform of a party; it is difficult to predict who might coalesce around the demand, what kind of political subject might emerge in relation to its advocacy. Who might be called to the project remains an open question.

Just as demands are more directional—to recall Trott's term—than prefigurative of a postwork society, the antiwork political subject that might coalesce around the demand or set of demands is less likely to be a vanguard than a coalition. In this sense, these demands might best be characterized not only as directional, but also as "articulatable"—that is, capable of being linked together. Although utopian demands do not present a systematic program or vision—they are not a means to some preconfigured end—broader political visions can be enabled as different constituencies find points of common interest. As demands manage to intersect and groups link together, broader social visions can emerge, not as a prerequisite of these articulations but as their product. To draw on Ernesto Laclau's description, demands might be "put together to create some kind of more feasible social imaginary," not a perfect state of emancipation and ultimate fulfillment, but more-global visions constructed around particularized items (Zournazi 2003, 123–24). Demands are more dispersed than ideologies or platforms, a partiality that does not lend itself to the traditional model of a vanguard or even a party. So the political result is not imagined as a series of local Bellamy Clubs, dedicated as they were to disseminating that author's broader vision, but as an assemblage of political desires and imaginaries out of which alternatives might be constructed.

CONCLUSION

The cultivation of utopian hope, as both Bloch and Nietzsche would have it, is an ambitious project: it is no easy thing to be in time this way, straddling past, present, and future, nurturing cognitive and affective investments in both the lived present as it has emerged from the past and its possible futures. Certainly each of the utopian forms we have considered has its own particular limitations. Indeed, the fundamental paradox of this most paradoxical of practices may be that by instantiating it in a form, utopian hope is at once brought to life and diminished. Perhaps the most that we can expect is that hopefulness will still haunt these forms as an enticement or a beckoning to want and to think otherwise.

This chapter began with a rehearsal of the argument against the utopianism of the demands for basic income and shorter hours. Having arrived at the end of the discussion, we may want to at least entertain a different conclusion: perhaps in light of utopia's functions and in comparison to other utopian forms—not to mention by the standard of the hopeful subject gleaned from Bloch and Nietzsche—the problem with these utopian demands is not that they are too utopian but that they are not utopian enough, that their futures are not as richly imagined and their critiques not as fully developed as those of the other utopian forms. Although this may be the case, as I have also tried to suggest, the incompleteness of the utopian demand does not necessarily diminish its force; more-fragmentary forms might better preserve utopia as process and project rather than end or goal, and might open utopia's critiques and visions to multiple insights and directions.

By allowing rather than evading the charge of utopianism that may be levied against such demands, we can begin to recognize their potential as tools of utopian thinking and practice. Conceiving such demands as modes of utopian expression that function to elicit utopian praxis—that is, as tools that can promote distancing from and critical thinking about the present and imaginative speculation about and movement toward a possible future—allows us to reconsider the nature and function of political demands by highlighting their performative effects: how they serve to produce the modes of critical consciousness that they seem merely to presuppose, to elicit the political desires that they appear simply to reflect, and to mobilize and organize the collective agency of which they might seem to be only an artifact. That is, perhaps under the rubric of this more expansive conception of utopianism, we can better appreciate the potential efficacy of such demands. Rather than hopelessly naive or merely impractical, these demands—including the ones for shorter hours or basic income—are potentially effective mechanisms by which to advance critical thinking, inspire political imagination, and incite collective action. Perhaps the greater danger is not that we might want too much, but that we do not want enough. By this reckoning, feminists should consider becoming not less but more demanding.

> The question of the right to a full life has to be divorced
> completely from the question of work.
>
> JAMES BOGGS, *THE AMERICAN REVOLUTION*

I want to end with two brief clarifications of my larger argument, followed by one supplement to it. The latter consists of a way to conceive the demands for basic income and shorter hours as elements of a broader political project. But before we get there, two aspects of the analysis call for further explication: first, the prescription of a politics (a postwork politics) to counter the power of an ethic (the work ethic); and second, the defense of limited demands as tools for radical change. The one requires some attention to the distinction between politics and ethics that the analysis has only presumed so far; the other concerns the specific understanding of the relationship between reform and revolution that informs the argument.

POLITICS AND CHANGE

I will begin here: why counter the power of the work ethic with a postwork politics and not with a postwork ethic? One could, after all, imagine the contours of a postwork ethic as something distinct from a postwork morality—a matter, to cite Virno's formulation, of "common practices, usages and customs, not the dimension of the must-be" (2004, 49). Deleuze marks the distinction this way: ethics are immanent to different modes of existence, whereas morals are imposed from above (1988, 23). But despite the ways that the terrain of ethics can be helpfully distinguished from that of traditional morality, I am still more interested in the possibilities of a politics than in the construction of a counterethic. Certainly the relationship between ethics and politics is a close one, with both modes of thinking and acting focusing on the question of how we might live together, both operating in private and public spheres and suffusing at once structures and subjectivities. Indeed, postwork politics and postwork ethics are mutually constitutive, each part of what produces and sustains the other. Nonetheless, because ethics remains more closely tethered than politics to the register of individual belief and choice, my argument prioritizes politics, understood in terms of collective action and fields of institutional change, over ethics, with its focus on practices of the self and encounters with the other. My preference for political rather than ethical remedies might then be understood as a polemical defense of a certain kind of structuralist impulse, a way to keep our focus trained on collective rather than individual action and on the task of changing the institutions and discourses that frame individual lives and relations.

Whereas the distinction between politics and ethics remains meaningful to me for the purposes of this project, the distinction between reform and revolution—which my affirmation of utopian visions together with my defense of restricted demands, would seem to confound —is more problematic. Of course the reform-revolution division has a long, storied history within Marxism, and the status of wage demands has often served as one of its traditional staging grounds. The choice of either reform or revolution continues to haunt some of the conflicts between anticapitalist pragmatists and radicals today, even if the terms of such debates are not posed as boldly as they were in the period of the Second International. From one still-familiar perspective, the idea of revolution is at best a distraction and at worst a diversion from the struggle for change; from the other, the commitment to reform represents a capitulation to the existing terms of that struggle. Whereas one supposedly betrays the present to a far-off future, the other is accused of sacrificing the future to the exigencies of a narrowly conceived present.

The utopian demand is meant to cut through such formulas. It is not that the utopian demand is a reformist alternative to the manifesto's revolutionary program, but that the demand refuses this traditional dichotomy. The radical potential of such relatively modest demands lies in two qualities that we reviewed in the previous chapter: their directionality and performativity. Selma James evokes the first of these in terms of the difference between preparing to lose the fight against capital, but with the hope of salvaging some concessions from the wreck of that defeat, and striving to succeed, while at the same time recognizing that "in struggling to *win*, plenty can be gained along the way (Dalla Costa and James 1973, 1). The demands that emerge out of the latter strategy are likely to be utopian demands, demands that, at their best, simultaneously speak to and direct us beyond the confines of the present. Antonio Negri alludes to the second quality in his claim about the potential generativity of reforms. As he explains it, the distinction between utopian and reformist temporalities breaks down under the conditions of biopolitical production: "Nowadays, each and every reform is radically transformative because we live on an ontological terrain, because our lives are pitched immediately on an ontological level" (Casarino and Negri 2008, 109). As reformist projects with revolutionary aspirations, utopian demands can point in the direction of broader horizons of change, open up new avenues for critical thought and social imagination, and assist in the construction of political subjects who may be better able to think and to want something different. Although the demands for basic income and shorter hours may be proposals for concrete reform rather than systematic transformation, conceiving such demands in relation to their aspirational trajectories and ontological effects confounds facile distinctions between reformist and revolutionary change.

PUBLICIZING AND POLITICIZING SOCIAL REPRODUCTION

As I noted earlier, one way to understand the wages for housework movement and analysis is as part of a larger effort both to map and to problematize the vexed relationship between social reproduction and capital accumulation. In the case of wages for housework, social reproduction was identified with the unwaged household labor necessary to reproduce waged work. One problem with this formulation was that, because housework was so closely identified with the institution of the family and associated with a limited range of domestic tasks, the site of the conflict was too narrowly conceived and the remedies that could and have been offered for the problem the advocates publicized and politicized—including work-life balance initiatives and commodified domestic services—have served more to sustain the existing system than to point us in the direction of something new. An alternative formulation would need to broaden the concept of social reproduction to capture more accurately and pose more effectively the terms of the conflict between processes of valorization and the reproduction of the subjects and socialities upon which they depend.

To locate another way to publicize and politicize this contradiction and hail its potential antagonists, let me revisit the demand for basic income and two different explanations of its legitimacy. One possible rationale for basic income presents it as a payment for our participation in the production of value above and beyond what wages can measure and reward. Such an accounting closely follows a classic Marxist strategy: we can organize together as producers to demand our rewards as such. The advantage of this formulation is its legibility, the familiar terms on which it claims benefits for members of a society; one disadvantage, at least from the perspective of this project, is that it continues to build on productivist mandates, insisting that we are entitled to income on the basis of our contributions to production. So I want to consider an alternative: what if basic income were to be seen as income not for the common production of value, but for the common reproduction of life? There are two shifts here that draw on different sources. First, the switch from production to reproduction as the relevant field of contribution draws upon a Marxist feminist analytic that prioritizes reproduction as the point of entry into the terrain of social production. Second, the move from value to life as its primary product builds on an antiproductivist logic of intervention—in this case, one that claims that it is more than unwaged domestic work that makes capital accumulation possible, that this accumulation draws on much more for its conditions of possibility and, moreover, has far broader effects. Whereas the first rationale builds on capital's own logic, posing basic income as a reward for our productivity, the second represents more of a break with this familiar warrant, demanding not income for the production that is necessary to sustain social worlds, but income to sustain the social worlds necessary for, among other things, production. The virtue of the latter approach is that it invokes a broader notion of social reproduction than the wages for housework analysis typically offered. Taking a cue from this second rationale, I want to consider "life" as a possible counterpoint to work. More specifically, I want to explore the political project of "life against work" as a general rubric within which to frame the kinds of antiwork critiques and postwork imaginaries represented here by the demands for basic income and shorter hours. As a way to publicize and politicize the relationship between social reproduction and capital accumulation, life against work offers what is certainly an expansive, but also a potentially potent, formulation of the terrain of conflict.

But can the category of life and the juxtaposition of life against work present a strong enough antagonism to the existing organization of social production and reproduction? Before we continue, I want to take note of two potential limitations of the formulation. The first offers a caution about the potential for life against work to be recuperated into the logic of commodity culture. If, for example, this life—despite my claims about its more expansive connotations—is something whose contents we would be satisfied merely to purchase in the time left to us after work, and then enjoy in the privacy of our homes, then its use would be limited indeed. A second possible drawback has to do with the way that life outside of work already figures in what Peter Fleming calls the "just be yourself" managerial discourses that, in purporting to draw upon and cash in on more of the "authentic" worker's self, seek "to put some life back into work by appropriating life itself" (2009, 40). In light of such corporate strategies, the danger is that organizing around the notion of life could be too easily coopted by management initiatives and subordinated to their purposes, in which case life would function less against work than as a further basis for its hegemony.[1]

GETTING A LIFE

Certainly these remain risks for a project that poses the antagonism along lines that are at once very broad and also difficult to discern. But as a way to explore further the possibilities of life against work, I want to turn here to a more specific articulation of the rubric that might cast its advantages and disadvantages in a different light. The political project of life against work can also be posed in familiar colloquial terms—in this case, as the mandate to "get a life."[2] As the authors of "The Post-Work Manifesto" declare, "it is time to get a life" (Aronowitz et al. 1998, 40), and in the brief discussion that follows, I want to speculate about how this popular directive might serve to frame a broad and expansive political project.

Let me explain by touching briefly on the three terms of the injunction in reverse order, beginning with the concept of life. The first point to emphasize is that the notion of life referenced in the slogan is not innocent, and it is thus very different from the one deployed in anti-abortion discourse. I mean this in two senses. First, rather than a pure biological life, this life that we would get is nonetheless the object and target of biopower; indeed, the project of life against work is a way to establish the terms of a biopolitical contest, not to recover some lost or imperiled innocence. Second, the life that we might set against work does not pose a simple opposition from a position of exteriority: life is part of work, and work is part of life. Life as an alternative to work does not pretend to be something more authentic and true, which we can find somewhere outside of work. Instead, it must be continually invented in the struggle to mark distinctions between fields of experience that nonetheless remain intertwined.

Neither is it adequately captured by the concept of life more typical of vitalist philosophies, a point that a consideration of the article "a" can illustrate: it is not *the* life that we are encouraged to get, not life as essential common denominator, but *a* life. It is not for this reason bare life that is invoked, but rather, as James Boggs describes it in the epigraph, "a full life" (1963, 47); it is a life filled with qualities that we are urged toward. This is not to say that it is an individual life. Rather, to draw on Deleuze's description, it is a life of singularities rather than individualities (1997, 4), a life that is common to and shared with others without being the same as theirs.[3] Finally, the injunction is not to get *this* life or *that* life; there is an assumption, by my reading of the phrase, that there will be different lives to get. To borrow another formulation from Deleuze, the indefinite article serves here as "the index of a multiplicity" (5); to say that we should get a life is not to say what its contents might be.

As for the third part of the popular challenge, the activity of "getting" introduces a temporality to the mandate, one that points toward a different future. It is not a call to embrace the life we have, the life that has been made for us—the life of a consumer or a worker, to recall the earlier cautions about what might suffice as a life—but the one that we might want. Deleuze evokes something that may be comparable to this through the distinction between the virtual and the actual: "A life," he explains, "contains only virtuals"; this virtual, however, "is not something that lacks reality, but something that enters into a process of actualization by following the plane that gives it its own reality" (1997, 5). To adapt the insight to my somewhat different purpose here, a life is what each of us needs to get; one cannot get a life if its terms are only dictated from the outside. That said, getting a life is also a necessarily collective endeavor;

one cannot get something as big as a life on one's own. And, moreover, though it is a life that would be ours, as a life rather than a commodity, as a web of relations and qualities of experience rather than a possession, it is not something we can be said precisely to own or even to hold. This kind of getting implies a fundamentally different mode of appropriation. The concept of life is not just expansive in this respect, it is also excessive. For Weber, it is the wealth of possibilities that the work ethic diminishes; for Nietzsche, it is what ascetic ideals disavow, but also what can potentially disrupt ascetic modes of containment. A life, by this measure, always exceeds what we have, and its getting is thus necessarily an incomplete process. In short, rather than burdening life with a fixed content—that is, with too many assumptions about what might count as a life beyond work—the possibility of the provocation to get a life lies in its capacity to pose a political project that it does not stipulate and to open a postwork speculative horizon that it cannot fix in advance. My claim is that these commitments to difference, futurity, and excess might render the political project of getting a life less amenable to those forces that would reduce, contain, or appropriate it.

Perhaps more important from the point of view of my argument, the collective effort to get a life can serve as a way both to contest the existing terms of the work society and to struggle to build something new. Seen in this light, the political project of getting a life is both deconstructive and reconstructive, deploying at once negation and affirmation, simultaneously critical and utopian, generating estrangement from the present and provoking a different future. Or, to put it in terms of the concepts around which the book was most broadly organized, it is a project that refuses the existing world of work that is given to us and also demands alternatives.

Notes

....

Introduction

1. Indeed, as Michael Denning notes, it is by now "a commonplace to note our reluctance to represent work in our popular stories. A Martian who hijacked the stock of the average video store would reasonably conclude that humans spent far more of their time engaged in sex than in work" (2004, 91–92).

2. Whereas work was once a phenomenon worthy of scrutiny, "contemporary political theory," Russell Muirhead observes, "has had more to say about pluralism, toleration, virtue, equality of opportunity, and rights than it has about the character of work" (2004, 14).

3. In a review of sociological work on the intersection of work and identity, Robin Leidner concludes that despite the widespread interest in identity across the social sciences and the humanities, "relatively few contemporary theorists have put work at the center of their analyses of identity in late or post modernity" (2006, 424).

4. Workers could thus be represented by the figure of the servant, as in one famous passage from *The Second Treatise on Civil Government*, in which Locke insists that the labor that entitles an individual to private property includes "the turfs my servant has cut" (1986, 20).

5. Cultural representations of the world of work are not only relatively rare but are also often slow to change. Daniel Rodgers gives the example of the continuing use of a cartoon image of a blacksmith to represent workers in the context of an industrial economy in which very few such figures could be found (1978, 242). In the 1960s, James Boggs made a similar point about the problem of clinging to outdated economic imaginaries when he argued that to tell the postindustrial unemployed "that they must work to earn their living is like telling a man in the big city that he should hunt big game for the meat on his table" (1963, 52).

6. Taken together, the two strategies risk replicating the traditional choice between either valuing work or valuing family, in relation to which various "work-family balance" programs remain the most-cited—but, it seems to me, singularly in-

adequate—solution to the conflicts generated by the two spheres' competing claims on our loyalties.

7. Harry Cleaver offers a similar argument against the labor-work distinction (2002).

8. The notion of "relations of rule" is adapted from Dorothy Smith's (far richer) category of "relations of ruling" (1987, 3).

9. Here, it should be noted, the concepts of living labor and work are rendered more compatible if living labor is conceived not as an interior essence or normative standard, but as a potential for specifically political agency. In this way, the concept serves not as a critical lens so much as "a source of the auto-valorization of subjects and groups, as the creation of social cooperation," as the potential to construct alternatives (Negri 1996, 171). See also Jason Read's similar approach to the category (2003, 90–91).

10. Different but compatible approaches to class as process include Joan Acker's revisiting of class from a feminist perspective (2000), Stanley Aronowitz's insistence on a class theory that places the emphasis on social time over social space (2003), and William Corlett's model of "class action" as a process of labor's self-determination (1998).

11. A relationship that might have been captured by a quantitative logic, measured by the distance between the one in front and the one behind, is revealed as something that must be grasped also in qualitative terms, as attitude, affect, feeling, and symbolic exchange.

12. Indeed, as one radical feminist famously declared, with a combination of daring and grandiosity not uncommon to 1970s feminism, "if there were another word more all-embracing than *revolution* we would use it" (Firestone 1970, 3).

13. Here I obviously part company with more orthodox Arendtian—let alone Nietzschean—analyses that would exclude work from the proper business of the political.

14. To be sure, to affirm the value of this latter agenda focused on freedom is not to discount the ongoing importance of the former committed to equality.

15. I will generally use the label "Marxist feminism" to describe a wide variety of feminisms, including my own, despite the fact that I sometimes draw on sources more typically identified (and often even self-identified) as socialist feminist. The distinction between Marxist feminism and socialist feminism is not always clear. Often they are distinguished by period, with Marxist feminism preceding the development of socialist feminism, and the latter described as a synthesis of Marxism and radical feminism developed in the 1970s. The term "socialist" is also sometimes used as a way to designate a more expansive and inclusive project, one committed to political-economic analysis, but not necessarily to Marxism per se. I prefer the term "Marxist feminism" for two reasons: first, because my own work and many of its points of reference, including the domestic-labor and wages for housework literatures, are indebted to Marxist theoretical traditions; and second, because I am skeptical about the contemporary relevance of the term "socialist," a point I will expand upon below.

16. The late 1960s to the early 1980s marks the period of Marxist feminism's maximum influence within US feminist theory. Today the project lives on, often under other labels, and explores, among other things, how the present organization of both waged and unwaged work—including current instances of the class, gender, race, and transnational divisions of labor—are implicated in the construction and maintenance of class, gender, racial, and national differences and hierarchies.

17. Both Marxists and feminists, as Barbara Ehrenreich explained her understanding of the socialist feminist project in 1976, "seek to understand the world—not in terms of static balances, symmetries, etc. (as in conventional social science)—but in terms of antagonisms" (1997, 66).

18. Perhaps the contemporary literature that most directly addresses social reproduction as a feminist analytic, in this case on the terrain of political economy, comes out of Canada. For some good examples, see Bakker and Gill (2003), Bezanson and Luxton (2006), and Luxton and Corman (2001).

19. "Social reproduction can thus be seen to include various kinds of work—mental, manual, and emotional—aimed at providing the historically and socially, as well as biologically, defined care necessary to maintain existing life and to reproduce the next generation" (Laslett and Brenner 1989, 383).

20. That is, in terms of "the new forms of organization and relations between people which we define as socialism" (Berkeley-Oakland Women's Union 1979, 356), but also sometimes in the more expansive terms of what another group identified as socialist, feminist, and antiracist revolution (Combahee River Collective 1979, 366).

21. Although since it is less a demand for change than a demand for the enforcement of existing policies, it is important to note that even demanding the enforcement of the wage and hours laws already on the books would make an enormous difference, especially to the lives of low-wage workers. See Annette Bernhardt et al. (2009).

22. Another example is the demand for universal healthcare without any ties to employment, although that demand's critique of work per se might be less direct than the critiques posed by the demands for basic income and shorter hours.

23. The demand for less work, as Jonathan Cutler and Stanley Aronowitz explain it, is unusual in its capacity to position workers to make further demands: "No other bargaining demand simultaneously enhances bargaining position" (1998, 20).

1. Mapping the Work Ethic

1. It is worth emphasizing that Weber confines his analysis to Western European and US capitalist social formations (1958, 52).

2. For an elaboration of this argument about the relation between production and subjectivity in Marxism, see Jason Read (2003).

3. For a development of this distinction, see Fredric Jameson's discussion of the difference between an antinomy and a contradiction (1994, 1–7).

4. According to Weber's account of Luther's conception of the calling, "the fulfill-ment of worldly duties is under all circumstances the only way to live acceptably to God"; thus, "every legitimate calling has exactly the same worth in the sight of God" (1958, 81).

5. This abstraction from the concrete qualities of work is accompanied within ascetic Puritanism by an abstraction of the notion of brotherly love: Christians can obey the commandment not just through the concrete care of specific individuals, but indirectly, through waged work—that is, through "labor in the service of impersonal social usefulness" (Weber 1958, 109).

6. Weber's argument is organized in classic social-scientific format: successive chapters lay out the problem and the hypothesis, followed by discussions of the dependent and independent variables, and then the findings and conclusion.

7. None of the goals—the certainty of an afterlife, social mobility, or self-fulfillment—are new; they coexist in various forms with varying degrees of emphasis in each of the three periods I want to isolate. All three versions—the Protestant, indus-trial, and postindustrial work ethics—are hybrids, rendered here as ideal types defined by the goal that tends to dominate the discourse of the work ethic in any one period.

8. The postindustrial work ethic returns in this way to the Protestant ethic's notion of work as a calling, thereby partially relieving it once again of a degree of the tangible instrumentality it had acquired in the industrial period, when it was coded as a means to economic mobility.

9. This general confounding of means and ends continues to haunt present under-standings of work. Is it an end in itself, or a means to other ends? Does one work, for example, to support a family or support a family in order to make meaning-ful one's investments in work? That is, do people work because they have fami-lies, or do they organize their lives around the familial model of sociality because they work? Is work a means to self-expression and self-development, or are these instead means by which one can make sense of and justify the time and energy one puts into work?

10. Seymour Martin Lipset observes that there is a long-standing tendency for an older generation to believe that the work ethic is not as strong in the younger generation (1992, 45).

11. Part of the story of the changing status of waged work that Fraser and Gordon recount centers on its increasing association with masculinity and whiteness, points that I will take up later in this chapter.

12. What was perhaps more difficult to maintain under the conditions of industrial production and Fordist regularization is perhaps easier to imagine under the conditions of postindustrial production and post-Fordist "flexploitation" (Gray 2004). With the increasing individualization of work (Castells 2000, 282)—in terms, for example, of a varied menu of schedules and contracts (Beck 2000, 54, 55)—work is even more likely to be conceived as a field of individual experience and responsibility.

13. It bears emphasizing here that the work ethic is not merely an ideology in the classic sense of a set of ideas about the value of work that are explicitly pronounced and intentionally propagated. The work ethic is also, as in Louis Althusser's notion of ideology, a set of ideas that inhere in apparatuses and are inscribed in ritualized practices (1971, 166). Althusser notes that in the industrial period of "mature capitalism," the church lost its position as the dominant ideological state apparatus and was replaced by the school (152). Although the school maintains its importance in reproducing the submission of the worker today the work ethic is dependent on neither the church nor the school for its reproduction. Rather, as Michael Burawoy suggests, we need to attend to the ways that consent to its demands is generated at the point of production (1979), via modes of subjectification generated through what Catherine Casey calls the "hidden curriculum" of work (1995, 74)—not just from the ideas that managers ask workers to recite and affirm, but from the practices and relationships, rewards and penalties, that work and workplaces structure.

14. Weber underscores the role that the work ethic plays in enabling exploitation. Rather than just rationalizing the exploitation of preconstituted subjects, it helps to fashion exploitable subjects. But the rewards of the disciplinary subjectivity constituted by the discourse of the work ethic, it should be emphasized, are not just economic; they are also, and more properly, social and political. The possible decline of the work ethic, the fearful consequences of which are periodically debated in the popular press, would lead, according to such accounts, not only to the economic but to the moral decline of the nation. Thus in one such text from the 1980s, the fear that US workers, increasingly given over to laziness and pleasure seeking, would not be able to compete with the industrious Japanese prompted the author to recommend a variety of measures to shore up the work ethic, including teaching it as propaganda in schools and investing in various make-work programs designed to strengthen the ethic (Eisenberger 1989, 224–25, 248). Proposals for disciplinary make-work—to be imposed on welfare recipients, prisoners, and juvenile offenders, to name a few groups—bring us back to that strange confounding of means and ends: rather than promoting the work ethic to make sure that we do the work that needs doing, work is created as a way to instill a work ethic (see also Beder 2000, 139–41). Here we can see more clearly that economic utility is not always what is at stake: work is associated with a host of socially and politically functional behaviors. Thus it is not only employers who have a stake in the work ethic; it is understood to be functional for a variety of regimes of social order and cooperation.

15. Weber did acknowledge the coexistence of competing ethics of work—not only traditionalism, but also, in a passing reference, "the class morality of the proletariat and the anti-authoritarian trade union," against which the dominant ethic protects those willing to work (1958, 167).

16. Today one can hear the echoes of this moral panic over the work ethic in some of the discourses about gay and lesbian marriage, particularly from those who

denigrate certain queer cultures by linking different patterns of supposedly pro-miscuous intimacies with so-called hedonistic consumer lifestyles and worry that those not ensconced in legible families have, to draw on Lee Edelman's (2004) critical account of such logics, no future for which to sacrifice in the present and, to borrow a concept from Judith Halberstam's critique of such narratives, no reproductive time (2005) around which to regulate their lives productively. Here I would just note a point that I will develop as an argument in another context below: the work ethic also seems to inform the responses of others who contest such assertions, but do so by mirroring their logic—in this case, by insisting that the benefits of marriage and family should be extended by means of a more inclusive family ethic to those now excluded from its supposed beneficial effects as a mode of social discipline.

17. Indeed, multiple versions of the work ethic are generated at the intersections of class, race, ethnicity, and gender, as these hierarchies are constructed, defended, and also contested; dissemination is thus also a process of further differentiation and hybridization.

18. As the quote suggests, Gilman's contribution to the domestic-science movement is interesting for the way that, as Ehrenreich and English observe, she took the argument about the importance of rationalizing domestic production much fur-ther, arguing that the private home should no longer serve as its locus (Ehrenreich and English 1975, 25–26). This willingness to extend an insight to its logical conclusion, running roughshod over custom and habit in the process, is reminis-cent of the kind of relentless logic that radical feminists from the 1970s periodi-cally used to such usefully disquieting effect.

19. For a classic example of the literature on the ethic of care, see Noddings (1984). For an important revision of this project that confronts the problem of gender essentialism head on and presents an alternative approach to both the ethics and the politics of care, see Tronto (1993). For a contribution to this literature that seeks to conceive care as a social phenomenon rather than an individual at-tribute, and to imagine the logic of care as an immanent ethical practice as opposed to a moral imperative, see Precarias a la Deriva (2006).

20. Madeline Bunting makes a similar point (2004, 169–70).

21. As Colin Cremin observes, flexible workers are not only expected to achieve employment, but to sustain their fitness for work, their "employability" (2010, 133).

22. Thus, for example, in a book based on interviews with executives at a number of companies that emphasize customer service, the interviewees claim repeatedly that hiring good employees is not about finding people with the right skills, it is about hiring people with the right attitudes (Wiersema 1998).

23. Studies report that across the employment spectrum, attitudes are often more important to managers than aptitude. See, for example, Barnes and Powers (2006, 4–5); Beder (2000, 196); Callaghan and Thompson (2002).

24. Talwar reports that the same equation of appearance with professionalism ap-pears in the codes of fast-food management (2002, 100).

2. Marxism and the Refusal of Work

1. For a few examples, see some of the actions in relation to the figure of San Precario in Italy (Tari and Vanni 2005; De Sario 2007), the Spanish groups Precarias a la Deriva (2006) and Dinero Gratis (http://www.sindominio.net/ eldinerogratis/index.html), the Euromarches (Mathers 1999; Gray 2004), and mobilizations around EuroMayDay (http://www.euromayday.org/).

2. See also Maria Milagros López's rich and interesting discussion of emerging postwork subjectivities in postindustrial Puerto Rico, decried by some as a kind of "entitlement attitude" on the part of recipients of state support, but which López examines as "forms of life and work that presume the saliency of the present and which claim rights, needs, entitlements, enjoyment, dignity, and self-valorization outside the structure of wages" (1994, 113).

3. These utopian visions, as I will explain further in chapter 5, are not blueprints for a perfect future, but rather—in keeping with more modest and serviceable conceptions of utopian thinking—attempts to imagine different possibilities and to anticipate alternative modes of life. As inspiring visions, they are designed both to advance the critique of daily life under capital and to stimulate desire for, imagination of, and hope in the possibility of a different future.

4. Ivan Illich offers another example of this kind of critique with his defense of a subsistence economy guided by an ethic of "convivial austerity." We cannot, Illich claims, live autonomously or act creatively "where a professionally engineered commodity has succeeded in replacing a culturally shaped use-value" (1978, 9).

5. On the relation between abstract and concrete labor see also Postone (1996, 353) and Vincent (1991, 97–98).

6. In a rereading of this famous section of *The German Ideology*, Terrell Carver claims that the original draft of the coauthored text indicates that Engels wrote the section, to which Marx made some small additions—including an earlier reference to "a critical critic," the very figure that *The German Ideology* is directed against, and the addition of "after dinner," which serves to belittle the practice of criticizing—that had the effect of making it into an ironic take on the kind of pastoral, pre-industrial utopias to which Marx objected (Carver 1998, 106).

7. Originally associated with the Operaismo, post-Operaismo and Autonomia movements in Italy, autonomist Marxism also developed within several other groups and movements, including the Midnight Notes Collective, Zerowork, the feminist group Lotta Feminista, and the movement for wages for housework. The authors I draw on most frequently in this account include some associated with both autonomist Marxism's early articulation and its later developments including Antonio Negri (also in his later collaboration with Michael Hardt), Paolo Virno, and, in the next chapter, Mariarosa Dalla Costa; some who have been inspired by and have built on elements of the tradition, including Harry Cleaver, Nick Dyer-Witheford, and Jason Read; and, finally, authors of specific

texts that, although developed independently, are nonetheless compatible with autonomist Marxism's orientation and project, most notably Moishe Postone (1996) and Jean-Marie Vincent (1991).

8. On autonomist Marxism as part of a much broader tradition of Marxist interpretation and scholarship, see Dyer-Witheford (1999, 62–64).

9. What I am calling a humanist work ethic bears some resemblance to two of the iterations discussed in the previous chapter: the Protestant work ethic and the laborist ethic. The humanist ethic shares the Protestant ethic's endorsement of work as an end in itself and as the center of life but is also selective about which forms of work merit such devotion. Unlike the Protestant ethic—which, by sanctioning all work regardless of what it produces or how it is organized, left no room for judging the quality of the work—the humanist ethic I will describe both celebrates the potential virtues of work and poses a critical standard by which the experience of the work can be assessed. The laborist ethic also poses a challenge to the Protestant ethic, by insisting on the ethical value of labor as part of its critique of labor's exploitation: the worthy practices of labor—the source of all value—deserve adequate recognition and recompense. Similarly, the humanist work ethic is also designed to facilitate rather than disallow the critique of work; it is thus an ethic that can be used against the traditional function of the work ethic, to deliver workers to their more effective exploitation. Like the laborist ethic, the humanist ethic invites our judgments about the quality of work, but whereas the laborist ethic of the industrial period traditionally focused on the problem of labor's exploitation and the quantity of its compensation, the postindustrial humanist work ethic focuses more on the critique of alienation and questions about the quality of work.

10. On human-resource management, see Bernstein (1997), Storey (1989), and Strauss (1992).

11. For an overview of some of these different managerial strategies, see Macdonald and Sirianni (1996, 5–11). Other popular managerial strategies involve drawing on models of disciplinary collectivity that are not typically associated with modern workplace hierarchies in order to replace antagonistic or nonproductive forms of collectivity—from union-based solidarities to corporate cultures that resist change—with more productive, less "worklike" modes of cooperation. Thus relations among co-workers and between workers and management are sometimes described as "like" a family, in terms of teams, or as relations of consumption and exchange between internal buyers and sellers (see Casey 1995, 92–101).

12. On work intensification's accompanying claims about enrichment and participation in a variety of different employment sectors, see Baldoz, Koeber, and Kraft. (2001), Bunting (2004), Macdonald and Sirianni (1996), McArdle et al. (1995), Parker and Slaughter (1988), Rinehart (2001), Shaiken, Herzenberg, and Kuhn. (1986), and Taplin (1995). On the intensification associated with flexible work options, see Kelliher and Anderson (2010).

13. On the importance of linking the demand for the qualitative change of work with the demand for its quantitative reduction, see also Cleaver (2000, 130).

14. Despite efforts to expand what counts legally and culturally as a family beyond the traditional heterosexual patriarchal model, the family's status as a private site responsible for much of the work of care has been more resistant to change (on this point see, for example, Brenner 2000, 135).

3. Working Demands

1. Although the intellectual and political project of wages for housework continues after this period, my focus is confined to this early period of its development for reasons I will explain below.

2. For an example of this taxonomy of feminist theory, see Jaggar (1983); for an important critique of this model, see Sandoval (2000, 41–64).

3. Here I would include my own earlier reading of wages for housework that sees it—inadequately, I now think—as representative of a kind of Marxist feminist theory upon which some later socialist feminisms improved (Weeks 1998).

4. This inattention to difference could characterize the dialectical model as well. Where the familial model elides difference and denies conflict, the dialectical model absorbs and subsumes them.

5. Robyn Wiegman observes that the "equation between subjectivity and feminist knowledge" is also grounded in feminism's historical insistence on the imbrication of the personal and the political, and with it, the methodological emphasis on experience and the political priority of consciousness-raising (2000, 813).

6. Margaret Benston, in an essay originally published in 1969, presented what was arguably the first installment in the domestic labor debate (1995). By the time Maxine Molyneux published her call to move "Beyond the Domestic Labour Debate" in 1979, she reports that over fifty articles had been published on the topic (1979, 3). For some additional analyses of and highlights from the debate, see Bubeck (1995), Vogel (2000), the introduction and essay by Malos (1995a, 1995b), and the volume she edited (1995c).

7. As Ellen Malos describes it, once "the debate shifted to the question of how to determine the 'value' of work in the household in a marxist sense, a kind of confrontational theoretical paralysis developed which dislocated the political agenda" (1995b, 216).

8. The text was published as a pamphlet, the second edition of which includes four texts: an introduction by James, dated July 1972; the title essay by Dalla Costa, completed in December 1971, first published in Italian in 1972 as "Donne e sovversione sociale" (Women and the Subversion of the Community), and translated the same year into English by Dalla Costa and James; an essay by James, "A Woman's Place," first published in 1953; and a brief "Letter to a Group of Women," signed by Dalla Costa, James, "and many others." My discussion is confined to the first two essays, as they are most relevant to the development of the wages for housework perspective. Besides this pamphlet, I draw most

heavily, though not exclusively, on the following contributions to the wages for housework literature: Federici (1975), Cox and Federici (1976), and James (1976).

9. On the relation between wages for housework and autonomist Marxism, see Cleaver (2000). On the relationship between the Italian wages for housework movement and specific groups associated with the autonomist tradition (including Potere Operaio and Midnight Notes), see Dalla Costa (2002). In an interview conducted in the 1980s, Antonio Negri claimed that "without the women's movement, *Autonomia* would never have gotten off the ground, in Italy or anywhere in Europe" (Jardine and Massumi 2000, 80; see also Negri 1988, 236). Feminist analyses were also arguably important to the development of the the-ory of the social worker, conceived as a new form of collectivity that cuts across the divides between productive and reproductive, and waged and unwaged, labor. Alisa Del Re observes that feminist analyses from the 1970s anticipated and provided tools for later understandings of post-Fordist labor. "Today," she noted in 2000, "when I hear of the feminization of labor, affective labor or immaterial labor, I laugh: it feels like they are joking because we used to say these things in the Seventies, when we imagined that there is a form of labor that is neither accountable nor measured and yet is what makes us reproduce the labor power and allows for material production to take place, something without which material production is impossible" (2005, 54).

10. Demands for an income independent of work have long been advocated by au-tonomists. For example, see Baldi (1972, 4), Zerowork (1975, 2), Dyer-Witheford (1999, 194–201), Hardt and Negri (2000, 403), and Berardi (2009, 213–14).

11. See, for example, Caroline Freeman's insistence, in a comment directed at Selma James, that the household does not resemble a factory, and that the identifica-tion of the two only obscures reality (1995, 143).

12. Again, in this respect Dalla Costa and James diverge rather dramatically from the more orthodox contributors to the domestic labor debate—who, when they failed to fit domestic labor within the theory of commodity production as Marx described it, concluded that domestic labor, which produces use values in the home, is not a form of productive labor and thus not a component of capitalist production proper. We must remember, one proponent of this position noted, that "Marx's definition of productive labour in the capitalist mode of produc-tion is made from the standpoint of capital," not from the point of view of those whose labor reproduces it, still less from the perspective of some revolutionary alternative. Hence, "it is not Marx's theory of value which marginalizes domestic labour, but the capitalist mode of production" (P. Smith 1978, 213, 215). From capital's perspective, which the more orthodox contributors see as identical to Marx's perspective in *Capital*, domestic labor is unproductive. Dalla Costa agrees that this was in fact Marx's position (Dalla Costa and James 1973, 30–31); she is simply unwilling to accept either that it is a viable position today or that a Marxist perspective would be content simply to mirror capitalist logics.

13. James, for example, argues that in and of themselves, demands like those for free child care and equal pay are inadequate both as strategy and as vision: "By

themselves these are not just co-optable demands. They are capitalist planning" (Dalla Costa and James 1973, 14, n. 3). Proponents of such demands "don't aim to destroy the capitalist social relation but only to organize it more rationally," a stance that "the extra-parliamentary left in Italy would call . . . a 'socialist' as distinct from a revolutionary position" (2). Similarly, Federici distinguishes between asking the state to provide child care or meals and—the strategy she defends—demanding that it pay for the arrangements that people choose for themselves (1995, 193).

14. This insistence on the singular importance of economic practices is, for example, clearly at work in James's claim in a later text that work is not just one feminist issue among many, but rather *the* issue: "In fact and in consciousness, the work we do, women and men, is the essence of our slavery" (1985, 13).

15. When we see wages for housework as a tool for orienting ourselves in relation to a set of social structures, or a tool for cognitive mapping, one common critique—that its categories are too abstracted from the lives and meanings of individuals to be able to capture the singularity of their experience—seems both correct and largely beside the point. Thus, it may be, as one critic argues, that Marxist feminist theories of the relationship between capitalism and patriarchy cannot do justice to the daily realities of motherhood, that "reproductive work is far too alienating a concept for such a personal and intimate experience" (Luttrell 1984, 45). Indeed, if the categories of reproductive labor or social reproduction were deployed in an attempt to represent the richness of individual experience, I might agree with claims about their deficiency. But deployed in the service of a structural mapping strategy, they are meant to serve a rather different purpose, for which a certain distance from personal experience and the cultural meanings in relation to which it is framed might be a useful thing. The analyses ask us to attend to the fact that whether it is a source of pleasure or pain, of delight or drudgery, the waged-labor economy depends on a privatized and gendered system of reproductive labor that it does not adequately recognize or support.

16. The demand as perspective and provocation could also be called a standpoint: a collective political project with both epistemological and ontological valences (see Weeks 1998, 8–10).

17. The description is borrowed from Naomi Scheman (2001, 332).

18. Interestingly, in one of the texts, needs and desires are described in terms of different temporalities: there is an immediacy to wanting, but needs are described as something yet to be determined, something only the future could reveal. First, advocates of wages for housework claim, women have to establish in and through the struggle for a wage who they are as feminist subjects. Then, once the wage is won, "we could begin to find out what *our* needs are" (Edmond and Fleming 1975, 7).

19. That the demand for wages for housework could perpetuate rather than challenge the gender division of labor was a risk that Dalla Costa notes in her initial assessment of the demand (Dalla Costa and James 1973, 34).

20. See, for example, van Parijs (1992); Gray (2004, 109–10); and The Basic Income Earth Network (http://www.basicincome.org/bien/). Groups demanding basic income have also been active in a number of countries, with the movements in South Africa and Brazil being among the best known.

21. For some of the terms of this debate, see Pateman (2003).

22. Nancy Folbre makes the argument that children should be recognized as public goods (2001, 111).

23. Hardt and Negri explain it this way: whereas in earlier periods capital provided the model of productive cooperation in the factory, now it harnesses forms of and capacities for cooperation produced in the social factory (2009, 140–41).

24. To those who worry that some people might forgo waged work entirely if they had a basic income, and become free riders on the productive efforts of others, proponents of the demand point out that those unwaged reproductive workers who had supported the free riding of those who do little or no such work will now receive an income too. Claus Offe explains: "The 'positive' injustice from which non-working recipients would benefit [through a basic income] is partly offset by an abolition of the 'negative' injustice from which many non-receiving 'workers' suffer today" (2008, 14).

25. Daniel Raventós (2007) stresses freedom as self-sovereignty, whereas Philippe van Parijs (van Parijs et al. 2001) emphasizes a more libertarian notion of freedom. For descriptions of these options, as well as some alternatives, see Pateman (2003) and Offe (2008).

26. For examples of a range of the positions on the debate about basic income, see van Parijs et al. (2001).

27. In his history of the rise and fall of guaranteed income proposals in the United States in the 1960s and 1970s, Steensland argues that one of the critical factors in their defeat was the threat they were seen to pose to cultural ideas about work and social reciprocity—that is, the idea that the "benefits" of a guaranteed income would "enable recipients to reap the benefits of citizenship without contributing to the common good" (2008, 229).

4. "Hours for What We Will"

1. For an interesting exception, see Hunnicutt's history (1996) of Kellogg's six-hour day, first instituted in the 1930s and maintained until the mid-1980s. The gendered history of the Kellogg case is interesting both because women were the strongest supporters of the six-hour day and because the progressive feminization of the shorter shift played a role in its devaluation and eventual defeat.

2. Hochschild recognizes other possible reasons as well, including a need or desire for money, pressures on workers to demonstrate their commitment through the number of hours they work, and ultimately, fear of losing their jobs. But, arguing that "all these sources of inhibition did not fully account for the lack of resistance Amerco's working parents showed to the encroachments of work time on family life," she emphasizes instead her own explanation (1997, 197–98).

3. It should be noted that Hochschild defends both reduced hours (though she

does not take up the prospect of a six-hours movement per se) and various forms of flextime.

4. See Luxton for a similar argument about the importance of linking work-time activism to questions about the gender division of domestic labor (1987, 176–77).

5. For a critical analysis of the gendered and racialized politics of welfare, see Mink (1998).

6. I take the term "controlling image" from Patricia Hill Collins (1991).

7. Broder (2002) discusses this link as well.

8. I draw here in part on Drucilla Cornell's (1998) discussion of freedom.

9. Indeed, many of the negative responses to postwork demands, like the demand for shorter hours, are themselves interesting. Lynn Chancer, for example, argues that the incredulity that the demand for a basic income so often elicits is itself peculiar and worthy of investigation (1998, 81–82). David Macarov describes the typical reactions to his own doubts about both the merits of linking welfare to work and the necessity and desirability of work as a mixture of disbelief, amusement, derision, and anger—a set of responses that underscores for him the power of traditional work values (1980, 206–208).

10. In addition to amending the Fair Labor Standards Act to reduce the standard workweek to, in this case, thirty-five hours (above which overtime pay would be mandated), Jerry Jacobs and Kathleen Gerson propose two additional reforms that could also help to ensure that work-time reduction would address the needs of both the overworked and the underemployed. First, requiring employers to provide benefits for all workers proportional to the hours they work would not only expand the pool of entitled employees, it would also eliminate another incentive for employers to underemploy some workers so they do not qualify for benefits, and extend the hours of other workers who already qualify. Second, eliminating the so-called white-collar exemption would extend the protections of the Fair Labor Standards Act to the roughly more than 25 percent of the workforce employed in those executive, administrative, and professional positions that are now exempt from its wages and hours provisions (Jacobs and Gerson 2004, 183–85; see also Linder 2004, 6). See also Schultz and Hoffman (2006) on these and other strategies—including economic incentives, negotiated solutions, and private industry initiatives—by which work time in the United States might be reduced.

11. On this point, see also Christopherson (1991, 182–84).

5. The Future Is Now

1. Popper's book was written in Britain during the fight against European fascism and, as he notes, "with the expectation that Marxism would become a major problem." In the preface to a later edition, Popper recognizes that the critique of Marxism is "liable to stand out as the main point of the book" (1950, vii).

2. It bears noting that Popper's and Fukuyama's critiques of utopian dreams of and struggles for a better world are presented neither under the auspices of a crude materialism (both recognize the potential power of ideas in political affairs) nor

in the name of realpolitik (as reason and progress, not interest and power, are their guiding ideals). As we will see, their problems with this kind of idealism lie elsewhere.

3. Interestingly, both Popper and Fukuyama center their arguments on historicism, with Hegel and Marx prominently represented. But although such evolutionary theories of historical development appear as the enemy of liberalism in Popper's account—insisting as they do that social orders come and go, and predicting the advent of new forms—they play a central role in Fukuyama's defense of liberalism. The historicism of Hegel and Marx so maligned by Popper is celebrated once it is clear, to Fukuyama at least, that liberalism and not communism is the *telos* of this historical drama.

4. Despite Popper's "firm conviction" that the "irrational emphasis on emotion and passion leads ultimately to what I can only describe as crime," he later admits that his own style could be accurately described as "emotional" (1950, 419, vii).

5. The difference between Popper's and Fukuyama's treatments of the passions is reminiscent of the way they are viewed by two theorists who bookend another epoch in the history of liberal political theory: Thomas Hobbes and John Stuart Mill. In contrast to Hobbes, Mill insists that the greater danger to both individual and society lies not in an overabundance of passions and desires, but in their attenuation (1986, 70).

6. On the production of feminist literary utopias, see the overviews in H. Rose (1988) and Russ (1981).

7. It seems to me that this retreat from the affirmative or propositional dimension of critical work sits uneasily in relation to political theory's disciplinary history and canonical commitments to a model of critique that encompasses both deconstructive and reconstructive moments.

8. This distrust of utopianism persists within some parts of the Marxist tradition. Even among those who would affirm utopianism, some do so in only the most cautious manner. Thus, for example, Immanuel Wallerstein begins his defense of utopian thinking with a standard critique of utopias as by definition "dreams of a heaven that could never exist on earth" and, hence, "breeders of illusions and therefore, inevitably, of disillusions" (1998, 1). His analysis and prescriptions are based, in contrast, on "sober, rational, and realistic" analysis, for which he feels the need to invent a new term, "utopistics," one presumably untainted by the history of the old term (1). Because he is, like Popper, concerned about utopias leading us astray from reason narrowly understood, in speaking out on behalf of utopianism, Wallerstein thus advocates only the most domesticated notion of it, shorn of much of its passion and imagination.

9. One of Bloch's favorite moves is to turn interrogatives into nouns (including, for example, the "Where To" and "What For"), thereby transforming an instrumental piece of familiar grammar into an enigmatic concept with a denser but still open-ended reality. Sometimes this works to open doors to new ways of thinking; at other times, the rhetoric falls flat.

10. On this point, see Tom Moylan's useful analysis of Bloch's thought and politics (1997, 108–18).

11. Bloch's version of the process ontology of being is notable for its animating force. In contrast to those who would identify a particular human drive as the transhistorical motor of history, humans are, according to Bloch, subject to a multiplicity of drives, none of which are timeless or fixed (1995, 1: 50). Hunger figures in Bloch's analysis as a kind of minimal ontological force, the "oil in the lamp of history" (1: 69) that animates the "no" to deprivation and the "yes" to a better life (1: 75). As a thoroughly historically variable, hunger "interacts as socially developed and guided need with the other social, and therefore historically varying needs which it underlies and with which, for this very reason, it is transformed and causes transformation" (1: 69). Although he presents hunger as a version or expression of the drive to self-preservation, it is not reducible to other, more familiar notions of self-preservation. In Bloch's version, "self-preservation, human preservation in no way seeks the conservation of that which has already been drawn and allotted to the self." Rather, self-preservation as hunger is what urges humans forward to extend themselves and become more.

12. To borrow a formulation from Deleuze's reading of Nietzsche, "the world is neither true nor real but living" (Deleuze 1983, 184).

13. "Affect" is, I would argue, a more fitting description than "emotion" for this dimension of Bloch's notion of hope. Not only is emotion, as the capturing and rendering legible of affect (Massumi 1995, 88), too narrow a formulation but affect—understood as a capacity for affecting and being affected (Massumi quoted in Zournazi 2003, 212)—can better register the expansive quality of hope that I want to emphasize.

14. Rather than describe hope as the opposite of fear and anxiety, as Bloch tends to do, I want to pose hopefulness as their complement or, better yet, their antidote.

15. The model of the abstract utopia, Bloch complains, "has discredited utopias for centuries, both in pragmatic political terms and in all other expressions of what is desirable; just as if every utopia were an abstract one" (1995, 1: 145).

16. We can also use Bloch's distinction between abstract and concrete utopias to draw further distinctions between hoping on the one hand and both wishfulness and nostalgia on the other hand. As was the case with the contrast between abstract and concrete utopias, these distinctions turn on the quality of the relationship to the present. Wishing or wishfulness can be described as an abstract mode of thinking the future, and nostalgia as an abstract memory practice. Although one is focused forward and the other looks backward, wishfulness and nostalgia are equally abstract in the Blochian sense: one seeks escape from the present in a fantastic future, the other in an idealized past.

17. For an analysis of the political fortunes of fear in US politics, see Corey Robin's account of the history of what he calls "fear American style" (2004).

18. Although I will focus on *ressentiment*, in light of our earlier mention of Left melancholy, it is worth noting here that there are family resemblances between

the affective temporalities of the subject of *ressentiment* and that of melancholy. Freud describes the melancholic subject—and, in at least these terms, the mourner as well—as displaying a "profoundly painful dejection, cessation of interest in the outside world, loss of the capacity to love," as well as an "inhibition of activity" (1957, 244).

19. In this sense, the distinction between affirmation as acceptance and willful affirmation in Nietzsche's thought resembles Bloch's distinction between automatic optimism and militant optimism. Characterized by "a will which refuses to be outvoted by anything that has already become" (1995, 1: 147), militant optimism is opposed to optimism of either the naive or teleological variety; it is as impatient with wishfulness as it is with nostalgia. Militant or "founded optimism" is thus opposed both to the "cheap credulity" of automatic optimism and to the automatic belief in progress (1: 199–200).

20. This is the kind of dislocation and disintegration of self that Julian West, Bellamy's character in *Looking Backward*, experiences after waking to a new social world more than a hundred years in the future: "moments," as Julian describes it, "when my personal identity seems an open question" (2000, 113). However, Bellamy also does much to assure the reader that the experience was otherwise ontologically assimilable, with a portrayal of a future that was in many respects soothingly familiar.

21. This attention to the function of utopias, beyond their form and content, is common in the utopian studies literature. For two good examples, see Levitas (1990) and McKenna (2001).

22. Suvin's (1972, 374) elaboration of this estrangement function of science fiction and the literary utopia draws on the work of Viktor Shklovsky and Bertolt Brecht.

23. As Vincent Geoghegan formulates this function of the classic utopian form, it "interrogates the present, piercing through existing societies' defensive mechanisms—common sense, realism, positivism and scientism" (1987, 2).

24. Foregrounding the utopian form's capacity for critical distancing, Edward Bellamy titled his famous 1888 novel about a utopian future set in the year 2000 not *Looking Forward*, but *Looking Backward* (2000).

25. The word play in More's original term "utopia"—which could sound like *outopos* or *eutopos*, meaning either no place or good place—might also be read in relation to the distinctive coupling of negation and affirmation that characterizes the form.

26. For a reading of Marin on neutralization, see Jameson (1977).

27. This was one of Bloch's fundamental claims, that the traditional conception of utopia, as a blueprint of an alternative society, is too restrictive, that utopian expressions assume a multiplicity of forms: "To limit the utopian to the Thomas More variety, or simply to orientate it in that direction, would be like trying to reduce electricity to the amber from which it gets its Greek name and in which it was first noticed" (1995, 1: 15).

28. To emphasize the importance of these utopian texts as critical perspectives is not

to deny their effects as provocations. Bellamy's *Looking Backward* inspired the formation of more than 160 Bellamy Clubs committed to achieving the utopian vision in the United States, along with a political party and publications (see Miller 2000, v–vi).

29. Sally Kitch's (2000) critique of feminist utopianism is a recent instance of this kind of argument, one that reduces utopianism to blueprints of perfect worlds and then dismisses it *tout court*.

30. These ways of managing a utopia's content can be matched by comparable formal techniques of closure that render the reader passive. The too easy refutation by Socrates in the early sections of the *Republic* of Thrasymachus's objections to the founding assumptions of the utopian state, a silencing that left Socrates with a rather more manageable set of interlocutors, stands as an early example of this technique. Bellamy deploys a comparable maneuver. In the penultimate chapter of *Looking Backward* (2000), not only do the protagonist and the daughter of his host declare their love for one another, but we discover that the daughter, Edith, who happens to share the name of the fiancée he left behind in the past, is in fact the great-granddaughter of his lost love. Thus loss is recoded by means of a synthesis that neatly preserves that which it surpasses, as Edith the idle socialite is replaced by her more worthy descendant, Edith the incarnation of productive domesticity. Peter Fitting describes this as an example of a method that reinscribes the reader within the dominant social order "which represents itself, like the traditional work of art, as whole and meaningful, without flaws or contradiction" (1987, 33). As Angelika Bammer argues: "To the extent that utopias insist on closure, both on the level of narrative structure and in their representation of a world complete unto itself, their transformative potential is undermined by the apparatus of their self-containment" (1991, 18).

31. Sargent defines the critical utopia as "a non-existent society described in considerable detail and normally located in time and space that the author intended a contemporaneous reader to view as better than contemporary society but with difficult problems that the described society may or may not be able to solve and which takes a critical view of the utopian genre" (1994, 9). Moylan describes it in these terms: "A central concern in the critical utopia is the awareness of the limitations of the utopian tradition, so that these texts reject utopia as blueprint while preserving it as dream. Furthermore, the novels dwell on the conflict between the originary world and the utopian society opposed to it so that the process of social change is more directly articulated. Finally, the novels focus on the continuing presence of difference and imperfection within utopian society itself and thus render more recognizable and dynamic alternatives" (1986, 10–11). Phillip Wegner argues that one can also find these elements in earlier examples of utopian fiction (2002, 99–100).

32. For another approach to the critical utopia, see Erin McKenna's "process-model" of utopia (2001, 3).

33. By this estimation, perhaps, as Jameson observes, "an 'achieved' Utopia—a full representation—is a contradiction in terms" (1982, 157).

34. It should be noted that Althusser makes a distinction that I do not between utopian and nonutopian manifestoes, in terms of whether there is a disjunction between the agency of the text and that of the political subject it addresses. *The Communist Manifesto* (Marx and Engels 1992) is, by his account, nonutopian (1999, 26–27; see also Puchner 2006, 30).

35. On the foundational role of More's *Utopia*, see Wegner (2007, 116–17); on the *Manifesto*, see Puchner (2006, 11–12).

36. Manifestoes come in a variety of forms; they are directed to different audiences, intervene in different fields of inquiry and endeavor, and are committed to different goals. There are artistic manifestoes, political manifestoes, organizational manifestoes, and theoretical manifestoes, which ask us to create, organize, and think differently. Radical feminist manifestoes from the 1970s, for example, range from the more narrowly programmatic—like those that are essentially organizational charters and solicitations for membership—to the more immediately practical that function essentially as party platforms with specific demands for modest reform, and the more visionary and more properly utopian that call for a more dramatic rupture with the status quo. Not all include a utopian element; to count as utopian, they must focus not only on what they are against but gesture toward—announce, describe, or urge us in the direction of— an alternative.

37. There are, of course, exceptions to this iconic model of the manifesto. Donna Haraway's "A Manifesto for Cyborgs" (1985), for example, appropriates the manifesto form while rejecting some of its classic rhetorical tendencies and political inclinations. Just as authors of the critical utopias of the 1970s demonstrated an awareness of the limitations of the traditional literary utopia, Haraway's contribution could be described as a critical manifesto.

38. Although the demands that are sometimes included in manifestoes can be the repositories of the texts' utopian content, they are also often treated as an opportunity for authors to assert their practical credentials and prove their seriousness of purpose. In such cases, the list can serve to assure readers that there is indeed a viable method to the madness, in the guise of a clear means to a concrete end. In contrast, the utopian demand absorbs the utopian content into the demand itself.

39. Some proponents of another demand—for reparations for slavery—emphasize in similar terms the demand's potential to provoke political agency. As Randall Robinson puts it, "the issue here is not whether or not we can, or will, win reparations. The issue rather is whether we will fight for reparations, because we have decided for ourselves that they are our due" (2000, 206).

Epilogue

1. This is a danger that Peter Fleming investigates interestingly in relation to some of the different ways that we might seek to secure "a life" by "reclaiming it from work so that self-identity (or personal authenticity) might be achieved" (2009,

149), some of which—he defends a strategy associated with the refusal of work that struggles for "freedom from work" (164)—hold more potential than others.

2. I explored the injunction to get a life briefly elsewhere in relation to some different concerns (Weeks 2007). I am grateful to the Duke Women's Studies Graduate Scholars Colloquium, and especially Fiona Barnett and Michelle Koerner, for a stimulating discussion of the essay and for helping me to think further about what it might mean to get a life.

3. John Rajchman links Deleuze's concept of life to a conception of society "in which what we have in common is our singularities and not our individualities —where what is common is 'impersonal' and what is 'impersonal' is common" (2001, 14).

References

Abramovitz, Mimi. 1988. *Regulating the Lives of Women: Social Welfare Policy from Colonial Times to the Present*. Boston: South End.

Acker, Joan. 2000. "Revisiting Class: Thinking from Gender, Race, and Organizations." *Social Politics* 7 (2): 192–214.

Althusser, Louis. 1971. "Ideology and Ideological State Apparatuses (Notes towards an Investigation)." In Louis Althusser, *Lenin and Philosophy and Other Essays*, translated by Ben Brewster, 127–86. New York: Monthly Review Press.

——. 1999. *Machiavelli and Us*. Edited by Francois Matheron. Translated by Gregory Elliott. London: Verso.

Arendt, Hannah. 1958. *The Human Condition*. Chicago: University of Chicago Press.

——. 1961. "What Is Freedom?" In Hannah Arendt, *Between Past and Future: Eight Exercises in Political Thought*. New York: Viking.

Aronowitz, Stanley. 1985. "Why Work?" *Social Text* 12:19–42.

——. 2003. *How Class Works: Power and Social Movement*. New Haven: Yale University Press.

Aronowitz, Stanley, and William DiFazio. 1994. *The Jobless Future: Sci-Tech and the Dogma of Work*. Minneapolis: University of Minnesota Press.

Aronowitz, Stanley, Dawn Esposito, William DiFazio, and Margaret Yard. 1998. "The Post-Work Manifesto." In *Post-Work: The Wages of Cybernation*, edited by Stanley Aronowitz and Jonathan Cutler, 31–80. New York: Routledge.

Bakker, Isabella, and Stephen Gill, eds. 2003. *Power, Production, and Social Reproduction: Human In/security in the Global Political Economy*. Houndmills, England: Palgrave Macmillan.

Baldi, Guido. 1972. "Theses on Mass Worker and Social Capital." *Radical America* 6 (3): 3–21.

Baldoz, Rick, Charles Koeber, and Philip Kraft, eds. 2001. *The Critical Study of Work: Labor, Technology, and Global Production*. Philadelphia: Temple University Press.

Bammer, Angelika. 1991. *Partial Visions: Feminism and Utopianism in the 1970s.* New York: Routledge.

Barbash, Jack. 1983. "Which Work Ethic?" In *The Work Ethic—A Critical Analysis,* edited by Jack Barbash, Robert J. Lampman, Sar A. Levitan, and Gus Tyler, 231–61. Madison, Wis.: Industrial Relations Research Association.

Barnes, Nora Ganim, and Colleen E. Powers. 2006. "Beyond the Labor Shortage: Poor Work Ethic and Declining Customer Satisfaction." *Business Forum* 27 (2): 4–6.

Baron, Ava. 1991. "An 'Other' Side of Gender Antagonism at Work: Men, Boys, and the Remasculinization of Printers' Work, 1830–1920." In *Work Engendered: Toward a New History of American Labor,* edited by Ava Baron, 47–69. Ithaca: Cornell University Press.

Baudrillard, Jean. 1975. *The Mirror of Production.* Translated by Mark Poster. St. Louis: Telos.

Bauman, Zygmunt. 1976. *Socialism: The Active Utopia.* New York: Holmes and Meier.

——. 1998. *Work, Consumerism and the New Poor.* Buckingham, England: Open University Press.

Beck, Ulrich. 2000. *The Brave New World of Work.* Translated by Patrick Camiller. Cambridge: Polity.

Beder, Sharon. 2000. *Selling the Work Ethic: From Puritan Pulpit to Corporate PR.* London: Zed.

Beechey, Veronica, and Tessa Perkins. 1987. *A Matter of Hours: Women, Part-Time Work and the Labor Market.* Minneapolis: University of Minnesota Press.

Bell, Daniel. 1976. *The Cultural Contradictions of Capitalism.* New York: Basic.

Bellamy, Edward. 2000. *Looking Backward, 2000–1887.* New York: Penguin.

Benhabib, Seyla. 1991. "Feminism and Postmodernism: An Uneasy Alliance." *Praxis International* 11 (2): 137–50.

Benhabib, Seyla, and Drucilla Cornell. 1987. "Introduction: Beyond the Politics of Gender." In *Feminism as Critique,* edited by Seyla Benhabib and Drucilla Cornell, 1–15. Minneapolis: University of Minnesota Press.

Bennett, Jane. 2002. "The Moraline Drift." In *The Politics of Moralizing,* edited by Jane Bennett and Michael J. Shapiro, 11–26. New York: Routledge.

Benston, Margaret. 1995. "The Political Economy of Women's Liberation." In *The Politics of Housework,* new ed., edited by Ellen Malos, 100–109. Cheltenham, England: New Clarion.

Berardi, Franco [Bifo]. 1980. "Anatomy of Autonomy." Translated by Jared Becker, Richard Reid, and Andrew Rosenbaum. *Semiotext(e)* 3 (3): 148–70.

——. 2009. *The Soul at Work: From Alienation to Autonomy.* Translated by Francesca Cadel and Giuseppina Mecchia. Los Angeles: Semiotext(e).

Berk, Sarah Fenstermaker. 1985. *The Gender Factory: The Apportionment of Work in American Households.* New York: Plenum.

Berkeley-Oakland Women's Union. 1979. "Principles of Unity." In *Capitalist Patriarchy and the Case for Socialist Feminism,* edited by Zillah Eisenstein, 355–61. New York: Monthly Review Press.

Bernhardt, Annette, et al. 2009. "Broken Laws, Unprotected Workers: Violations of Employment and Labor Laws in America's Cities." http://nelp.3cdn.net/ 319982941a5496c741_9qm6b92kg.pdf.

Bernstein, Paul. 1997. *American Work Values: Their Origin and Development*. Albany: State University of New York Press.

Bezanson, Kate, and Meg Luxton, eds. 2006. *Social Reproduction: Feminist Political Economy Challenges Neo-Liberalism*. Montreal: McGill-Queen's University Press.

Blanchot, Maurice. 1986. "Marx's Three Voices." *New Political Science* 7 (1): 17–20.

Bloch, Ernst. 1970. *A Philosophy of the Future*. Translated by John Cumming. New York: Herder and Herder.

———. 1995. *The Principle of Hope*. 3 vols. Translated by Neville Plaice, Stephen Plaice, and Paul Knight. Cambridge: MIT Press.

Blum, Linda M. 1991. *Between Feminism and Labor: The Significance of the Comparable Worth Movement*. Berkeley: University of California Press.

Boggs, James. 1963. *The American Revolution: Pages from a Negro Worker's Notebook*. New York: Monthly Review Press.

Boris, Eileen. 1999. "When Work Is Slavery." In *Whose Welfare?*, edited by Gwendolyn Mink, 36–55. Ithaca: Cornell University Press.

Bourdieu, Pierre. 1998. "A Reasoned Utopia and Economic Fatalism." *New Left Review* 227:125–30.

Bowman, John R., and Alyson M. Cole. 2009. "Do Working Mothers Oppress Other Women? The Swedish 'Maid Debate' and the Welfare State Politics of Gender Equality." *Signs* 35 (1): 157–84.

Boydston, Jeanne. 1990. *Home and Work: Housework, Wages, and the Ideology of Labor in the Early Republic*. New York: Oxford University Press.

Brenner, Johanna. 2000. "Utopian Families." *Socialist Register* 36:133–44.

Broder, Sherri. 2002. *Tramps, Unfit Mothers, and Neglected Children: Negotiating the Family in Nineteenth Century Philadelphia*. Philadelphia: University of Pennsylvania Press.

Brody, Jennifer DeVere. 2008. *Punctuation: Art, Politics, and Play*. Durham: Duke University Press.

Brown, Wendy. 1995. *States of Injury: Power and Freedom in Late Modernity*. Princeton: Princeton University Press.

———. 1999. "Resisting Left Melancholy." *boundary 2* 26 (3): 19–27.

———. 2005. *Edgework: Critical Essays on Knowledge and Politics*. Princeton: Princeton University Press.

Bubeck, Diemut Elisabet. 1995. *Care, Gender, and Justice*. Oxford: Oxford University Press.

Bunting, Madeleine. 2004. *Willing Slaves: How the Overwork Culture Is Ruling Our Lives*. London: Harper Collins.

Burawoy, Michael. 1979. *Manufacturing Consent: Changes in the Labor Process under Monopoly Capitalism*. Chicago: University of Chicago Press.

Callaghan, George, and Paul Thompson. 2002. " 'We Recruit Attitude': The

Selection and Shaping of Routine Call Centre Labour." *Journal of Management Studies* 39 (2): 233–54.

Campaign for Wages for Housework. 2000. "Wages for Housework." In *Dear Sisters: Dispatches from the Women's Liberation Movement*, edited by Rosalyn Baxandall and Linda Gordon, 258. New York: Basic.

Carver, Terrell. 1998. *The Postmodern Marx*. University Park: Pennsylvania State University Press.

Casarino, Cesare, and Antonio Negri. 2008. *In Praise of the Common: A Conversation on Philosophy and Politics*. Minneapolis: University of Minnesota Press.

Casey, Catherine. 1995. *Work, Self and Society: After Industrialism*. London: Routledge.

Castells, Manuel. 2000. *The Rise of Network Society*. 2nd ed. Oxford: Blackwell.

Caws, Mary Ann. 2001. "The Poetics of the Manifesto: Nowness and Newness." In *Manifesto: A Century of Isms*, edited by Mary Ann Caws, xix–xxxi. Lincoln: University of Nebraska Press.

Chancer, Lynn. 1998. "Benefiting from Pragmatic Vision, Part I: The Case for Guaranteed Income in Principle." In *Post-Work: The Wages of Cybernation*, edited by Stanley Aronowitz and Jonathan Cutler, 81–127. New York: Routledge.

Christopherson, Susan. 1991. "Trading Time for Consumption: The Failure of Working-Hours Reduction in the United States." In *Working Time in Transition: The Political Economy of Working Hours in Industrial Nations*, edited by Karl Hinrichs, William Roche, and Carmen Sirianni, 171–97. Philadelphia: Temple University Press.

Cleaver, Harry. 1992. "The Inversion of Class Perspective in Marxian Theory: From Valorisation to Self-Valorisation." In *Open Marxism*, edited by Werner Bonefeld, Richard Gunn, and Kosmas Psychopedis, 2:106–44. London: Pluto.

——. 2000. *Reading Capital Politically*. 2nd ed. Leeds, England: Anti/Theses.

——. 2002. "Work Is *Still* the Central Issue! New Words for New Worlds." In *The Labour Debate: An Investigation into the Theory and Reality of Capitalist Work*, edited by Ana C. Dinerstein and Michael Neary, 135–48. Aldershot, England: Ashgate.

——. 2003. "Marxian Categories, the Crisis of Capital, and the Constitution of Social Subjectivity Today." In *Revolutionary Writing: Common Sense Essays in Post-Political Politics*, edited by Werner Bonefeld, 39–72. New York: Autonomedia.

Cobble, Dorothy Sue. 2004. *The Other Women's Movement: Workplace Justice and Social Rights in Modern America*. Princeton: Princeton University Press.

Collins, Patricia Hill. 1991. *Black Feminist Thought: Knowledge, Consciousness, and the Politics of Empowerment*. New York: Routledge.

Combahee River Collective. 1979. "A Black Feminist Statement." In *Capitalist Patriarchy and the Case for Socialist Feminism*, edited by Zillah Eisenstein, 362–72. New York: Monthly Review Press.

Corlett, William. 1998. *Class Action: Reading Labor, Theory, and Value*. Ithaca: Cornell University Press.

Cornell, Drucilla. 1998. *At the Heart of Freedom: Feminism, Sex, and Equality*. Princeton: Princeton University Press.

Costea, Bogdan, Norman Crump, and Kostas Amiridis. 2008. "Managerialism, the Therapeutic Habitus and the Self in Contemporary Organizing." *Human Relations* 61 (5): 661–85.

Cox, Nicole, and Silvia Federici. 1976. *Counter-Planning from the Kitchen: Wages for Housework, A Perspective on Capital and the Left*. Brooklyn, N.Y.: New York Wages for Housework Committee.

Cremin, Colin. 2010. "Never Employable Enough: The (Im)possibility of Satisfying the Boss's Desire." *Organization* 17 (2): 131–49.

Cutler, Jonathan, and Stanley Aronowitz. 1998. "Quitting Time: An Introduction." In *Post-Work: The Wages of Cybernation*, edited by Stanley Aronowitz and Jonathan Cutler, 1–30. New York: Routledge.

Dalla Costa, Mariarosa. 1975. "A General Strike." In *All Work and No Pay: Women, Housework, and the Wages Due*, edited by Wendy Edmond and Suzie Fleming, 125–27. Bristol, England: Falling Wall.

——. 1988. "Domestic Labour and the Feminist Movement in Italy since the 1970s." *International Sociology* 3 (1): 23–34.

——. 2002. "The Door to the Garden." Translated by Arianna Bove and Pier Paolo Frassinelli. http://www.generation-online.org/p/fpdallacosta1.htm.

Dalla Costa, Mariarosa, and Selma James. 1973. *The Power of Women and the Subversion of the Community*. 2nd ed. Bristol, England: Falling Wall.

De Angelis, Massimo. 1995. "Beyond the Technological and the Social Paradigms: A Political Reading of Abstract Labour as the Substance of Value." *Capital & Class* 57:107–34.

De Sario, Beppe. 2007. " 'Precari su Marte': An Experiment in Activism against Precarity." *Feminist Review* 87:21–39.

Del Re, Alisa. 1996. "Women and Welfare: Where is Jocasta?" Translated by Maurizia Boscagli. In *Radical Thought in Italy: A Potential Politics*, edited by Paolo Virno and Michael Hardt, 99–113. Minneapolis: University of Minnesota Press.

——. 2005. "Feminism and Autonomy: Itinerary of Struggle." Translated by Arianna Bove. In *The Philosophy of Antonio Negri*, vol. 1, *Resistance in Practice*, edited by Timothy S. Murphy and Abdul-Karim Mustapha, 48–72. London: Pluto.

Deleuze, Gilles. 1983. *Nietzsche and Philosophy*. Translated by Hugh Tomlinson. New York: Columbia University Press.

——. 1988. *Spinoza: Practical Philosophy*. Translated by Robert Hurley. San Francisco: City Light.

——. 1997. "Immanence: A Life. . . ." Translated by Nick Millett. *Theory, Culture & Society* 14 (2): 3–7.

D'Emilio, John, and Estelle B. Freedman. 1988. *Intimate Matters: A History of Sexuality in America*. New York: Harper and Row.

Denning, Michael. 2004. *Culture in the Age of Three Worlds*. London: Verso.

Disch, Lisa J., and Jean M. O'Brien. 2007. "Innovation Is Overtime: An Ethical Analysis of 'Politically Committed' Academic Labor." In *Feminist Waves, Feminist Generations: Life Stories from the Academy*, edited by Hokulani K. Aikau, Karla A. Erickson, and Jennifer L. Pierce, 140–67. Minneapolis: University of Minnesota Press.

Dyer-Witheford, Nick. 1999. *Cyber-Marx: Cycles and Circuits of Struggle in High-Technology Capitalism*. Urbana: University of Illinois Press.

Eagleton, Terry. 1999. "Utopia and Its Opposites." In *Necessary and Unnecessary Utopias*, edited by Leo Panitch and Colin Leys, 31–40. Rendlesham, England: Merlin.

Edelman, Lee. 2004. *No Future: Queer Theory and the Death Drive*. Durham: Duke University Press.

Edmond, Wendy, and Suzie Fleming. 1975. "If Women Were Paid for All They Do." In *All Work and No Pay: Women, Housework, and the Wages Due*, edited by Wendy Edmond and Suzie Fleming, 5–12. Bristol, England: Falling Wall.

Ehrenreich, Barbara. 1997. "What Is Socialist Feminism?" In *Materialist Feminism: A Reader in Class, Difference, and Women's Lives*, edited by Rosemary Hennessy and Chrys Ingraham, 65–70. New York: Routledge.

———. 2001. *Nickel and Dimed: On (Not) Getting By in America*. New York: Henry Holt.

Ehrenreich, Barbara, and Deirdre English. 1975. "The Manufacture of Housework." *Socialist Revolution* 26:5–40.

Eisenberger, Robert. 1989. *Blue Monday: The Loss of the Work Ethic in America*. New York: Paragon.

Eisenstein, Zillah. 1979. "Developing a Theory of Capitalist Patriarchy and Socialist Feminism." In *Capitalist Patriarchy and the Case for Socialist Feminism*, edited by Zillah Eisenstein, 5–40. New York: Monthly Review Press.

———. 1981. *The Radical Future of Liberal Feminism*. New York: Longman.

Elson, Diane. 1979. "The Value Theory of Labour." In *Value: The Representation of Labour in Capitalism*, edited by Diane Elson, 115–80. Atlantic Highlands, N.J.: Humanities Press.

English, Deirdre, Barbara Epstein, Barbara Haber, and Judy MacLean. 1985. "The Impasse of Socialist-Feminism: A Conversation." *Socialist Review* 79:93–110.

Fagan, Colette. 1996. "Gendered Time Schedules: Paid Work in Great Britain." *Social Politics* 3 (1): 72–106.

Federici, Silvia. 1995. "Wages against Housework." In *The Politics of Housework*, new ed., edited by Ellen Malos, 187–94. Cheltenham, England: New Clarion.

Feminist Review Collective. 1986. "Editorial." In "Socialist-Feminism: Out of the Blue." Special issue, *Feminist Review* 23 (1): 3–10.

Feminists. 1973. "The Feminists: A Political Organization to Annihilate Sex Roles." In *Radical Feminism*, edited by Anne Koedt, Ellen Levine, and Anita Rapone, 368–78. New York: Quadrangle.

Firestone, Shulamith. 1970. *The Dialectic of Sex: The Case for Feminist Revolution*. New York: Farrar, Straus and Giroux.

Fitting, Peter. 1987. "Positioning and Closure: On the 'Reading-Effect' of Contemporary Utopian Fiction." In *Utopian Studies 1*, edited by Gorman Beauchamp, Kenneth Roemer, and Nicholas D. Smith, 23–36. Lanham, Md.: University Press of America.

——. 1990. "The Turn from Utopia in Recent Feminist Fiction." In *Feminism, Utopia, and Narrative*, edited by Libby Falk Jones and Sarah Webster Goodwin, 141–58. Knoxville: University of Tennessee Press.

Fleming, Peter. 2009. *Authenticity and the Cultural Politics of Work: New Forms of Informal Control.* Oxford: Oxford University Press.

Fleming, Suzie. 1975. "Family Allowance: The Woman's Money." In *All Work and No Pay: Women, Housework, and the Wages Due*, edited by Wendy Edmond and Suzie Fleming, 89–92. Bristol, England: Falling Wall.

Folbre, Nancy. 2001. *The Invisible Heart: Economics and Family Values.* New York: New Press.

Fortunati, Polda. 1975. "The Housewife." In *All Work and No Pay: Women, Housework, and the Wages Due*, edited by Wendy Edmond and Suzie Fleming, 13–19. Bristol, England: Falling Wall.

Foucault, Michel. 1977. *Language, Counter-Memory, Practice: Selected Essays and Interviews.* Translated by Donald F. Bouchard and Sherry Simon. Ithaca: Cornell University Press.

——. 1979. *Discipline and Punish: The Birth of the Prison.* Translated by Alan Sheridan. New York: Vintage.

——. 1983. "The Subject and Power." In Hubert L. Dreyfus and Paul Rabinow, *Michel Foucault: Beyond Structuralism and Hermeneutics*, with an afterword by Michel Foucault, 2nd ed., 208–26. Chicago: University of Chicago Press.

——. 2003. *'Society Must be Defended': Lectures at the Collège de France, 1975–76.* Translated by David Macey. New York: Picador.

Fraser, Nancy, and Linda Gordon. 1994. "A Genealogy of 'Dependency': Tracing a Keyword of the U.S. Welfare State." *Signs* 19 (2): 309–36.

Freedman, Carl. 2001. "Science Fiction and Utopia: A Historico-Philosophical Overview." In *Learning from Other Worlds: Estrangement, Cognition, and the Politics of Science Fiction and Utopia*, edited by Patrick Parrinder, 72–97. Durham: Duke University Press.

Freeman, Carla. 2000. *High Tech and High Heels in the Global Economy: Women, Work, and Pink-Collar Identities in the Caribbean.* Durham: Duke University Press.

Freeman, Caroline. 1995. "When Is a Wage Not a Wage?" In *The Politics of Housework*, new ed., edited by Ellen Malos, 142–48. Cheltenham, England: New Clarion.

Freud, Sigmund. 1957. "Mourning and Melancholia." In Sigmund Freud, *The Standard Edition of the Complete Psychological Works of Sigmund Freud*, 14:243–58, translated by James Strachey. London: Hogarth.

Friedan, Betty. 1963. *The Feminine Mystique.* New York: W. W. Norton.

———. 1997. *Beyond Gender: The New Politics of Work and Family*. Edited by Brigid O'Farrell. Washington: Woodrow Wilson Center.

Froines, Ann. 1992. "Renewing Socialist Feminism." *Socialist Review* 22 (2): 125–31.

Fromm, Erich. 1961. *Marx's Concept of Man*. New York: Frederick Ungar.

Fukuyama, Francis. 1989. "The End of History?" *National Interest* 16 (summer): 3–18.

Genovese, Eugene D. 1974. *Roll, Jordan, Roll: The World the Slaves Made*. New York: Pantheon.

Geoghegan, Vincent. 1987. *Utopianism and Marxism*. New York: Methuen.

Gheaus, Anca. 2008. "Basic Income, Gender Justice and the Costs of Gender-Symmetrical Lifestyles." *Basic Income Studies* 3 (3): 1–8.

Gilman, Charlotte Perkins. 1992. *Herland and Selected Stories*. New York: Penguin.

———. 2002. *The Home, Its Work and Influence*. Walnut Creek, Calif.: AltaMira Press.

Gini, Al. 2000. *My Job, Myself: Work and the Creation of the Modern Individual*. New York: Routledge.

Glazer, Nona Y. 1993. *Women's Paid and Unpaid Labor: The Work Transfer in Health Care and Retailing*. Philadelphia: Temple University Press.

Glenn, Evelyn Nakano. 1999. "The Social Construction and Institutionalization of Gender and Race: An Integrative Framework." In *Revisioning Gender*, edited by Myra Marx Ferree, Judith Lorber, and Beth B. Hess, 3–43. Thousand Oaks, Calif.: Sage.

Goodwin, Sarah Webster. 1990. "Knowing Better: Feminism and Utopian Discourse in *Pride and Prejudice*, *Villette*, and 'Babette's Feast.'" In *Feminism, Utopia, and Narrative*, edited by Libby Falk Jones and Sarah Webster Goodwin, 1–20. Knoxville: University of Tennessee Press.

Gordon, Linda. 1992. "Family Violence, Feminism, and Social Control." In *Rethinking the Family: Some Feminist Questions*, rev. ed., edited by Barrie Thorne with Marilyn Yalom, 262–86. Boston: Northeastern University Press.

Gorz, André. 1999. *Reclaiming Work: Beyond the Wage-Based Society*. Translated by Chris Turner. Cambridge: Polity.

Gray, Anne. 2004. *Unsocial Europe: Social Protection or Flexploitation?* London: Pluto.

Greenwood, Ernest. 1966. "The Elements of Professionalization." In *Professionalization*, edited by Howard M. Vollmer and Donald L. Mills, 9–19. Englewood Cliffs, N.J.: Prentice-Hall.

Gutman, Herbert G. 1977. *Work, Culture, and Society in Industrializing America*. New York: Vintage.

Halberstam, Judith. 2005. *In a Queer Time and Place: Transgender Bodies, Subcultural Lives*. New York: New York University Press.

Haraway, Donna. 1985. "A Manifesto for Cyborgs: Science, Technology, and Socialist Feminism in the 1980s." *Socialist Review* 80:65–107.

Hardt, Michael, and Antonio Negri. 2000. *Empire*. Cambridge: Harvard University Press.

———. 2009. *Commonwealth*. Cambridge: Harvard University Press.

Hartsock, Nancy C. M. 1983. *Money, Sex, and Power: Toward a Feminist Historical Materialism*. Boston: Northeastern University Press.

Hays, Sharon. 1996. *The Cultural Contradictions of Motherhood*. New Haven: Yale University Press.

———. 1998. "Reconsidering the 'Choice': Do Americans Really Prefer the Workplace over the Home?" *Contemporary Sociology* 27 (1): 28–32.

———. 2003. *Flat Broke with Children: Women in the Age of Welfare Reform*. Oxford: Oxford University Press.

Hemmings, Clare. 2005. "Telling Feminist Stories." *Feminist Theory* 6 (2): 115–39.

Hennessy, Rosemary. 2000. *Profit and Pleasure: Sexual Identities in Late Capitalism*. New York: Routledge.

Henwood, Doug. 1997. "Talking about Work." *Monthly Review* 49 (3): 18–30.

Higbie, Toby. 1997. "Crossing Class Boundaries: Tramp Ethnographers and Narratives of Class in Progressive Era America." *Social Science History* 21 (4): 559–92.

Higgins, Kathleen Marie. 1987. *Nietzsche's Zarathustra*. Philadelphia: Temple University Press.

Hochschild, Arlie. 1983. *The Managed Heart: Commercialization of Human Feeling*. Berkeley: University of California Press.

———. 1989. *The Second Shift: Working Parents and the Revolution at Home*. New York: Viking.

———. 1997. *The Time Bind: When Work Becomes Home and Home Becomes Work*. New York: Metropolitan.

Hunnicutt, Benjamin Kline. 1988. *Work without End: Abandoning Shorter Hours for the Right to Work*. Philadelphia: Temple University Press.

———. 1996. *Kellogg's Six-Hour Day*. Philadelphia: Temple University Press.

Huntington, Samuel P. 1996. *The Clash of Civilizations and the Remaking of the World Order*. New York: Simon and Schuster.

Illich, Ivan. 1978. *The Right to Useful Unemployment and Its Professional Enemies*. London: Marion Boyars.

Jacobs, Jerry A., and Kathleen Gerson. 2004. *The Time Divide: Work, Family, and Gender Inequality*. Cambridge: Harvard University Press.

Jaggar, Alison M. 1983. *Feminist Politics and Human Nature*. Totowa, N.J.: Rowman and Allanheld.

James, Selma. 1975. *Sex, Race and Class*. Bristol, England: Falling Wall.

———. 1976. *Women, the Unions, and Work; Or . . . What Is Not to Be Done and the Perspective of Winning*. Bristol, England: Falling Wall.

———. 1985. *Strangers and Sisters: Women, Race and Immigration*. Bristol, England: Falling Wall.

Jameson, Fredric. 1971. *Marxism and Form*. Princeton: Princeton University Press.

———. 1973. "The Vanishing Mediator: Narrative Structure in Max Weber." *New German Critique* 1:52–89.

———. 1977. "Of Islands and Trenches: Neutralization and the Production of Utopian Discourse." *Diacritics* 7 (2): 2–21.

——. 1982. "Progress versus Utopia: or, Can We Imagine the Future?" *Science Fiction Studies* 9 (2): 147–58.

——. 1991. *Postmodernism, or, The Cultural Logic of Late Capitalism*. Durham: Duke University Press.

——. 1994. *The Seeds of Time*. New York: Columbia University Press.

——. 2001. " 'If I Find One Good City I Will Spare the Man': Realism and Utopia in Kim Stanley Robinson's Mars Trilogy." In *Learning from Other Worlds: Estrangement, Cognition, and the Politics of Science Fiction and Utopia*, edited by Patrick Parrinder, 208–32. Durham: Duke University Press.

——. 2005. *Archaeologies of the Future: The Desire Called Utopia and Other Science Fictions*. New York: Verso.

Jardine, Alice, and Brian Massumi. 2000. "Interview with Toni Negri." *Copyright* 1:74–89.

Jenness, Valerie. 1993. *Making It Work: The Prostitutes' Rights Movement in Perspective*. New York: Aldine De Gruyter.

Joreen. 1973. "The BITCH Manifesto." In *Radical Feminism*, edited by Anne Koedt, Ellen Levine, and Anita Rapone, 50–59. New York: Quadrangle.

Kelley, Robin D. G. 1994. *Race Rebels: Culture, Politics, and the Black Working Class*. New York: Free Press.

——. 2002. *Freedom Dreams: The Black Radical Imagination*. Boston: Beacon.

Kelliher, Clare, and Deirdre Anderson. 2010. "Doing More with Less? Flexible Working Practices and the Intensification of Work." *Human Relations* 63 (1): 83–106.

Kessler-Harris, Alice. 1990. *A Woman's Wage: Historical Meanings and Social Consequences*. Lexington: University Press of Kentucky.

Kitch, Sally L. 2000. *Higher Ground: From Utopianism to Realism in American Feminist Thought and Theory*. Chicago: University of Chicago Press.

Kolakowski, Leszek. 1978. *Main Currents of Marxism: Its Rise, Growth, and Dissolution*. Vol. 2. Translated by P. S. Falla. Oxford: Clarendon Press of Oxford University Press.

Kornbluh, Felicia. 1997. "To Fulfill their 'Rightly Needs': Consumerism and the National Welfare Rights Movement." *Radical History* 69:76–113.

Lafargue, Paul. 1898. *The Right to Be Lazy: Being a Refutation of the "Right to Work" of 1848*. Translated by Harriet E. Lothrop. New York: International Publishing.

Laslett, Barbara, and Johanna Brenner. 1989. "Gender and Social Reproduction: Historical Perspectives." *Annual Review of Sociology* 15:381–404.

Lazzarato, Maurizio. 1996. "Immaterial Labor." In *Radical Thought in Italy: A Potential Politics*, edited by Paolo Virno and Michael Hardt, 133–47. Minneapolis: University of Minnesota Press.

Lebowitz, Michael A. 1992. *Beyond Capital: Marx's Political Economy of the Working Class*. New York: St. Martin's.

Lehr, Valerie. 1999. *Queer Family Values: Debunking the Myth of the Nuclear Family*. Philadelphia: Temple University Press.

Leidner, Robin. 1993. *Fast Food, Fast Talk: Service Work and the Routinization of Everyday Life*. Berkeley: University of California Press.

———. 1996. "Rethinking Questions of Control: Lessons from McDonald's." In *Working in the Service Society*, edited by Cameron Lynne Macdonald and Carmen Sirianni, 29–49. Philadelphia: Temple University Press.

———. 2006. "Identity at Work." In *Social Theory at Work*, edited by Marek Korczynski, Randy Hodson, and Paul Edwards, 424–63. Oxford: Oxford University Press.

Leigh, Carol. 1997. "Inventing Sex Work." In *Whores and Other Feminists*, edited by Jill Nagle, 225–31. New York: Routledge.

Lenin, V. I. 1989. "The Immediate Tasks of the Soviet Government." In V. I. Lenin, *Lenin's Economic Writings*, edited by Meghnad Desai, 221–59. Atlantic Highlands, N.J.: Humanities Press International.

Levitas, Ruth. 1990. *The Concept of Utopia*. London: Philip Allan.

———. 1997. "Educated Hope: Ernst Bloch on Abstract and Concrete Utopia." In *Not Yet: Reconsidering Ernst Bloch*, edited by Jamie Owen Daniel and Tom Moylan, 65–79. London: Verso.

Linder, Marc. 2004. *"Time and a Half's the American Way": A History of the Exclusion of White-Collar Workers from Overtime Regulations, 1868–2004*. Iowa City: Fānpìhuà.

Lipset, Seymour Martin. 1992. "The Work Ethic, Then and Now." *Journal of Labor Research* 13 (1): 45–54.

Locke, John. 1986. *The Second Treatise on Civil Government*. Amherst, N.Y.: Prometheus.

Logan, Shirley Wilson. 2002. " 'What Are We Worth': Anna Julia Cooper Defines Black Women's Work at the Dawn of the Twentieth Century." In *Sister Circle: Black Women and Work*, edited by Sharon Harly and the Black Women and Work Collective, 146–63. New Brunswick, N.J.: Rutgers University Press.

López, Maria Milagros. 1994. "Post-Work Selves and Entitlement 'Attitudes' in Peripheral Postindustrial Puerto Rico." *Social Text* 38:111–33.

Los Angeles Wages for Housework Committee. 1975. "Sisters Why March?" In *All Work and No Pay: Women, Housework, and the Wages Due*, edited by Wendy Edmond and Suzie Fleming, 123–24. Bristol, England: Falling Wall.

Luttrell, Wendy. 1984. "Beyond the Politics of Victimization." *Socialist Review* 73:42–47.

Luxton, Meg. 1987. "Time for Myself: Women's Work and the 'Fight for Shorter Hours.' " In *Feminism and Political Economy: Women's Work, Women's Struggles*, edited by Heather Jon Maroney and Meg Luxton, 167–78. Toronto: Methuen.

Luxton, Meg, and June Corman. 2001. *Getting By in Hard Times: Gendered Labour at Home and on the Job*. Toronto: University of Toronto Press.

Lyon, Janet. 1991a. *Manifestoes: Provocations of the Modern*. Ithaca: Cornell University Press.

———. 1991b. "Transforming Manifestoes: A Second-Wave Problematic." *Yale Journal of Criticism* 5 (1): 101–27.

Macarov, David. 1980. *Work and Welfare: The Unholy Alliance*. Beverly Hills: Sage.

Macdonald, Cameron Lynne, and Carmen Sirianni. 1996. "The Service Society and the Changing Experience of Work." In *Working in the Service Society*, edited by Cameron Lynne Macdonald and Carmen Sirianni, 1–26. Philadelphia: Temple University Press.

Malos, Ellen. 1995a. Introduction. In *The Politics of Housework*, new ed., edited by Ellen Malos, 1–33. Cheltenham, England: New Clarion.

———. 1995b. "The Politics of Household Labour in the 1990s: Old Debates, New Contexts." In *The Politics of Housework*, new ed., edited by Ellen Malos, 206–17. Cheltenham, England: New Clarion.

———, ed. 1995c. *The Politics of Housework*. Cheltenham, England: New Clarion.

Marx, Karl. 1964. *The Economic and Philosophic Manuscripts of 1844*. Translated by Martin Milligan. New York: International Publishers.

———. 1973. *Grundrisse: Foundations of the Critique of Political Economy*. Translated by Martin Nicolaus. New York: Vintage.

———. 1976. *Capital: A Critique of Political Economy*. Vol. 1. Translated by Ben Fowkes. New York: Vintage.

———. 1978. "Critique of the Gotha Program." In *The Marx-Engels Reader*, 2nd ed., edited by Robert C. Tucker, 525–41. New York: W. W. Norton.

———. 1981. *Capital: A Critique of Political Economy*. Vol. 3. Translated by David Fernbach. London: Penguin.

Marx, Karl, and Friedrich Engels. 1970. *The German Ideology, Part One*. Edited by C. J. Arthur. New York: International Publishers.

———. 1992. *The Communist Manifesto*. Edited and with an introduction by David McLellan. Oxford: Oxford University Press.

Massumi, Brian. 1995. "The Autonomy of Affect." *Cultural Critique* 31:83–109.

Mathers, Andy. 1999. "Euromarch—the Struggle for a Social Europe." *Capital & Class* 68:15—19.

May, Martha. 1987. "The Historical Problem of the Family Wage: The Ford Motor Company and the Five Dollar Day." In *Families and Work*, edited by Naomi Gerstel and Harriet Engel Gross, 111–31. Philadelphia: Temple University Press.

McArdle, Louise, et al. 1995. "Total Quality Management and Participation: Employee Empowerment or the Enhancement of Exploitation?" In *Making Quality Critical: New Perspectives on Organizational Change*, edited by Adrian Wilkinson and Hugh Willmott, 156–72. London: Routledge.

McGregor, Douglas. 1960. *The Human Side of Enterprise*. New York: McGraw-Hill.

McKay, Ailsa. 2001. "Rethinking Work and Income Maintenance Policy: Promoting Gender Equality through a Citizens' Basic Income." *Feminist Economics* 7 (1): 97–118.

McKay, Ailsa, and Jo Vanevery. 2000. "Gender, Family, and Income Maintenance: A Feminist Case for Citizens Basic Income." *Social Politics* 7 (2): 266–84.

McKenna, Erin. 2001. *The Task of Utopia: A Pragmatist and Feminist Perspective*. Lanham, Md.: Rowman and Littlefield.

McLellan, David. 1969. "Marx's View of Unalienated Society." *Review of Politics* 31 (4): 459–65.

Meagher, Gabrielle. 2002. "Is It Wrong to Pay for Housework?" *Hypatia* 17 (2): 52–66.

Mies, Maria. 1986. *Patriarchy and Accumulation on a World Scale: Women in the International Division of Labour.* London: Zed.

Mill, John Stuart. 1986. *On Liberty.* Amherst, N.Y.: Prometheus.

———. 1988. *The Subjection of Women.* Indianapolis: Hackett.

Miller, Walter James. 2000. "The Future of Futurism: An Introduction to *Looking Backward.*" In *Looking Backward, 2000–1887,* edited by Edward Bellamy, v–xiii. New York: Penguin.

Mills, C. Wright. 1951. *White Collar: The American Middle Classes.* New York: Oxford University Press.

Mills, Jane. 1989. *Womanwords: A Dictionary of Words about Women.* New York: Free Press.

Mink, Gwendolyn. 1998. *Welfare's End.* Ithaca: Cornell University Press.

Molyneux, Maxine. 1979. "Beyond the Domestic Labour Debate." *New Left Review* 116:3–27.

Morris, William. 1999. "Useful Work Versus Useless Toil." In William Morris, *William Morris on Art and Socialism,* edited by Norman Kelvin, 128–43. Mineola, N.Y.: Dover.

Moylan, Tom. 1986. *Demand the Impossible: Science Fiction and the Utopian Imagination.* New York: Methuen.

———. 1997. "Bloch against Bloch: The Theological Reception of *Das Prinzip Hoffnung* and the Liberation of the Utopian Function." In *Not Yet: Reconsidering Ernst Bloch,* edited by Jamie Owen Daniel and Tom Moylan, 96–121. London: Verso.

———. 2000. *Scraps of the Untainted Sky: Science Fiction, Utopia, Dystopia.* Boulder, Colo.: Westview.

Muirhead, Russell. 2004. *Just Work.* Cambridge: Harvard University Press.

Muñoz, José Esteban. 2007. "Queerness as Horizon: Utopian Hermeneutics in the Face of Gay Pragmatism." In *A Companion to Lesbian, Gay, Bisexual, Transgender, and Queer Studies,* edited by George E. Haggerty and Molly McGarry, 452–63. Malden, Mass.: Blackwell.

Nadasen, Premilla. 2002. "Expanding the Boundaries of the Women's Movement: Black Feminism and the Struggle for Welfare Rights." *Feminist Studies* 28 (2): 271–301.

Negri, Antonio. 1988. *Revolution Retrieved: Writings on Marx, Keynes, Capitalist Crisis and New Social Subjects (1967–83).* Translated by the Red Notes Collective. London: Red Notes.

———. 1991. *Marx Beyond Marx: Lessons on the* Grundrisse. Translated by Harry Cleaver, Michael Ryan, and Maurizio Viano. Brooklyn, N.Y.: Autonomedia.

———. 1996. "Twenty Theses on Marx: Interpretation of the Class Situation Today." Translated by Michael Hardt. In *Marxism beyond Marxism,* edited by Saree Makdisi, Cesare Casarino, and Rebecca E. Karl, 149–80. New York: Routledge.

———. 2005. *Books for Burning: Between Civil War and Democracy in 1970s Italy*. Translated by Timothy S. Murphy, Arianna Bove, Ed Emory, and Francesca Novello. New York: Verso.

Neubeck, Kenneth J., and Noel A. Cazenave. 2001. *Welfare Racism: Playing the Race Card against America's Poor*. New York: Routledge.

Nietzsche, Friedrich. 1966. *Beyond Good and Evil*. Translated by Walter Kaufmann. New York: Vintage.

———. 1967. *On The Genealogy of Morals*. Translated by Walter Kaufmann. New York: Vintage.

———. 1968. *The Will to Power*. Translated by Walter Kaufmann and R. J. Hollingdale. New York: Vintage.

———. 1969. *Thus Spoke Zarathustra*. Translated by R. J. Hollingdale. New York: Penguin.

———. 1974. *The Gay Science*. Translated by Walter Kaufmann. New York: Vintage.

Noddings, Nel. 1984. *Caring: A Feminine Approach to Ethics and Moral Education*. Berkeley: University of California Press.

Offe, Claus. 2008. "Basic Income and the Labor Contract." *Basic Income Studies* 3 (1): 1–30 (http://www.bepress.com/bis/vol3/iss1/art4).

Parker, Mike, and Jane Slaughter. 1988. *Choosing Sides: Unions and the Team Concept*. Boston: South End.

Pateman, Carole. 1988. *The Sexual Contract*. Stanford: Stanford University Press.

———. 2003. "Freedom and Democratization: Why Basic Income Is to Be Preferred to Basic Capital." In *The Ethics of Stakeholding*, edited by Keith Dowding, Jurgen De Wispelaere, and Stuart White, 130–48. London: Palgrave Macmillan.

———. 2006. "Democratizing Citizenship: Some Advantages of a Basic Income." In *Redesigning Distribution: Basic Income and Stakeholder Grants as Alternative Cornerstones for a More Egalitarian Capitalism*, edited by Bruce Ackerman, Anne Alstott, and Philippe van Parijs, 101–19. London: Verso.

Pearce, Kimber Charles. 1999. "The Radical Feminist Manifesto as Generic Appropriation: Gender, Genre, and Second Wave Resistance." *Southern Communication Journal* 64 (4): 307–15.

Peters, Tom. 1997. "The Brand Called You." *Fast Company* 10:83–94.

Peterson, Spike V. 2003. *A Critical Rewriting of Global Political Economy: Integrating Reproductive, Productive and Virtual Economies*. New York: Routledge.

Pfaelzer, Jean. 1990. "Response: What Happened to History?" In *Feminism, Utopia, and Narrative*, edited by Libby Falk Jones and Sarah Webster Goodwin, 191–200. Knoxville: University of Tennessee Press.

Popper, Karl. 1947–48. "Utopia and Violence." *Hibbert Journal* 46:109–116.

———. 1950. *The Open Society and Its Enemies*. Rev. ed. Princeton: Princeton University Press.

Postone, Moishe. 1996. *Time, Labor, and Social Domination: A Reinterpretation of Marx's Critical Theory*. Cambridge: Cambridge University Press.

Power of Women Collective. 1975. "The Home in the Hospital." In *All Work and No*

Pay: Women, Housework, and the Wages Due, edited by Wendy Edmond and Suzie Fleming, 69–88. Bristol, England: Falling Wall.

Precarias a la Deriva. 2006. "A Very Careful Strike—Four Hypotheses." *Commoner* 11:33–45.

Puchner, Martin. 2006. *Poetry of the Revolution: Marx, Manifestos, and the Avant-Gardes*. Princeton: Princeton University Press.

Rajchman, John. 2001. Introduction. In Gilles Deleuze, *Pure Immanence: Essays on A Life*, translated by Anne Boyman, 7–23. New York: Zone.

Raventós, Daniel. 2007. *Basic Income: The Material Conditions of Freedom*. Translated by Julie Wark. London: Pluto.

Read, Jason. 2003. *The Micro-Politics of Capital: Marx and the Prehistory of the Present*. Albany: State University of New York Press.

Rinehart, James. 2001. "Transcending Taylorism and Fordism? Three Decades of Work Restructuring." In *The Critical Study of Work: Labor, Technology, and Global Production*, edited by Rick Baldoz, Charles Koeber, and Philip Kraft, 179–95. Philadelphia: Temple University Press.

Robeyns, Ingrid. 2001. "An Income of One's Own: A Radical Vision of Welfare Policies in Europe and Beyond." *Gender and Development* 9 (1): 82–89.

Robin, Corey. 2004. *Fear: The History of a Political Idea*. Oxford: Oxford University Press.

Robinson, Randall. 2000. *The Debt: What America Owes to Blacks*. New York: Penguin.

Rodgers, Daniel T. 1978. *The Work Ethic in Industrial America: 1850–1920*. Chicago: University of Chicago Press.

Roediger, David R. 1991. *The Wages of Whiteness: Race and the Making of the American Working Class*. London: Verso.

Roediger, David R., and Philip S. Foner. 1989. *Our Own Time: A History of American Labor and the Working Day*. London: Verso.

Roof, Judith. 1997. "Generational Difficulties; or, The Fear of a Barren History." In *Generations: Academic Feminists in Dialogue*, edited by Devoney Looser and E. Ann Kaplan, 69–87. Minneapolis: University of Minnesota Press.

Roschelle, Anne R. 1999. "Gender, Family Structure, and Social Structure: Racial Ethnic Families in the United States." In *Revisioning Gender*, edited by Myra Marx Ferree, Judith Lorber, and Beth B. Hess, 311–40. Thousand Oaks, Calif.: Sage.

Rose, Hilary. 1988. "Dreaming the Future." *Hypatia* 3 (1): 119–37.

Rose, Michael. 1985. *Re-Working the Work Ethic*. London: Batsford.

Ross, Andrew. 2003. *No-Collar: The Humane Workplace and Its Hidden Costs*. New York: Basic.

Rousseau, Jean-Jacques. 1988. "On Social Contract." In Jean-Jacques Rousseau, *Rousseau's Political Writings: New Translations, Interpretive Notes, Backgrounds, Commentaries*, edited by Alan Ritter and Julia Conway Bondanella, and translated by Julia Conaway Bondanella, 84–173. New York: W. W. Norton.

Rowbotham, Sheila, Lynne Segal, and Hilary Wainwright. 1979. *Beyond the Fragments: Feminism and the Making of Socialism*. London: Merlin.

Russ, Joanna. 1981. "Recent Feminist Utopias." In *Future Females: A Critical Anthology*, edited by Marlene S. Barr, 71–85. Bowling Green, Ohio: Bowling Green State University Press.

Salzinger, Leslie. 2003. *Genders in Production: Making Workers in Mexico's Global Factories*. Berkeley: University of California Press.

Sandoval, Chela. 2000. *Methodology of the Oppressed*. Minneapolis: University of Minnesota Press.

Sargent, Lyman Tower. 1994. "The Three Faces of Utopianism Revisited." *Utopian Studies* 5 (1): 1–37.

Scheman, Naomi. 2001. "Non-Negotiable Demands: Metaphysics, Politics, and the Discourse of Needs." In *Future Pasts: The Analytic Tradition in Twentieth-Century Philosophy*, edited by Juliet Floyd and Sanford Shieh, 315–37. Oxford: Oxford University Press.

Schleuning, Neala. 1990. *Idle Hands and Empty Hearts: Work and Freedom in the United States*. New York: Bergen and Garvey.

Schor, Juliet. 1997. "Utopias of Women's Time." In *Feminist Utopias in a Postmodern Era*, edited by Alkeline van Lenning, Marrie Bekker, and Ine Vanwesenbeeck, 45–53. Tilburg, the Netherlands: Tilburg University Press.

Schultz, Vicki, and Allison Hoffman. 2006. "The Need for a Reduced Workweek in the United States." In *Precarious Work, Women, and the New Economy: The Challenge to Legal Norms*, edited by Judy Fudge and Rosemary Owens, 131–51. Portland, Ore.: Hart.

Seidman, Michael. 1991. *Workers against Work: Labor in Paris and Barcelona during the Popular Fronts*. Berkeley: University of California Press.

Shaiken, Harley, Stephen Herzenberg, and Sarah Kuhn. 1986. "The Work Process under More Flexible Production." *Industrial Relations* 25 (2): 167–83.

Sirianni, Carmen, and Cynthia Negrey. 2000. "Working Time as Gendered Time." *Feminist Economics* 6 (1): 59–76.

Smith, Dorothy E. 1987. *The Everyday World as Problematic: A Feminist Sociology*. Boston: Northeastern University Press.

Smith, Paul. 1978. "Domestic Labour and Marx's Theory of Value." In *Feminism and Materialism: Women and Modes of Production*, edited by Annette Kuhn and AnnMarie Wolpe, 198–219. London: Routledge and K. Paul.

Solanas, Valerie. 1991. *The SCUM Manifesto*. London: Phoenix.

Somigli, Luca. 2003. *Legitimizing the Artist: Manifesto Writing and European Modernism, 1885–1915*. Toronto: University of Toronto Press.

Spivak, Gayatri Chakravorty. 2000. "From Haverstock Hill Flat to U.S. Classroom, What's Left of Theory?" In *What's Left of Theory? New Work on the Politics of Literary Theory*, edited by Judith Butler, John Guillory, and Kendall Thomas, 1–39. New York: Routledge.

Stacey, Judith. 1996. *In the Name of the Family: Rethinking Family Values in the Postmodern Age*. Boston: Beacon.

Steensland, Brian. 2008. *The Failed Welfare Revolution: America's Struggle over Guaranteed Income Policy*. Princeton: Princeton University Press.

Stillman, Peter G. 2001. "'Nothing Is, But What Is Not': Utopias as Practical Political Philosophy." In *The Philosophy of Utopia*, edited by Barbara Goodwin, 9–24. London: Frank Cass.

Storey, John. 1989. "Introduction: From Personnel Management to Human Resource Management." In *New Perspectives on Human Resource Management*, edited by John Storey, 1–18. London: Routledge.

Strauss, George. 1992. "Human Resource Management in the USA." In *The Handbook of Human Resource Management*, edited by Brian Towers, 27–48. Oxford: Blackwell.

Suvin, Darko.1972. "On the Poetics of the Science Fiction Genre." *College English* 34 (3): 372–82.

Talwar, Jennifer Parker. 2002. *Fast Food, Fast Track: Immigrants, Big Business, and the American Dream*. Boulder, Colo.: Westview.

Taplin, Ian M. 1995. "Flexible Production, Rigid Jobs: Lessons from the Clothing Industry." *Work and Occupations* 22 (4): 412–38.

Tari, Marcello, and Ilaria Vanni. 2005. "On the Life and Deeds of San Precario, Patron Saint of Precarious Workers and Lives." *Fibreculture*, no. 5 (http://journal.fibreculture.org/issue5/vanni_tari.html).

Taylor, Barbara. 1983. *Eve and the New Jerusalem: Socialism and Feminism in the Nineteenth Century*. New York: Pantheon.

Theobald, Robert. 1966. Preface. In *The Guaranteed Income: Next Step in Economic Evolution?*, edited by Robert Theobald, 15–25. New York: Doubleday.

Thompson, E. P. 1976. "Romanticism, Moralism and Utopianism: The Case of William Morris." *New Left Review* 99:83–111.

———. 1991. "Time, Work-Discipline and Industrial Capitalism." In E. P. Thompson, *Customs in Common*, 352–403. London: Merlin.

Townley, Barbara. 1989. "Selection and Appraisal: Reconstituting 'Social Relations'?" In *New Perspectives on Human Resource Management*, edited by John Storey, 92–108. London: Routledge.

Tronti, Mario. 1980. "The Strategy of Refusal." *Semiotext(e)* 3 (3): 28–35.

Tronto, Joan C. 1993. *Moral Boundaries: A Political Argument for an Ethic of Care*. New York: Routledge.

Trott, Ben. 2007. "Walking in the Right Direction?" *Turbulence* 1:14–15.

Tyler, Gus. 1983. "The Work Ethic: A Union View." In *The Work Ethic—A Critical Analysis*, edited by Jack Barbash, Robert J. Lampman, Sar A. Levitan, and Gus Tyler, 197–210. Madison, Wis.: Industrial Relations Research Association.

Van Parijs, Philippe. 1992. "Competing Justification of Basic Income." In *Arguing for Basic Income: Ethical Foundations for a Radical Reform*, edited by Philippe van Parijs, 3–43. London: Verso.

Van Parijs, Philippe, et al. 2001. *What's Wrong with a Free Lunch?* Edited by Joshua Cohen and Joel Rogers. Boston: Beacon.

Vercellone, Carlo. 1996. "The Anomaly and Exemplariness of the Italian Welfare State." Translated by Michael Hardt. In *Radical Thought in Italy: A Potential*

Politics, edited by Paolo Virno and Michael Hardt, 81–96. Minneapolis: University of Minnesota Press.

Vincent, Jean-Marie. 1991. *Abstract Labour: A Critique*. Translated by Jim Cohen. New York: St. Martin's.

Virno, Paolo. 1996. "Virtuosity and Revolution: The Political Theory of Exodus." Translated by Ed Emory. In *Radical Thought in Italy: A Potential Politics*, edited by Paolo Virno and Michael Hardt, 189–210. Minneapolis: University of Minnesota Press.

———. 2004. *A Grammar of the Multitude*. Translated by Isabella Bertoletti, James Cascaito, and Andrea Casson. Los Angeles: Semiotext(e).

Virno, Paolo, and Michael Hardt. 1996. "Glossary of Concepts." In *Radical Thought in Italy: A Potential Politics*, edited by Paolo Virno and Michael Hardt, 261–64. Minneapolis: University of Minnesota Press.

Vogel, Lise. 2000. "Domestic Labor Revisited." *Science & Society* 64 (2): 151–70.

Wallerstein, Immanuel. 1998. *Utopistics: Or, Historical Choices of the Twenty-First Century*. New York: New Press.

Washington, Booker T. 1971. *Up From Slavery: An Autobiography*. Williamstown, Mass.: Corner House.

Weber, Max. 1946. "Science as a Vocation." In Max Weber, *From Max Weber: Essays in Sociology*, translated and edited by H. H. Gerth and C. Wright Mills, 129–56. New York: Oxford University Press.

———. 1958. *The Protestant Ethic and the Spirit of Capitalism*. Translated by Talcott Parsons. New York: Charles Scribner's Sons.

Weeks, Kathi. 1998. *Constituting Feminist Subjects*. Ithaca: Cornell University Press.

———. 2007. "Life within and against Work: Affective Labor, Feminist Critique, and Post-Fordist Politics." *Ephemera* 7 (1): 233–49.

Wegner, Phillip E. 2002. *Imaginary Communities: Utopia, the Nation, and the Spatial Histories of Modernity*. Berkeley: University of California Press.

———. 2007. "Here or Nowhere: Utopia, Modernity, and Totality." In *Utopia, Method, Vision: The Use Value of Social Dreaming*, edited by Tom Moylan and Raffaella Baccolini, 113–29. Bern, Switzerland: Peter Lang.

West, Candace, and Don H. Zimmerman. 1991. "Doing Gender." In *The Social Construction of Gender*, edited by Judith Lorber and Susan A. Farrell, 13–37. Newbury Park, Calif.: Sage.

Wiegman, Robyn. 2000. "Feminism's Apocalyptic Futures." *New Literary History* 31 (4): 805–25.

Wiersema, Fred, ed. 1998. *Customer Service: Extraordinary Results at Southwest Airlines, Charles Schwab, Lands' End, American Express, Staples, and USAA*. New York: Harper Business.

Williams, Joan. 2000. *Unbending Gender: Why Family and Work Conflict and What to Do about It*. Oxford: Oxford University Press.

Willis, Paul. 1977. *Learning to Labor: How Working Class Kids Get Working Class Jobs*. New York: Columbia University Press.

Wilson, William Julius. 1996. *When Work Disappears: The World of the New Urban Poor*. New York: Alfred A. Knopf.

Winkiel, Laura. 1999. "The 'Sweet Assassin' and the Performative Politics of SCUM Manifesto." In *The Queer Sixties*, edited by Patricia Juliana Smith, 62–85. New York: Routledge.

Wollstonecraft, Mary. 1996. *A Vindication of the Rights of Woman*. Mineola, N.Y.: Dover.

Young, Iris. 1981. "Beyond the Unhappy Marriage: A Critique of Dual Systems Theory." In *Women and Revolution*, edited by Lydia Sargent, 43–69. Boston: South End.

Zerilli, Linda. 2005. *Feminism and the Abyss of Freedom*. Chicago: University of Chicago Press.

Zerowork, eds. 1975. Introduction. *Zerowork* 1:1–6.

Zournazi, Mary. 2003. *Hope: New Philosophies for Change*. New York: Routledge.

Zuboff, Shoshana. 1983. "The Work Ethic and Work Organization." In *The Work Ethic—A Critical Analysis*, edited by Jack Barbash, Robert J. Lampman, Sar A. Levitan, and Gus Tyler, 153–81. Madison, Wis.: Industrial Relations Research Association.

Index

....

class: class composition, 19, 94; laborist work ethic and, 59–60; "leading role of the proletariat," 93–94, 127; as outcome, 16–19; process notion of, 19–20; subjectification function of work and, 9; subordination, insubordination, and work ethic, 57–61; working class as category, 94–95; work in relation to, 16–20

Cleaver, Harry, 91, 95, 97, 236n7

clothing and professional discourse, 73–74

Cobble, Dorothy Sue, 154

cognitive mapping, 130–31, 245n14

"cold stream" Marxism, 188–89

Cold War anti-utopianism, 178–79

Collins, Patricia Hill, 247n6

command and obedience. See domination and subordination

The Communist Manifesto (Marx and Engels), 85, 214–16, 252n34

concrete utopias, 195–97, 202–3, 212–13, 216, 221, 249n16

concrete vs. abstract labor, 87–88, 90–91

consumer politics models and decline of work-based activism, 4

consumption: production, relationship to, 8, 88–89, 146; production connected to, in socialist humanism, 88–89; professionalism discourse and, 74; refusal of work and "carefree consumption," 98–99; shorter hours and, 169–70; work ethic and, 47–51, 75. See also asceticism

"convivial austerity," 241n4

Cooper, Anna Julia, 65

cooperation and social production, 91–92

Corlett, William, 236n10

Cornell, Drucilla, 123, 247n8

Cox, Nicole, 122

COYOTE ("Call Off Your Old Tired Ethics"), 67–68

creative activity: freedom as creative practice, 22; Illich on convivial austerity and, 241n4; materialism and, 18–19; refusal of work and, 99–100; shorter hours and, 169; social labor and, 102–3; work ethic and, 82

Cremin, Colin, 240n21

critical utopias, 208, 210–11, 251n31

"culture of poverty" discourses, 64

Cutler, Jonathan, 237n23

Dalla Costa, Mariarosa, 119–30, 133–36, 141, 243n8, 244n12

daydreams, 190–94

Delany, Samuel, 211

Deleuze, Gilles, 201, 227, 232, 249n12, 253n3

Del Re, Alisa, 137, 244n9

demands and demanding: better work, 104–9; directional demands, 220–21; enforcement of wage and hours laws, 237n21; "getting a life," 231–33; as perspective, 128–31, 139–45; as provocation, 131–36, 145–46; slavery reparations, 252n39; utopian, 176, 218–24. *See also* basic income demand; time and shorter hours demand; wages for housework

denaturalizing effect of wages for housework demand, 130

Denning, Michael, 23, 235n1

dependence vs. autonomy, work ethic and, 51–57

desire: basic income demand and, 146; education of, 207; family and, 165; *ressentiment* and, 185–86; wages for housework and, 134–35; work ethic and, 54, 75–76. *See also* asceticism

desire, utopian. *See* utopias

dialectic contradiction vs. antagonism, 96

dialectic model of feminist theory, 115

DiFazio, William, 76–77

difference, utopia and, 211–12

directional demands, 220–21, 228–29

Disch, Lisa, 72
disciplinary subjectivity, work ethic and, 53–55, 239n14
Dispossessed (Le Guin), 211
distancing, utopian, 205–8, 250n24
division of labor vs. class, 17–18. *See also* gender division of labor
domestic production and reproduction: demystification of, 129; domestic labor debate, 118–20, 244n12; gendered work ethic and, 63; hired domestic workers, 172–74; recognition of, as work, 66–67; refusal of work and, 109, 124; shorter hours and, 162–64; as unproductive, from capital's perspective, 244n12. *See also* wages for housework
domination and subordination: beyond exploitation, 20–21; conflict of individual and control, 55–56; work ethic and autonomy vs. command, 51–57; work ethic and subordination vs. insubordination, 57–61
dreams, day vs. night, 190–94
dual-systems model and Fordism vs. post-Fordism, 28
Du Bois, W. E. B., 62

Eagleton, Terry, 211
economic imaginaries, outdated, 235n5
Edelman, Lee, 240n16
Ehrenreich, Barbara, 237n17
eight-hour movement, 162, 169
Eisenstein, Zillah, 66
Elson, Diane, 97
employment contracts, dominance and submission in, 20–21
empowerment of workers in human-resources approach, 107
"The End of History?" (Fukuyama), 178–81
enforcement of wage and hours laws, demand for, 237n21
Engels, Friedrich: *The Communist Man-*

ifesto, 85, 214–16, 252n34; *The German Ideology*, 18–19, 85, 241n6; materialist methodology, 18–19; utopianism and, 187, 222
equality vs. freedom, 20–23
estrangement, utopian function of, 205–8, 213–14, 218, 250n22
eternal return doctrine (Nietzsche), 194, 199–202
ethical discourse of work. *See* work ethic
exchange values vs. use values, 87–88, 90–91
exclamation points, in manifestoes, 214–15
exclusion, racialized work ethic and, 61–63
exit concept, 100
exodus concept, 100
exploitation: domination and subordination as beyond, 20–21; exploitable subjects made at the point of production, 10–11; gendered, in domestic space, 25; socialist modernization and, 83; work ethic and exploitable subjects, 51, 53–55, 239n14

Fair Labor Standards Act, 247n10
family: care work and, 243n14; as component of wage system, 121; Fordism and family-based model, 27; income and family membership, 143–44; Lehr's *Queer Family Values*, 167–68; separate spheres ideology, critiques of, 129; shorter hours demand based on, 155–61; wages for housework demand and, 116; work ethic and family ethic, 164–66; work-family balance discourse, 156, 235n6; work hours constructed in reference to, 163–64
family ethic: gendered work ethic and, 63–64; social welfare policy and, 165; work ethic and, 165–66, 240n16

modernization, socialist, 82–86, 92, 97
Molyneux, Maxine, 243n6
More, Thomas, 208, 250n25
Morris, William, 12, 53
Moylan, Tom, 183, 210, 251n31
Muirhead, Russell, 104–5, 108, 235n2
Muñoz, José, 213

National Welfare Rights Organization, 80, 138, 144
need: desire vs., 134–35; expansion of, 102–3; as justification for work, 4, 7, 44, 80; temporality of, 245n18; wages for housework demand and, 134–35
Negri, Antonio, 90–96, 99–100, 102, 141, 229, 244n9, 246n23
neoconservative discourse, 181
neoliberal anti-utopianism, 179–81
Nietzsche, Friedrich, 91, 194, 198–203, 233
normative theory and utopianism, 184–85
the "Not-Yet-Become," 189
the "Not-Yet-Conscious," 190–93
novum (Bloch), 194, 196–97, 216

O'Brien, Jean, 72
Offe, Claus, 246n24
"On Social Contract" (Rousseau), 209
The Open Society and Its Enemies (Popper), 178–81
optimism, automatic vs. militant, 250n19
overman (Nietzsche), 194, 199, 201–2
overtime, 164

parenting as reproductive labor, 141. *See also* child rearing; family
participation income, 139
part-time work, 164
Pateman, Carole, 20–21, 144
performance measurement issue in post-Fordist context, 70–71
performative quality of utopian provocation, 206–7

personality, 71, 73
Peters, Tom, 71–72
Pfaelzer, Jean, 206
pink-collar workers, 66–67, 73–74
political theory: on freedom, 22–23; marginalization of work within, 2–4, 23; work as political problem of freedom, 35
politics vs. ethics, postwork, 227–29
Popper, Karl, 178–81, 186, 247nn1–2, 248nn3–5
postindustrial, post-Fordist production: alienation critique and, 89; basic income demand and, 142; dependency and, 52–53; family ethic and, 64; "flexploitation," 238n12; production and consumption, relationship between, 50–51; production and reproduction, relationship between, 140–42; production vs. reproduction, 28; professionalism discourse, 71–75; wages for housework demand and, 140; work ethic and, 46, 60, 69–71
Postone, Moishe, 7–8, 15, 84–85, 102
poststructuralism and utopianism, 184
poststructuralist feminism, 115
"The Post-Work Manifesto" (Aronowitz et al.), 161–62, 168, 231
postwork politics vs. postwork ethic, 227–29
postwork society and utopian possibility, 30
poverty discourses, 64
The Power of Women and the Subversion of the Community (Dalla Costa and James), 119, 128, 243n8
power relations, history of struggle vs., 27
precarity movements, European, 80
predestination, 45
The Principle of Hope (Bloch), 187
privatization of work, 3–4
process ontology of being, 189, 249n11
production: exploitable subjects made

Schleuning, Neala, 88

scum Manifesto, 217

secularization of the work ethic, 46–47

Seidman, Michael, 79

self-affirmation, 201–2

self-control, valorization of, 164

self-development of employees, 71–72

self-discipline, 48, 73

self-fulfillment as postindustrial work ethic promise, 46

self-preservation, 249n11

self-realization and socialist humanism, 86

self-valorization: autonomy and, 95–96; laborist work ethic and, 59; refusal of work and, 32, 100, 103

separate spheres ideology: critiques of, 129–30; shorter hours and, 158–59; wages for housework and, 140

separation, in autonomous Marxism, 95–96, 100

sex work, 67–68

Shklovsky, Viktor, 250n22

Shor, Juliet, 163

shorter hours. *See* time and shorter hours demand

slavery reparations demand, 252n39

Smith, Dorothy, 236n8

social factory, 120–23, 127–28, 140, 142

socialism: domestic work and, 125–26, 244n13; Lenin and, 83–84; liberal anti-utopianism and anticommunism, 177; utopian politics and problems with, 29–30

socialist feminism. *See* Marxist feminism

socialist humanism, 82, 85–89, 92, 97

socialist modernization, 82–86, 92, 97

social mobility as industrial work ethic promise, 46

social production: family as site of, 123; Marx on cooperation and, 91–92; modernization and, 86; productive power of, 102–3; wages for housework and, 148

social reproduction. *See* reproductive labor and social reproduction

social wage, 139

Socrates, 251n30

Solanas, Valerie, 217

Spivak, Gayatri, 91

stakeholder grants, 139

standardization, professionalism as, 74

Steensland, Brian, 138, 246n27

Stillman, Peter, 211

style, professional discourse and, 73–74

subjectivities: autonomous Marxism and, 93; demands and the antiwork political subject, 223–24; exploitable subjects made at the point of production, 10–11; fearful vs. hopeful subject, 198; Nietzsche's overman, 201–2; subjectification function of work, 8–9; Taylor, individuals, and, 56; utopian desubjectivization, 205; Weber on construction of capitalist subjectivities, 39–40; work ethic and exploitable subjects, 51, 53–55, 239n14. *See also* the individual

subordination. *See* domination and subordination

surplus value, production of: absolute vs. relative, 153; domestic labor and, 119–20; self-valorization vs., 95; social reproduction vs., 27; sovereign individual subject of exploitation and, 51; wage and, 122

Suvin, Darko, 205, 250n22

Talwar, Jennifer Parker, 240n24

Taylor, Barbara, 113, 136, 149

Taylor, Frederick W., 56, 71–72

Taylorism and post-Taylorism: commitment from post-Taylorist workers, 69–70; dual-systems model and, 28; independence and, 55–56; Lenin and, 84; management and, 71–73; mass

"work-family balance," 235n6

working class, autonomous Marxism on, 93–95

working hours, Marx on, 98–99. *See also* time and shorter hours demand

work society, 5–8, 101–2

work values. *See* work ethic

worldly asceticism, 47–51, 89, 103

Young, Iris, 17–18

Zerilli, Linda, 22–23

KATHI WEEKS is associate professor of women's studies at
Duke University.

Library of Congress Cataloging-in-Publication Data
Weeks, Kathi
The problem with work : feminism, Marxism, antiwork
politics, and postwork imaginaries / Kathi Weeks.
p. cm.
"A John Hope Franklin Center Book."
Includes bibliographical references and index.
ISBN 978-0-8223-5096-5 (cloth : alk. paper)
ISBN 978-0-8223-5112-2 (pbk. : alk. paper)
1. Work—Social aspects. 2. Work-life balance.
3. Feminism. 4. Socialism. I. Title.
HD4904.W37 2011
331.2—dc23   2011021966